Ethics and Governance in Sport

What is, or what should be, the function of sport in a globalized, commercialized world? Why does sport matter in the twenty-first century? In *Ethics and Governance in Sport: The future of sport imagined*, an ensemble of leading international experts from across the fields of sport management and ethics calls for a new model of sport that goes beyond the traditional view that sport automatically encourages positive physical, psychological, social, moral, and political values.

Acknowledging that sport is beset by poor practice, corruption, and harmful behaviors, it explores current issues in sport ethics, governance and development, considering how good governance and the positive potentials of sport can be implemented in a globalized sporting landscape. *Ethics and Governance in Sport* suggests a future model of sport governance based on well-substantiated projections, and argues that identifying the root causes of harmful behavior, those things that are characteristic of sport, and engaging sport managers, policy-makers, and leaders of sport organizations, are essential if sport is to thrive.

The book's interdisciplinary examination of sport, encompassing philosophy, sociology, economics, management, and sport development, and its forward-looking approach, makes it important reading for advanced students, researchers, and policy-makers with an interest in the place and development of modern sport. Its clear messages invite self-reflection and discussion, especially within sports organizations.

Yves Vanden Auweele is Professor (Em.) in Sport Psychology at Katholieke Universiteit Leuven (KULeuven, Belgium). Since 1980 he has taught psychology to physical education, psychology, and medicine students. He has published on stress and abuses in sport, on psychology for physical educators, and on sport for development. He was coordinator of the European Masters Program for Exercise and Sport Psychology, President of the Belgian Society of Sport Psychology, and member of the Managing Council of the European Federation of Sport Psychology (FEPSAC). He was also involved in a sport and development project (2002–2014) with the University of the Western Cape (South Africa). He is still an active member of the Cultural and Scientific Committee of Panathlon International and was senior author of the Panathlon Declaration of Ethics in Youth Sport.

Elaine Cook is a doctoral candidate at the University of Toronto (Canada), and a member of the Panathlon Cultural and Scientific Committee (CSC). Her research explores coach behaviors and interventions designed to influence coach behaviors in such a way that athletes flourish. Elaine is also a certified Solution-Focused Coach (CSFC).

Jim Parry was Head of the Department of Philosophy, University of Leeds, UK, and is now Visiting Professor at the Faculty of PE and Sport, Charles University in Prague. He has been International Professor of Olympic Studies, Autonomous University of Barcelona 2003, University of Ghent 2009, Gresham College, London 2012, Russian International Olympic University, Sochi 2013–2015, and International Olympic Academy, Greece 1986–2015. He is co-author of *The Olympic Games Explained*, 2005, *Sport and Spirituality*, 2007, and *Olympic Ethics and Values in Contemporary Society*, 2012; and co-editor of *Ethics and Sport*, 1999, *Theology, Ethics and Transcendence in Sport*, 2010, *An Introduction to the Phenomenological Study of Sport*, 2012, *Olympic Ethics and Philosophy*, 2012, and *Fields of Vision: The Arts in Sport*, 2014.

Routledge Research in Sport, Culture and Society

Ethics and Governance in Sport

The future of sport imagined

Edited by
**Yves Vanden Auweele, Elaine Cook
and Jim Parry**

Taylor & Francis Group

LONDON AND NEW YORK

First published 2016
by Routledge

2 Park Square, Milton Park, Abingdon, Oxon OX14 4RN
711 Third Avenue, New York, NY 10017, USA

Routledge is an imprint of the Taylor & Francis Group, an informa business

First issued in paperback 2017

British Library Cataloguing-in-Publication Data
A catalogue record for this book is available from the British Library

Library of Congress Cataloging in Publication Data
Ethics and governance in sport : the future of sport imagined / edited by
Yves Vanden Auweele, Elaine Cook and Jim Parry.
pages cm
Includes bibliographical references and index.
1. Sports–Moral and ethical aspects. 2. Sports administration–Moral and
ethical aspects. I. Vanden Auweele, Yves, 1941- II. Cook, Elaine.
III. Parry, S. J. (S. Jim)
GV706.3.E83 2016
796.01–dc23
2015018413

ISBN: 978-1-138-93180-0 (hbk)
ISBN: 978-1-138-08791-0 (pbk)

Typeset in Times New Roman
by Cenveo Publisher Services

In dedication of Vic De Donder, respected president of the Cultural and Scientific Committee of Panathlon International, who died before he could celebrate the release of this book. His passion to strive for more ethics in sport was the stimulus to produce this book.

Contents

Preface

As President of Panathlon International, a service-club whose goal is to examine, promulgate, and defend the values of sport intended as a means toward the development and the advancement of the individual, and as a vehicle of solidarity between people and peoples, I am proud to present this volume to the international world of sport science. It may be considered as the culmination of years of intensive activities by our Cultural and Scientific Committee (CSC).

Since its foundation in 1951 in Venice, Panathlon has been constantly active in the field of ethical and cultural values. One example is the protection of children and youngsters in sport. The resolutions of the Panathlon Congresses of Avignon (1995) and Vienna (1997) inspired by the *Charter for the Rights of the Child in Sport* published in 1986 by the Public Education Department of the Geneva Canton (Switzerland), culminated in the *Panathlon Declaration on Ethics in Youth Sport* presented by an international team of experts on 24 September 2004 during a consensus conference in Ghent (Belgium). Since then, UNICEF, the International Olympic Committee (IOC), SportAccord, nearly all international sport federations, hundreds of national sport federations, the European Olympic Committee, national Olympic Committees, universities, provinces, and cities have endorsed this code of ethics, considering it as having a high moral value.

However, though work on the implementation of the Declaration is ongoing, Panathlon International desired to broaden its vision. Since 2012, a working group of its Cultural and Scientific Committee has been reflecting actively on the future of sport, the result of which is evident in this book, *Ethics and Governance in Sport: The future of sport imagined*, edited by the eminent scholars Yves Vanden Auweele (Belgium), who chaired the workgroup, Elaine Cook (Canada), and Jim Parry (UK). The book draws together the ideas of leading thinkers of three continents in the field, across various disciplines.

I wish to thank the members of our CSC, and in particular its President Vic De Donder (Belgium), for realizing one of our main goals: to promote study and research of the problems facing sport and its interrelations with society, and to communicate the results to the public in collaboration with schools, universities, and other cultural organizations. I hope this book will find its way to all stakeholders in the world of sport, for the benefit of all those who practice sport and believe that sport brings people together. Once again Panathlon "jungit ludis."

Giacomo Santini
President of Panathlon International

Contributors

Kola Adeosun is currently a final year Masters student in Sport and Development at Southampton Solent University (SSU). Alongside this, he is also an Associate Lecturer at Southampton Solent University (SSU) as well as an academic Fellow and Teaching Associate in Sport and Development at the Zambian Institute of Sport (ZIS). He was also Project Leader in the "Kicking AIDS Out" Jamaica research, Project Coordinator and Supervisor for the Coaching Innovation Program (CIP) at SSU, and Director of Youth Soccer Program Development.

Sandro Arcioni has a Doctoral Degree in Sport Sciences (Management) from the University Claude Bernard Lyon 1, France and a Postgraduate Master's Degree in Information Technology from EPFL, Lausanne, Switzerland. He is a teacher and researcher in non-profit organizations, Senior Vice President and founder of Mupex Sàrl, a consulting company, in Lausanne, Switzerland, a member of the Constitution and Arbitration Board (CAB) of Panathlon International (PI), Italy, and former president and founder of the Panathlon Club Gruyère, Switzerland. He is an expert in cyber-defense and specializes in good governance in sport.

Fred Coalter is Professor of Sports Policy at Leeds Metropolitan University (UK) and Visiting Professor at the University of Ulster. He is Fellow of the Academy of Leisure Sciences (USA) and a board member of the Mathare Youth Sport Association Sports and Community Leadership Academy, Nairobi. His research interests and related publications are in the sport-for-development area. His published work includes *Sport-in-Development: A Monitoring and Evaluation Manual* (UK Sport/UNICEF, 2006), *A Wider Social Role for Sport: Who's Keeping the Score?* (Routledge, 2007), and *Sport for Development: What game are we playing?* (Routledge, 2013).

Elaine Cook is a doctoral candidate at the University of Toronto (Canada) and a member of the Panathlon Cultural and Scientific Committee (CSC). Her research explores coach behaviors and interventions designed to influence coach behaviors in such a way that athletes flourish. Elaine is also a certified Solution-Focused Coach (CSFC).

Christo de Coning is a Professor Extraordinaire at the School of Public Leadership, University of Stellenbosch and the Faculty of Community and Health Sciences, University of the Western Cape (UWC) (South Africa). He is presently a part-time researcher at the Interdisciplinary Centre for Sport Science and Development (ICESSD) at UWC. He was awarded the Tim Noakes Scientific and Research Award for 2013 for his research on the socio-economic benefits of sport and recreation in March 2014. He specializes in policy, governance, and evaluation, and is an editor of the recently published *Evaluation Management in South Africa and Africa*. He is a founding member of the Foundation for Sport, Development and Peace, a non-profit organization in South Africa.

Peter Donnelly is Director of the Centre for Sport Policy Studies, and a Professor in the Faculty of Kinesiology and Physical Education at the University of Toronto (Canada). He has published a number of scholarly articles on topics ranging from sport policy and politics to mountaineering history. His books include: *Taking Sport Seriously: Social Issues in Canadian Sport* (1997, 2000, 2011) and *Inside Sports*; and two Canadian editions of *Sports in Society: Issues and Controversies* (both with Jay Coakley, 1999, 2004, 2009). Peter Donnelly was Editor of the *Sociology of Sport Journal* (1990–1994), and the *International Review for the Sociology of Sport* (2004–2006); and President of the North American Society for the Sociology of Sport (2000).

Hilary A. Findlay is Associate Professor in the Department of Sport Management, Brock University in Canada. She is also a founding partner of the Centre for Sport and Law, now known as the Sport Law and Policy Group, a sport law and policy consulting practice. Hilary researches and publishes primarily in the areas of the international regulation of sport, sport governance, and discriminatory practices across sport. She also continues to maintain a law practice specifically working with sport organizations.

Arnout Geeraert is a Post-doctoral Research Fellow at International and European Studies (LINES Institute, Leuven, Belgium). His current work explores the role of the European Union in achieving good governance in international sports and investigates elements of good governance in sports organizations in general. He studied International Politics and Social Sciences (PhD) at the University of Leuven and International and European Law at the University of Brussels. His research explored the role of the European Union in achieving good governance in international sports, taking a principal–agent perspective and focusing on the European Union as an *ex-post* control mechanism. He currently works for both Play the Game/Danish Institute for Sports Studies and LINES, and coordinates the work of an international consortium on good governance in sport

Frank Hendrickx obtained his Doctoral Law degree, a Baccalaureate in Philosophy at the Katholieke Universiteit Leuven (KULeuven, Belgium) and an LLM at the London School of Economics (UK). He worked as an attorney at the Antwerp and Brussels Bar. He is currently employed as a Professor of Labor and Sports Law at the Law Faculty of the Katholieke Universiteit Leuven (Belgium) and part-time chair holder in European labor law at Tilburg University (the Netherlands). He is Editor of the *International Encyclopaedia of Sport Law*, Editor-in-chief of the *European Labor Law Journal* and member of the editorial board of the *International Sports Law Journal*.

Jorid Hovden is Professor in Sport Sociology, Program Leader of Sport Studies and of the Master program in Sport Sciences in the Department of Sociology and Political Science, Norwegian University of Science and Technology (NTNU), Trondheim (Norway). She was Pro-rector of Finnmark University College, and Coordinator of the Research Group on Rural Women at Finnmark University College. She was President of the Norwegian Association for Women and Gender Studies.

Bengt Kayser is Professor at the Institute for Sport Sciences of the University of Lausanne (Switzerland) and has been discussing ethical issues regarding doping and anti-doping since 2005. He is particularly interested in alternatives to zero-tolerance policies and draws parallels with the global efforts against psychotropic drug use and modern alternative drug policies.

Marion Keim is Associate Professor at University of the Western Cape (UWC), South Africa, and directs the Interdisciplinary Centre of Excellence for Sports Sciences and Development (ICESSD). Her research and training interests include sport and community development, leadership, multiculturalism, conflict transformation, youth development and sport as a means for social transformation and peace building. She is Chairperson of the Foundation for Sport, Development and Peace, Training Advisor for Women for Peace Western Cape, and an Advocate of the High Court of South Africa, certified in Mediation and Sports Law. She is a member of the National Advisory Committee for Sport and Recreation, advisor for the Minister of Sport and Recreation, South Africa on Sport and Transformation and a member of the IOC Culture and Olympic Education Commission.

Gretchen Kerr is Professor and Associate Dean in the Faculty of Physical Education and Kinesiology at the University of Toronto (Canada). Gretchen Kerr serves as a Harassment Officer for Gymnastics Ontario and Gymnastics Canada, and has a wealth of teaching and research experience in child development and athlete-centered sport.

Stefan Kesenne is Professor Emeritus of Economics at the University of Antwerp (Belgium) and the Katholieke Universiteit Leuven (KULeuven, Belgium). His main interests are sports economics and labor economics. He has published in many international journals and is the author of the textbook *The Economic Theory of Professional Team Sports* (Edward Elgar, 2007). He is a founding member of the European Sports Economics Association (ESEA) and a member of the editorial board of the *Journal of Sports Economics*.

Wim Lagae is Associate Professor of Sports Marketing at the Katholieke Universiteit Leuven (Belgium) in the Faculty of Economics and Business, Campus Antwerp, and the Department of Human Kinesiology, Campus Leuven. He is part-time Associate Professor at Ghent University (Belgium). His research interests relate to sports sponsorship and marketing communications in professional road cycling and other spectator sports.

Mike McNamee is Professor of Applied Ethics at Swansea University, Wales, since 2008. He is author of *Morality Play: Sports, Virtues and Vices*, and *Sports Ethics: A Reader*; and has authored or edited 15 books in sport philosophy and ethics, and is editor of the Routledge series *Ethics and Sport*, with more than 20 titles. He is also founding editor of the journal *Sport, Ethics and Philosophy*. Mike was Founding Chair, British Philosophy of Sport Association, from 2002; President of the International Association for the Philosophy of Sport 2000–2001; and Executive Member of both the International Council for Sport Science and Physical Education and the European College of Sport Science.

William J. Morgan is a Full Professor of the University of Southern California. He received his PhD in 1977 from the University of Minnesota, with a major concentration in philosophy. He has published numerous peer-reviewed journal articles, book chapters, and two major books, as well as edited and co-edited several published anthologies. He has also presented numerous scholarly papers to national and international conferences. In 2006 his book, *Why Sports Morally Matter*, was runner-up for the best book award from the North American Society for the Sociology of Sport. In 1994 he was awarded the Distinguished Scholar Award by the International Association of the Philosophy of Sport, and elected as a Fellow to the American Academy of Kinesiology.

Oscar Mwaanga is an Associate Professor as well as a social entrepreneur and activist internationally renowned for Sport for Development and Peace (SDP). He has focused his work around sport as a tool for health promotion, for example movement games to educate about HIV/AIDS, obesity, and poverty. His e-work has targeted marginalized groups in sub-Saharan Africa (SSA) and the South of England. Oscar is recognized as one of the indigenous leaders of the Sub-Saharan Africa Sport for Development and Peace movement of the last decade, especially after founding EduSport Foundation, which is the first Sport for Development Peace organization in Zambia. He has also pioneered a number of world-renowned Sport for Development Peace initiatives, including Kicking AIDS Out (implemented in 30 countries), SDP peer leadership, and Go Sisters. His current projects, Fair Game Football and EduMove, are looking to address social justice in football and childhood obesity, respectively.

Jim Parry was Head of the Department of Philosophy, University of Leeds, and is now Visiting Professor at the Faculty of PE and Sport, Charles University in Prague. He has been International Professor of Olympic Studies, Autonomous University of Barcelona 2003, University of Ghent 2009, Gresham College, London 2012, Russian International Olympic University, Sochi 2013–2015, and International Olympic Academy, Greece,1986–2015. He is co-author of *The Olympic Games Explained*, 2005, *Sport and Spirituality*, 2007, and *Olympic Ethics and Values in Contemporary Society*, 2012; and co-editor of *Ethics and Sport*, 1999, *Theology, Ethics and Transcendence in Sport*, 2010, *An Introduction to the Phenomenological Study of Sport*, 2012, *Olympic Ethics and Philosophy*, 2012, and *Fields of Vision: The Arts in Sport*, 2014.

Karen Petry is Deputy Head of the Institute of European Sport Development and Leisure Studies at Cologne Sport University (Germany). She is responsible for research activities in European Sport Policy, Sport for Development, and Social Work and Sport. Karen lectures on the BA Sport, Outdoor Activities and Movement, the MA Sport Management, and the MA Sport Tourism. She is also Lecturer in the European Master Program "Health and Physical Activity" at the University of Rome (Italy). She is a member of the editorial board of the *Journal of Sport for Development*. Currently, Karen is leading the Monitoring and Evaluation activities of the sector program "Sport for Development" of the German Ministry for Economic Cooperation and Development, as well as a further education program in "Sport and Development" in cooperation with the German Olympic Sport Confederation (DOSB).

Roland Renson studied Physical Education, Physical Therapy and Social and Cultural Anthropology at Katkolieke Universiteit Leuven (KULeuven, Belgium), where he also obtained his PhD in 1973. He has taught courses on History of Physical Education, Sociology of Sport, Comparative Physical Education and Sport, Social Kinesiology, and Research Methods. He began research projects of the Flemish Games File in 1973, archives of gymnastics in 1980, and archives of modern sport in 1980. Spin-offs of these projects were the Flemish Folk Games Central (1980) and the Sports Museum Flanders (1983), which amalgamated into the Sportimonium in 2004, of which he is still chairperson. He was President of HISPA (1985–1989) and first president of ISHPES (1989–2003).

Marius Runkel completed a BA Sports Science program with an emphasis on health and management at the University of Bielefeld (Germany) in 2007 and finished his MSc Sport Management studies at the German Sport University Cologne (Germany) in 2013. His Master's thesis, titled "The involvement of NGOs implementing cycling as a tool for development in post-apartheid South Africa," was completed during a four-month stay in South Africa, Cape Town. He has more than three years of professional experience in sports marketing and management.

Marijke Taks is Professor of Sport Management at the University of Windsor, Ontario, Canada, and Adjunct Professor in the Department of Sport and Movement Sciences at Katkoliek Universiteit Leuven (KULeuven, Belgium).

She teaches courses in socio-economic aspects of sports, global issues in sport management, and sport marketing, both at the undergraduate and graduate level. Her research interests relate to impacts, outcomes, and leveraging of small and medium sized sport events.

Jan Tolleneer is Professor at Katholieke Universiteit Leuven (KULeuven, Belgium) and Ghent University (Belgium). He also teaches at the National Training Academy of Flanders, Belgium. He was a board member of the International Society for Comparative Physical Education and Sport (ISCPES) and of the International Society for the History of Physical Education and Sport (ISHPES). He teaches foundations of physical education, comparative studies, sports history, and sports ethics. He coordinates the Interfaculty Research Group Sport and Ethics at KU Leuven, Belgium.

Yves Vanden Auweele, PhD, is Professor (Em.) in Sport Psychology at Katholieke Universiteit Leuven (KULeuven, Belgium). Since 1980 he has taught psychology to students of physical education, psychology, and medicine. He has published on stress and abuses in sport, on psychology for physical educators, and on sport for development. He was coordinator of the European Masters Program for Exercise and Sport Psychology, President of the Belgian Society of Sport Psychology, and member of the Managing Council of the European Federation of Sport Psychology (FEPSAC). He was also involved in a sport and development project (2002–2014) with the University of the Western Cape (South Africa). He is still an active member of the Cultural and Scientific Committee of Panathlon International and was senior author of the Panathlon Declaration of Ethics in Youth Sport.

Daam Van Reeth is Professor at the Katholieke Universiteit Leuven (KULeuven, Belgium) in the Faculty of Economics and Business, Campus Brussels, and is Program Director of the Business Administration program. He teaches courses in Microeconomics and International Research in Economics. His research interests relate to the economics of sport, with a special focus on professional road cycling and media attention for sport. Research topics he worked on include TV demand for the Tour de France, doping perception, gender balance in sports coverage, and fantasy sports.

Bart Vanreusel is Professor in the Department of Human Kinesiology, Katholieke Universiteit Leuven (KULeuven, Belgium). His research, publications, teaching assignments, and policy commitments are in sociology of sport and physical activity, with an emphasis on public policies and sport, management of sport and leisure, sport and integration, sport, social change and development, and issues of participation.

Jan Vorstenbosch is Assistant Professor for Applied Ethics at Utrecht University (the Netherlands). He has published widely on the ethics of sports and is currently working on a book about normative theory of sports.

Abbreviations

ADRV(s)	anti-doping rule violation(s)
AFLD	Agence Française de Lutte contre le Dopage
AIGCP	Association Internationale des Groupes Cyclistes Professionnels
APRM	African peer review mechanism
ASO	Amaury Sports Organization
ATLAS	Athletic Talent Laboratory Analysis Systems
AU	African Union
CAS	Court of Arbitration for Sport
CICR	Comité International de la Croix Rouge
CIO	Comité International Olympique
CIRC	Cycling Independent Reform Commission
CJEU	Court of Justice of the EU
COC	Canadian Olympic Committee
CPA/APC	Cyclistes Professionnels Associés/Association of Professional Cyclists
CPP	critical participatory paradigm
CSR	corporate social responsibility
EASM	European Association for Sport Management
EC	European Commission (the executive branch of the EU)
ECHR	European Court of Human Rights
EIA	economic-impact analyses
EMT	early version of modernization theory
EPO	erythropoietin
EU	European Union
EUFA	Union of European Football Associations
FFP	Financial Fair Play
FIFA	Fédération Internationale de Football Association
FIFPro	World Players' Union
FILA	Fédération Internationale de Lutte Amateur
GCDP	Global Commission on Drug Policy
GSOs	global sport organizations
IAAF	International Association of Athletics Federations

ICESSD	Interdisciplinary Centre of Excellence for Sport Sciences and Development
IF(s)	International Sport Federation(s)
ILO	International Labor Organization
IOC	International Olympic Committee
IPCT	International Professional Cycling Teams
ISCO	International Standard Classification of Occupations
ISOs	international sport organizations
MDG(s)	Millennium Development Goal(s)
MPCC	Mouvement Pour un Cyclisme Crédible
MSE	mega sport events
NADO	national anti-doping organizations
NBA	National Basketball Association
NEPAD	New Partnership for Africa's Development
NF(s)	national sport federation(s)
NFL	National Football League (Canada)
NFLPA	National Football League Players' Association (Canada)
NGO(s)	non-governmental organization(s)
NMSE	non-mega sport events
NMT	new modernization theory
NOC(s)	National Olympic Committee(s)
NPE	Normative Power Europe
OATH	Olympic Advocates Together Honorability
OG	Olympic Games
PanAmJacs	Panamerican Junior Athletic Championships
PED(s)	performance-enhancing drug(s)
RBMES	results-based monitoring and evaluation system
RDP	(South African) Reconstruction and Development Program
SDG(s)	sustainable development goal(s)
SDPIWG	Sport for Development and Peace International Working Group
SiD	sport in development
SPD	Sport for Development and Peace
TFEU	Treaty on the Functioning of the European Union
THG	tetrahydrogestrinone (a designer anabolic steroid)
UCI	Union Cycliste Internationale
UCL	UEFA Champions League
UNDP	United Nations Development Program
UNHCR	United Nations High Commissioner for Refugees
USADA	US Anti-Doping Agency
WACA	World Anti-Corruption Agency
WADA	World Anti-Doping Agency
WSGA	World Sport Governance Agency
YOG	Youth Olympic Games

Introduction

*Yves Vanden Auweele, Elaine Cook and
Jim Parry*

Objectives and rationale

The idea of making projections on the future of sports in the twenty-first century began with an awareness that each generation has interpreted and structured sport in its own context and ideology, but also an awareness that a growing contrast between the positive, admirable ideals and values of sport that are often proclaimed, and the current and emerging challenges of questionable practices in sport, could not be ignored. An additional consideration was that we doubted the efficacy of a mere accumulation of ad hoc solutions for the various problems that arise from time to time, or appear in a refurbished form as a result of new trends and possibilities in our contemporary society. Instead, we have sought a fundamental re-thinking of the potentials, pitfalls, and challenges of the meaning and function of sport in the twenty-first century.

We are therefore not only considering concrete suggestions for improvement and innovation, but also a more fundamental re-conceptualization or re-thinking of sport in current society, taking into account, of course, the processes that brought us to the current situation. The editors suggest an unmasking, an exposure of the mainstream assumptions regarding the ethical implications of the governance and functioning of sport in current society. They consider the time ripe for a disclosure of the way in which accepted "truths" in sport have become established, but even more for a resonant reaction to alternatives and new ideas.

This idea did not appear out of thin air, since there are already a growing number of authorities (e.g. the Sport Commission of the European Parliament), organizations within and outside of the sport sector (Panathlon International; Play the Game, etc.) and, not least, sport scholars (e.g. the authors of this book) who are already exploring these ideas and projections into the future.

Panathlon International (www.panathlon.net), on whose behalf the editors accepted to coordinate this book, reckoned that it could do some pioneering work by helping to channel this desire, ambition, and tendency by drawing together the important ideas of leading thinkers in the field, across various disciplines, into one publication.

Operationalization

We defined and operationalized the aims of the book from *four perspectives*. First, as an attempt to analyze and describe the consequences of current trends and driving forces in both society and sport that lie behind current practices, values, beliefs, systems, and organizations in modern sport. We identified trends such as globalization, commercialization, sporting autonomy, sport as a means for development and peace, for democratization, shifts in the balance of power between superpowers and developing countries, and associated geopolitical tensions, social media, scientific progress in enhancing sport materials, coaching, emerging potentials of the body, new ideologies, politics, international terrorism and boycotts, and others.

Second, as an extrapolation of some current trends into future sport practice, sports management, sport law, etc. We asked "what if ..." an (unrestrained) autonomy of sport, (genetic) doping; a neo-liberal mindset; a lack of debate, discussion, and self-criticism; an interference of dominant nations and/or financially rich countries ... were to become generally accepted and condoned as mainstream or at least as unavoidable? What might sport become, as a result?

Third, as a stimulation to suggest ways of resisting or shaping current trends in a more (morally) acceptable direction, such as more democratic governance, corporate social responsibility, less eccentric financing, a more focused promotion of the workable elements that unlock the positive energy of sport, etc. Or, on the contrary, as an attempt to accept, embrace, refine, or justify current trends and practices with reasoned arguments. Why shouldn't we accept genetic doping, why shouldn't we accept current financial practices (salaries, transfers, bonuses, tax fiddling) of the global sport organizations (FIFA, IOC, IAAF, etc.) in the supply and demand rationale? Why shouldn't we applaud the financial input from sponsors, rich (oil) countries, the media, etc.? Why shouldn't we defend the autonomy of sport, with its own set of rules and regulations?

Finally, at a more speculative level, we might expect some authors to attempt a conceptualization of a totally new philosophy of sport, with original ideas and concepts, and possibly less attention to specific answers to currents tendencies.

The book includes five parts and 22 chapters

We grouped the contributions into five parts according to some major themes or perspectives addressed by the authors:

- timeline of projections into the future and related strategies: open-ended, short, medium or long term;
- good governance in sport;
- fairness in (financial) management;
- sport and body enhancement;
- re-conceptualization of sport and development.

Not even 22 contributions are able to cover the whole range of future projections, questions, problems, opinions, and realizations, and though some texts include contrasting information and perhaps too few texts reflect the Southern perspective, we think that this book offers nonetheless an inspiring set of critical and challenging ideas and suggestions on the future of sport, which will offer enough material to begin an enriching debate.

In a perfect world we would have liked to have had a more global representation of authors; however, we finally ended up with 28 authors from three continents (Europe, North America and Africa) and 11 countries: Belgium, Canada, Czech Republic, Germany, the Netherlands, Norway, South Africa, Switzerland, the UK, the USA, and Zambia.

This book will be useful for sport managers and authorities, the media, trainers and coaches, sport scientists, sponsors, athletes, and fans – in fact, for all stakeholders in the sport sector.

We emphasize five distinct points that may attract a wide range of readers:

1   No aggressive and fanciful opinions, but short and well-substantiated contributions, with clear messages that invite reflection and discussion.
2   An interdisciplinary socio-economic approach, including elements of philosophy, sociology, economics, marketing, management, sport and development, etc.
3   A balanced approach, without being hypercritical and overly cynical, or being overly romantic about the power of the positive potentials of sport.
4   A focus not only on ad hoc problems or solutions, but also on the underlying causes of problems and on suggestions for a more fundamental re-direction or re-thinking of sport; even exploring the idea of replacing sport by a broader movement culture. Most of the contributions have a definite speculative and prospective character.
5   A claim for a new culture of rights, relationships, and geo-political checks and balances in sport, similar to what is developing in the international trade and environmental protection sectors.

PART I

Re-thinking and implementing concepts and practices in the future of sport

Introduction

*Yves Vanden Auweele, Elaine Cook
and Jim Parry*

Suggestions regarding the "most appropriate time line" (open-ended, short-, medium-, or long-term strategies) to successfully implement changes in the future constitute the link between the chapters in this first part, dealing with, on first sight, very different concepts, practices, and solutions.

Mike McNamee (UK) prefers to set clear objectives and related plans within the realistic timeframe of a decade, prohibiting fanciful projections into the distant future. He bases this timeframe on a *Report on Ethical Threats to the Integrity of Sport in the UK*. Pressing issues that are addressed include corruption, Paralympic hyper-technologization, Olympic–Paralympic fusion, international migration of sports labor, breakdown of gender identity, inflation of athletes' rights, commodification of sports medicine and performance-enhancement doping.

Yves Vanden Auweele (Belgium) argues that the continuum of aberrant behaviors, ranging from inappropriate to criminal, may be symptoms of the same common causes: "side effects of commercialization and globalization." Combating causes instead of symptoms may require more difficult, longer-term, and wider ranging strategies, but in eventually reducing the roots of aberrant behavior it may be more efficient than developing separate ad hoc solutions for each aberrant behavior.

Jim Parry (UK) believes that a renewed Olympism still has a future. Despite the doom-sayers looking forward to the era of "post-Olympism," he argues that a re-theorized Olympism, appropriate for the ethics, politics, and economics of the twenty-first century, represents not only the best hope for the survival of elite sport as an ethical enterprise, but also still the best foundation for sport as an educational enterprise.

Jori Hovden (Norway) describes and advocates a fast-track discourse as a necessary and relevant point of departure to challenge and change male dominance and democratic deficit in sport organizations. The emphasis is on how the use of quota provisions may serve as an adequate and efficient political measure for closing the gender gap and realizing future democratization.

Elaine Cook and Gretchen Kerr (Canada) propose a shifting of the question from "how can harm be prevented?" to "how might sport experiences be optimized?" With a positive psychology philosophy (as an open-ended task), they make recommendations that illustrate an athlete-centered approach, purported to be the best way to reduce harm and to optimize the quality of the sport experience for young participants.

Finally, **Roland Renson** (Belgium) advocates, by analogy to the concept of bio-diversity, for ludo-diversity, to counteract the tendency toward a movement mono-culture. Ludo-diversity means the variation among all movement cultures, encompassing the domains of play, competition, physical culture, and movement expression, and their respective sub-fields such as games, sports, physical exercises, dance, and acrobatic performances.

1 Ethics and the integrity of sport
Issues for the next decade[1]

Mike McNamee

I am told that the newly minted phrase "horizon scanning" has been implemented with increasing frequency in the world of elite sports performance management. Scientists are contracted to scan the latest issues of research journals, from medicine to science and technology, in order to see what new breakthroughs in cognate fields might find their way into sports performance optimization. While it is an interesting example of the creativity of sports to adapt to cutting-edge knowledge and techniques, it is also an example of the increasingly deeper penetration of science into sport. Predicting future outcomes is not an exercise for the faint-hearted. Each effort should come with a warning that the variables cannot be controlled nor the predictions be especially reliable. Here, then, is an effort to estimate loosely – prediction is too strong a notion – how present ethical concerns may develop over the next decade and what original problems they may present the world of sports administration and governance, policy, and practice.

Corruption

There has been a long-standing tradition in the social sciences of sport, and in investigative sports journalism, to focus on matters of financial corruption in sports. Most recently, Joao Havelange was forced to resign his honorary position at FIFA, but there are few who doubt that he is but one example from the world of commodified sports. Scandals of this kind will doubtless continue to hit the headlines as they have done for decades. More interesting, however, is an issue that has been developing over the last few years concerning match-fixing and its relationship to unregulated, or loosely regulated, gambling operations. This particular configuration has been referred to as "narrow sport integrity" as opposed to a broader catalogue of ethical problems that can be grouped under the heading "wide sport integrity" (Cleret, McNamee, & Page, 2015).

In May 2013 the World Ministers of Sport and Physical Education met in Berlin to discuss three significant challenges in international sport policy prior to achieving a UNESCO declaration (www.unesco.org/new/en/social-and-human-sciences/themes/physical-education-and-sport/mineps-2013). One of the three concerned the fight against match-fixing, illegal betting, doping, and corruption in sport, including the capacity of national (NF) and international federations (IF) to effectively govern corrupt practices relating to their own sports. Clearly, major international sports federations have had enough difficulty keeping their own houses in order. Unregulated gambling and its relationship to match-fixing is far beyond the scope even of IFs, since it requires information-gathering across national boundaries, with police and other state agencies, and across international legal systems that permit more or less intrusion and surveillance.

Part of the management of this threat will be the development of much stronger governance structures. National Federations must play an active role, but the evolution of national and international agencies (e.g. Transparency International; Europol; Interpol) is essential in order to tackle what is a multi-stakeholder problem, both national and international. How this will be coordinated, and who will lead international coordination after the UNESCO declaration of May 2013, is a moot point. Different norms of tolerance and intolerance to unregulated gambling exist across the world. Developing coherent and committed global policies, practices, and quality assurance standards will be far from easy.

International migration of sports labor

In the sports sociology literature much has been made lately of the migration of sports labor in general terms with respect to the globalization of sports driven by media and commercial commodification of sports products. There has also been discussion of the rise of athletes born in one country but competing in and/or for another. Bale coined the memorable term "the brawn drain"[2] to capture it. Others have referred to it as the "muscle drain." More recently, however, there has also been discussion regarding the increase in employing overseas coaches; expatriate coaching.

The pros of expatriate coaching are, in principle, that it allows for the most competent coaches to be appointed. This can improve selection practices and training regimes, as well as, of course, performance outcomes. The UK, like many other countries, appointed former East German expert coaches at the fall of the Berlin Wall. Equally, high-profile sports such as football at club and national levels have long crossed national boundaries without much outcry; Ireland, Scotland, and Wales Rugby Union federations have hitherto appointed expatriate coaches and indeed head coaches; UK Athletics was led by a Dutch coach to considerable effect at the 2012 Games.

Apart from the obvious point of equality of opportunity, accounted for and modified by legal jurisdictions, is there anything ethically objectionable about this practice?

First, the issue of denying opportunities to national coaches is often raised. If an NF wishes to appoint a UK national coach, the pool from which they might reasonably choose is limited to the extent that expatriate coaches begin to proliferate, taking up roles that are relatively scarce. It is not clear that this need be a problem if, however, the NFs (perhaps mindful of public support/opprobrium) are clear that their policy is to appoint the best coach (whatever that might mean) for the job.

Whether the general public identifies with foreign coaches in the same way as they might with the athletes themselves is an interesting question worthy of exploration. It may be that concerns are only raised if and when the team fails to win or at least achieve its potential. Such scapegoating is likely to mask an under-lying xenophobia.

A third concern is more difficult to appraise. To what extent is it desirable to think of a national team as a standard bearer for its country, or individuals to act as role models? Many countries have drawn on the narrative of sports' fostering of national identity. If this is the case, then there may arise questions as to the coaches' understanding of the norms and values that comprise that identity, and indeed their identification with it.

Fourth, there might be widespread support for expatriate coaches who are winning, but it is an open question whether an (e.g.) Olympic Team coached only by expatriates would be acceptable to the host nation. The aspect of public engagement, identification, and support is especially important in the less commercialized sports that draw on major funding from the public purse via some national agency, funded by public taxation.

Fifth, for those countries that have strongly developed coaching pathways that mark out the long-term development of coaches from grass-roots to an interna-tional stage, how are non-native trained coaches to be evaluated in terms of expertise and expectations?

It is also clear that a similar debate surrounding the near absence of high-level coaches in, for example, the UK's Premier League or the American National Football League or National Basketball Association, or from Rugby Union's tri-nations league (Australia, New Zealand, South Africa) from ethnic minorities, or the preponderance of male coaches in female sports, raises very similar issues that are worthy of policy consideration rather than more sensationalist media-driven exposure.

Breakdown of binary gender identity and its impact on sport classification

Much of the sports world is divided by categories and classifications. The purposes of these categories or classifications are manifold. Perhaps above all they are designed to ensure fair and meaningful competition. Historically, catego-ries such as employment or social status came to be viewed as pernicious and discriminatory. Less contentious are categories for weight (e.g. boxing, wres-tling) or age. Not only can such categories ensure fair contests, they can also prevent harm to others by significant disparities in bodily capabilities or charac-teristics. More contentious are categories of ability/disability (see above) and gender, both of which have been raised to visibility in international athletics.

While the ambiguity of male/female categories is not lost on gender scholars, it took a long time for sports medical scientists to appreciate the nature and significance of ambiguous cases. Some women are known to exhibit extremely high levels of testosterone and are known to have a range of conditions referred to collectively as "hyper-androgenism." Caster Semenya, an 18-year-old from South Africa, won the 800-meter title in the 2009 World Championships by nearly 2.5 seconds. At least one finalist complained that she had competed against a "man." Semenya was subjected to a process of gender verification, which (while avoiding some of the awful precedents involving visual inspection of genitalia) has been the subject of widespread critique and condemnation. Her case was not a new one. While there are genuinely ambiguous and contested cases of gender identity (often referred to as "intersex athletes"), there have been historical cases of "gender fraud" as it might be called, notably in the 1936 Berlin Olympic Games where a male German athlete competed as a woman.

The IOC and IAAF set out a policy prior to the London 2012 Olympic Games that avoided visual inspections or chromosomal tests. Henceforth, women athletes "known or suspected" to have hyper-androgenism will be allowed to compete only if they agree to medical intervention, or if they are found to be "insensitive" to androgens. Notwithstanding criticisms of the process that led to the leaking of confidential data (failing to protect the anonymity of the athlete under question in the case of Caster Semenya), there has been much greater respect for the privacy of athletes of disputed gender. Equally, there has been greater multidisciplinary involvement, including not only sports physicians and lawyers, but also intersex community representatives.

What is more problematic, though, is the criticism of the hyper-androgenic marker used to distinguish those intersex athletes who may not compete in female sporting classes. The integrity of the test may be compromised by hormonal variations or complicated by other aspects of sexual development disorders that athletes may suffer from. Finally, there is the issue of whether a biological marker, as opposed to cultural or social ones relating to upbringing and their historical gender identity (i.e. the identity that they have been brought up in/with) is the more decisive criterion of identity. While the use of biological markers will be easier to identify and provide consensus, it does not follow that they are the most relevant.

Finally, there is of course the issue of whether gender-based sport is, at least in some cases, nothing more than a historical anachronism. This idea has been mooted often within the philosophy of sport. While, for example, speed and power events will inevitably favor males, all things considered, there are several sports where participation is mixed (e.g. equestrian sports) and gender thought to be an irrelevant variable. The fusion of these pre-existing categories may well be an interesting development for certain sports and could have implications at both ends of the sporting continuum between educational sport provision and the Olympic Games.

Inflation of athletes' rights

There is a celebrated short-hand in communitarian political theory that runs: "rights corrode practices" (see McIntyre, 1984). What this means, briefly put, is that if all individuals within any social practice (e.g. sports) press their claims hard enough, the practice itself will be rent asunder. Some might see this as hyperbole, but it is worth stressing that rights-talk has been on the rise for some decades now and several claims to would-be human rights have brought about controversial, and at times counter-intuitive, claims such as those by prisoners to vote, or pedophiles to their privacy, irrespective of the vileness of the actions that they may have perpetrated. How might this play out in elite sports?

To take a familiar example, consider the rights of athletes who might also be taking banned substances or employing banned methods under the WADA code. At present there are several cases pending at the European Court of Justice (ECJ) considering whether WADAs whereabouts policy, which is essential for out-of-competition testing, is an infringement under Article 8 of the European Convention on Human Rights. This right preserves, among other things, the right to a family life, which (it is argued) is threatened by year-round testing.

The status of certain elite athletes as workers means that unfair contract terms, restraint of trade, and right to work are subject to the treaties and laws of the European Union (EU). As workers, these elite athletes are also entitled to the protection of the Working Time Directive 2003 that requires a daily rest period of 11 hours, an additional weekly rest period of 24 hours, and an annual leave entitlement of 5.6 weeks. How athletes on publicly funded programs should be viewed becomes thus a critical issue.

How would being available for out-of-competition testing be possible under a strong interpretation of this right? Clearly, the strong advocacy of athletes' rights here has serious implication for the effectiveness of anti-doping policy. The EHCR has, however, a backlog amounting to thousands of cases. Would hearing such a case be considered a judicial or political priority? What changes in context might bring such a prioritization about? Were such a case held and the ruling to fall in favor of athletes' individual rights, then the implications for the effectiveness and deterrent effects of prosecuting anti-doping policy would be very significant.

Rights need not, however, be understood in an individualistic way. Collective rights intended to protect or to promote interests are equally worthy of note. Trades unions such as the Professional Players Federation in the UK (www.ppf.org.uk), European Elite Athletes Association (www.euathletes.org); Uni Global Union (www.uniglobalunion.org/Apps/uni.nsf/pages/sport_proEn) are becoming increasingly vocal about what they see as the unfair conditions of their professional sports workers. This may be seen as strengthening the hand of elite athlete workers. One might think that the increasing recognition of athletes' rights as workers would be a good thing. Yet if rights are to become more widely acknowledged, what else might follow? Another well-known dictum, this time from moral philosophy, runs: "rights correspond to duties/responsibilities (and vice versa)." This phrase has a political analogue too – consider the Boston Tea Party: no taxation (duty) without representation (right). What duties might athletes be forced to undertake if their rights are to be respected? One bold claim might run as follows: anti-doping is a quality assurance system designed for the right of protection of athletes to enjoy doping-free sport: thus athletes should be directly or indirectly responsible, i.e. have a duty, for its operation. What would athlete-sponsored anti-doping look like? How would the burden of a duty of responsibility be distributed? Could it be as effective? Would they be prepared to finance at least part of the system? How would its operations be compromised? What is clear is that athletes' claims to the protection or promotion of their interests within a rights framework ought to be balanced by a consideration of their duties to, for example, ensure fair sport, whether through anti-doping or anti-corruption practices. The role of agents in professional sports, however, has seen the advancement of only one side of this ethical and political problematic. The widely perceived lack of governance standards relating to sports agents' practices and the concomitant increase in players' salaries in certain sports is a factor that clearly exacerbates sports operating practices while promoting individual athletes' interests.

Increasing commercialization of sports medicine

There is a widespread dictum in medicine that the physician ought always to serve the patient's best interests. Ordinarily, this will entail informing the patient of their diagnosis, any complications, the treatment alternatives, recommending the best option, and allowing the patient to decide what they perceive to be in their best interests. There are some exceptions to this general medical norm: for example, those who are unable to determine what is in their own best interests. This category, in relation to sports, will comprise child and adolescent athletes or those rendered incapable of competent decision making. In the former case, gaining consent *may* be problematic. Legal considerations are not straightforward here. Legal precedent may favor either parent/guardian *or* the adolescent athlete according to the particulars of the case. In the latter case we might expect to find athletes with severe learning difficulties or athletes whose competence is temporarily undermined by some injury, such as concussion. In such cases, the medical team may take decisions on behalf of the athlete patient who may be considered incapable of *informed* consent.

The inauguration of the Youth Olympics in Singapore in 2010 is no more than the culmination of a trend that elite sports performances, generally speaking, are being produced by younger performers. The ethical difficulties are manifold (Parry, 2012). For example, early specialization may foreclose opportunities elsewhere; increasing early specialization is likely to expose the growing athlete to health risks; successful youth athletes, in some sports, are likely to become commodities in the way that highly promising young football stars have been over the last decade (despite FIFA's development of policies against the practice of contracting the potential cream of the coming crop of young stars under the age of 11).

These ethical problems have long been associated with talent identification. A recent complicating factor has been the rise of genetic medicine, which, whether through hype or the selective use of data, has led to the commercialization of genetic tests which are said to be predictive of athletic potential. There is little robust data to support these marketing claims. Nevertheless, websites have proliferated that entice consumers (one suspects "pushy parents" with gifted sports children) to test in order to predict athletic talent. Thus, for example, ATLAS (Athletic Talent Laboratory Analysis Systems) writes on its home page:

> Is it possible to develop a series of Performance Tests that could measure and predict athletic talent? The answer is **Yes**.
>
> (www.atlasgene.com/)

Alongside the eye-catching phrasing are other advertisements for talent identification programs and standardized testing equipment. At present there are some prospects for the therapeutic use of genetic medicine in sports (e.g. tissue repair; identification of vulnerability to hypertrophic cardiomyopathy associated with sudden death syndrome), but its efficacy for predicting athletic talent, which is a complex of genotype and phenotype (environmental) factors, is extremely limited due to the variability of the latter. The use of genetic medicine in sport, therefore, must proceed with respect to a precautionary principle.

A second, potentially related, issue pertains to the kinds of conflict of interests that can emerge when the sports physician or sports medicine team is employed directly by a club or franchise and fails to serve directly the patient and their best interests. The use of genetic screening or testing for conditions that may affect employment is almost certainly discriminatory under employment legislation and contrary to the European Bioethics Convention. The same might apply to non-genetic tests, where coaches or team managers may pressurize sports medicine teams to reveal confidential data on health or injury status. While this has been a long-standing problem in commercialized sports, it is likely to be exacerbated with the increasing sophistication of biotechnology in sports. At present there are limited governance frameworks to deal with these issues of conflict of interest.

Performance enhancement via doping

The issue of doping, or more precisely of anti-doping rule violations (ADRVs), has long bedeviled elite sport. It is not necessary to cover the general terrain, but with WADA's new Code, ratified in Johannesburg in November 2013, it is worth commenting on some specific contemporaneous issues.

First, the Lance Armstrong case was played out in the full gaze of the world's media. Among the many interesting issues it raised concerns about the length of time anti-doping organizations may trawl back to find evidence of ADRVs. Clearly, there is an issue of the integrity of samples that are stored. Not only is there a fixed amount of time that samples can be held for, there is also the problem of who can hold and test. Thus, for example, the IOC has jurisdiction during the Games, while WADA has at all other times. Given the extent of funding supplied by the IOC (50 percent) and the problem of retrieving funds from nation states, it is always likely that the IOC will lead on Games-related anti-doping. However, it clearly has a potential conflict of interest in that it has an interest both in clean Games and the public perception of such. A problem, however, that complicates this is the extent to which re-testing of samples is targeted. Whose samples? Should they be the object of new advances in testing protocols? How will the IOC and WADA mediate this?

Second, justice, where possible, should be swift. Is it meaningful to disqualify or take away titles and medals so many years after the performance? How can we promote others if we cannot be reasonably certain that they, who may not have had to provide an in-competition sample at the time, were clean themselves? If no sample exists in a scenario where gold, silver, and bronze medal winners are all declared as having committed ADRVs, ought we simply register a "no clear winner" result?

Third, while ADRVs have focused on physical enhancement methods and substances, the rise of neurocognitive enhancement will have the potential to enhance sports performances in disciplines that have a significant psychological component. Capacities such as increased memory, attentiveness, visual perception, and so on are likely to be mined by the application of therapeutic pharmacology to athletic populations. This is a strongly emerging dimension of Western medicine and while some sports (e.g. target sports) are obvious contenders for abuse, there is no reason to suspect that their use will be limited thereto.

Finally, there has been evidence of EPO abuse from at least one elite Kenyan athlete, just as there have been recent positive tests in Jamaican athletics, notably sprinting. The collision of two factors is of interest in these cases. First, there is the dominance of a sporting activity in a geographically concentrated area. Second, the area in question does not enjoy significant anti-doping investment and its structures for effective testing may not be as robust as other countries. The failure to catch doping cheats in certain sports/countries is perceived by athletes as an extremely important issue for sports justice. It is unlikely that the Athlete's Biological Passport system will be used extensively across sports because of its expense. The discrepancies of NADO and IF compliance to the WADA Code and, moreover, the limited conception of compliance in terms of crude quantitative measures (like numbers of samples taken) currently in place in anti-doping policy is widely recognized. The more efficient targeting of resources on an international level, and more substantial monitoring of anti-doping organizational performance, is critical for the integrity of sport.

Summary remarks

The issues presented here anticipate some problems concerning current trends and issues of an ethical kind across the world of sports. However, no attempt has been made here to offer a comprehensive view of ethical problems in elite sport, and this sample might have included many others, such as the increasing commercialization of sports medicine and the hyper-technologization of Paralympic sport.

Nevertheless, it presents certain key issues that are discussed in academic research in sports ethics and related social science fields. No-one can look into the future of sports with a high degree of reliability over one year, let alone a decade. Speculative judgment supported by reasoned argument and a reasonable body of evidence is the most that can be asked.

Notes

1 This chapter is a revised version of an unpublished report that was commissioned by UK Sport to anticipate changes in sport in the coming decade, focusing on integrity issues.
2 The phrase is a play on another – the "brain drain" – which was used during the Prime Ministership of Margaret Thatcher when academics, disgruntled with the economic and political direction the UK was taking, migrated elsewhere to ply their trade.

References

Cleret, L., McNamee, M.J., & Page, S. (2015). "Sports Integrity" needs sports ethics (and sports philosophers and sports ethicists too). *Sport, Ethics and Philosophy*, 9 (1).
McIntyre, A.C. (1984). *After virtue: A study in moral theory* (2nd ed.). London: Duckworth.
Parry, S.J. (2012). The Youth Olympic Games: Some ethical issues. *Sports, Ethics and Philosophy*, 6 (2), 138–154.

2 Restoring sport's integrity

Beyond ad-hoc solutions in challenging aberrations in sport[1]

Yves Vanden Auweele

Introduction

Within the context of this chapter, "integrity" will refer to the (re)application of values and norms in sport practice – such as wellness and well-being, fair play, solidarity, and health (Biddle, 2006) – that are generally promoted and considered positive.

The integrity of sport is said to be undermined first by a number of high-profile integrity violations. These include match-fixing and illegal betting, child trafficking, child labor, sexual abuse, and corruption (e.g. Brackenridge, 2006; Donnelly & Petherick, 2006; Forster & Pope, 2004; Giulianotti, 2006; Hong, 2006; Lenskyi, 2006; McNamee & Fleming, 2007; Morgan, 2006; Oxford Research A/S, 2010; Arnaut, 2006; UNICEF, 2010).

In addition to these abusive and criminal actions, other behaviors in sport have also been analyzed and described as inappropriate and poor practice, such as athletes cheating and doping, over-aggressive and intolerant trainers, and coaches and parents who place exaggerated pressure on young athletes for their own egocentric reasons (e.g. Parry, 2004; Roberts, 2004; Vanden Auweele, 2004).

Finally, there is an ever more glaring contrast reported between the enthusiasms and joys that mega sport events generate and the frequent reports of negative side-effects for the local population (see Taks, this volume).

There appears to be an amalgam of disturbing behaviors equal to the amalgam of standards, rules, ethical precepts and human and civil rights. It is this author's opinion, however, that the continuum of aberrant behaviors, ranging from inappropriate to criminal, may be symptoms of the same common grounds. Battling these common grounds may need more difficult, long-term strategies than to challenge each single problematic behavior with ad-hoc solutions; however, it may lead to a wider range of strategies that provide more effective solutions.

We will first identify some common grounds for behaviors that do not feel right. To substantiate this we will refer to research in sport economy, sociology, psychology, and ethics. We will then suggest some elements that target these aberrant behaviors' basic common grounds.

Common grounds of reported aberrant behaviors

Gradually and implicitly, some developments in society and the values which they externalize have coincided with some intrinsic characteristics of sport. The systemic and complex links of these societal developments with inherent sport factors, described already in the 1980s (Eitzen, 1988; Seifart, 1984), have acquired a self-evident central place in sports practice, and influence to a great extent the moral atmosphere and subsequently the moral behavior of all stakeholders in current sport (McNamee, 2008).

Sport-relevant developments in society

- The increasing importance of commercialization, sponsorship, marketing, merchandising, and the related mediatizing of society has resulted in an increasing commodification of sport.
- The globalization of the world has resulted in the development of Global Sports Organizations (GSOs) such as the IOC, FIFA, and IAAF, that have to manage a surplus of power and money.

Sport-intrinsic factors as susceptible receptors of these societal developments

- The basic egocentrism in sport.
- The possibility to acquire power and esteem via sport.
- The passion to explore one's own limits according to the adage "citius, altius, fortius" (faster, higher, stronger) and the pressure to win, whether coming from inside or outside the athlete.

The marriage of these societal and sport-intrinsic factors is not in principle in contradiction with sports' potential to unlock positive values. We certainly do not argue that this partnership automatically leads to aberrations. However, it turns out that it easily causes conflicts of interests and ethical dilemmas, and because of maladjusted procedures, structures and attitudes, the positive values usually end up on the losing side (Maesschalck & Vanden Auweele, 2010).

Commodification and globalization of sport as a challenge/ threat to its integrity

Over a few decades many sports organizations are said to have turned progressively from purely sport-oriented into commerce-oriented companies. Sport has become a commodity (Walsh & Giulianotti, 2001). According to an EU working group

(Arnaut, 2006) there is a danger that this overly commercial approach to sports will end up compromising important sporting values and undermining the social function of sport. Considering the power and impact of the GSOs (IOC, FIFA, IAAF, etc.) and elite clubs (AC Milan, Manchester United, etc.) serving as a model for the lower levels, one may assume that the same attitudes, orientations, and atmosphere filter through to other sport organizations and down to the grass-roots.

Without being exhaustive, we will elaborate some challenges to the integrity of sport linked to the globalization and the increased importance of commerce.

Competitive imbalance

The fact that sports organizations can have a far greater reach in a globalized world has resulted in a growing "asymmetrical" interdependence between sports organizations and the clubs within each sport organization. GSOs and elite clubs organize themselves in such a way that it becomes more and more difficult to be challenged by national sport bodies, by less professional clubs, and clubs with a more restricted market. This creates competitive imbalance and tension between sport in Western, emerging, and developing countries, between popular and less popular sports and between elite and less professional sport clubs. Investment in youth sport and talent development has become less important for them because they can buy the best players on the market (Arnaut, 2006).

Abuse and exploitation of children, i.e. child trafficking and child labor

Talent scouts and agents are recruiting young players in Africa and South America for the wealthy soccer clubs in Western Europe. Many of these children don't make it and the International Office of Migration reports that many of these children are abandoned and live in the streets and some are sexually exploited. In the sporting goods industry (e.g. sport shoes and clothing) the relocation of manufacturing jobs to developing countries had, as a side-effect, an increase in child labor due to extreme poverty (Donnelly & Petherick, 2006).

Gambling and match-fixing

Where revenues once were the means to sporting ends, it is now sport that is the means not only to financial success for the sports organizations, the media and the sponsors, but also to easy money for (legal and illegal) gamblers and Mafiosi (Forster & Pope, 2004; Oxford Research A/S, 2010).

Questionable management of the accumulation of a surplus of power and money

Because sport organizations are more frequently forced to combine sport regulatory and commercial functions, conflicts of interest between their actions and decisions have become all the more likely. This is a breeding ground for questionable management and corruption. GSOs have found themselves increasingly involved in off-field issues such as commercial disputes, legal controversies, and human rights violations (Arnaut, 2006).

The management of sports organizations, and in particular the GSOs, often appears at odds both with the behavior that they impose upon countries, member organizations, and individual athletes, and also with their self-prescribed positive role in global society as a means to preserve peace and human dignity. These GSOs secure substantial revenues from organizing mega sport events and take advantage of the bidding countries' eagerness to organize, playing nations against each other in order to maximize their profits (Forster & Pope, 2004; Kesenne, 2005; Taks, this volume).

The pressure of sponsors and media as a threat/challenge to sports' integrity

The fact that some sports (soccer, tennis, Formula 1, etc.) are global favorites with enormous consumer demand stimulates both sponsors and media to intensive bidding processes and to offering grandiose sums of money for rights.

Sponsors want maximum exposure and the media are dependent on ratings and viewing figures on which their financial success depends. They put pressure on nations, GSOs, clubs, trainers, parents, medical staff, etc. This may result in exaggerated nationalism and patriotism (e.g. Hong, 2006), in forcing too strict marketing and commercial favors at the disadvantage of local businesses, in interference with preparation for competitions, in the shortening of the recovery period after an injury, and in the condoning or trivializing of manifest emotional and physical abuses (Brackenridge, 2006; Coakley, 1998; Donnelly & Petherick, 2006; Forster & Pope, 2004; Morgan, 2006; Taks, this volume).

The conditioning of athletes' behavior

Commerce influences the value the athletes put on their sporting practice, their motivation, their objectives, and the way they use their bodies. Their bodies are considered to be instruments which must be optimized physically and mentally, preferably by legal means (nutritive supplements, mental training, etc.) but if necessary with illegal means (doping, etc.). The athletes' behavior has been shaped (conditioned) progressively toward the expectations of those who pay them, expectations regarding risk and substance-taking, pain tolerance and the expression of emotions (Bredemeier & Shields, 1986; McNamee, 2008; Roberts, 2004).

Sport-intrinsic factors as susceptible receptors of the commodification and globalization of sport

Many of the problems of modern sports can be traced to the economic level. However, these economic factors would not have had such an impact if they had not matched receptive intrinsic sport factors.

Egocentrism in sport

It is inherent to sports to be centered on oneself, to devote oneself to the team's interests in order to beat the opponent. However, egocentrism in sport isn't free-wheeling individualism. It is only legitimate insofar as it is displayed within a framework and strict rules which are agreed upon. These include spatial and temporal borders. During the game they guarantee the conditions for fairness; they protect against injuries and specify appropriate sanctions for breaking the rules. After the game all players, winners and losers, return to normal life.

Problems only arise when these limits are crossed. This is the case when specific game strategies and tactics are used without those restrictions or outside the context of play, i.e. outside the playground between fans or managers of competing clubs. To control or at least to reduce the uncertainty of competition and the related uncertainty of their income, athletes, trainers, and managers are prepared to use game tactics outside the game context (De Wachter, 1980; McNamee, 2008).

Ethical implications of the acquisition of power, honor, prestige, and self-esteem through sport

Next to the sponsors and media, other actors also have an interest in good sport results, and in organizing mega sport events, although for reasons beyond monetary gain.

Politicians know that sports attract the masses. Politicians cannot afford to neglect the basic needs and aspirations of their citizens, and as a result they invest considerably in sport. The expected return on investment is national pride and prestige (Hong, 2006). The seamy side is that as far as mega events are concerned, some nations are prepared to make far-reaching sacrifices in order to organize mega events. They are prepared to engage in private agreements (concealed bribes?) with the GSOs. They are also willing to sacrifice (displace) domestic financial responsibilities (education, medical services, transportation, etc.) and some human rights (e.g. forced relocation) in their country (Cornelissen & Swart, 2006; Mivelaz & Cahn, 2007; Pillay, Tomlinson, & Bass, 2009; Taks, this volume). Another constraint or threat to the integrity of sport is that in some nations the striving for nation-building turns into a passion of extreme patriotism, showing its power to neighboring countries via its number of medals (Hong, 2006).

Fans and supporters as sports consumers don't care about abuses, they want to be entertained; they not only encourage, they cheer, condemn, call names, demand the removal of players, trainers, referees, and managers (Dixon, 2007).

The passion of the athlete to explore his physical (citius, altius, fortius) and mental limits (resilience, toughness) runs parallel with the scientist's passion to explore and test the technological and scientific frontiers (Allison, 2005; Tamburrini, 2005). The pursuit of progress, improvement, and records has always been the driving force behind the search for legal as well as illegal advantages in sport. Technology and science try to improve the equipment, outfit, gear (bicycle, pole, swimming suit, etc.), as well as the body of the athlete (nutrition, drugs, pressure cabins, genetic technology, etc.). Though these innovations have undeniably resulted in some positive advancement, there are drawbacks. For some scientists, sport is an ideal testing ground and athletes are receptive subjects to test experimental devices and products (Tamburrini, 2005; see Part IV of this book).

What should be the leading principles of an integrity policy in sport?

The aim of this chapter is to move beyond complaints about the moral deficit of sports and to make some suggestions that offer a way out of the problems.

In response to the negative effects of globalization and commodification of sport, a redefined and ethically justified relationship between the sport sector and commercialization, media, and sponsors is needed to ensure that private aspirations no longer take precedence over common public ones (Morgan, 2006), and that the asymmetrical interdependences in sports are corrected (Arnaut, 2006). In our view, such a response could be realized via a *modern integrity management framework* that thoughtfully balances rules-based and values-based approaches, preventing serious integrity violations on the one hand, and stimulating understanding, commitment, and capacity for ethical decision-making on the other (Maesschalck & Vanden Auweele, 2010, 2013).

Some key concepts that are relevant in an integrity management framework are: *fairness, corporate social responsibility* (CSR) and *good governance*. Being aware of the Northern origin of these concepts and their related political discourses, movements, and actions, we must certainly adapt them to cultural differences and the specifics of the sport context (Giulianotti, 2006). In this regard, McNamee and Fleming (2007) have already done some pioneering work by including these key concepts in their theorized and conceptually informed method of an ethics audit in sports organizations. In other chapters in this book concrete examples of these three concepts are elaborated upon.

Fairness in integrity management should exclude exploitation of children and be conceived as a partnership based on dialogue, transparency, and respect that seeks greater equity and re-distribution of revenues, and preserves competitive balance, encourages player education and training, and fosters ties of sporting and financial solidarity.

CSR in sport should reinforce the public support for and interest in the organizations' decision-making, i.e. by assuming responsibility for the impact of its activities not only on its stakeholders, but also on the social context in which they operate; by promoting community growth and development; and by the elimination of practices that harm the public sphere.

Good governance should require that the relevant sports governing bodies *continuously* examine their own structures to ensure they are sufficiently representative and democratic and that their powers are not exercised in an unreasonable, discriminatory or arbitrary manner.

Conclusion

We acknowledge that, despite its low moral status, sports possess important features that have the potential to encourage social, moral, and political values crucial to a democratic polity. It is this *potential* that makes sports matter morally. There is no doubt whatsoever about the limits being overstepped when sexual abuse or illegal trafficking of children are concerned, when matches are fixed, or when drugs are sold in an unrestrained and uncontrolled manner. However, we also acknowledge that all actors in today's sport are challenged by difficult dilemmas and choices; that the behaviors described as poor practices may be related to intrinsic sport values, and that it isn't always clear where the lines have to be drawn or whether the limits are just strained or overstepped.

Our basic assumption is that the whole continuum of aberrant behavior, ranging from the inappropriate to the criminal, are symptoms of the same causes, which we have identified as an unhealthy match between the commodification and globalization of modern sport and an exaggerated egocentrism, an unrestrained passion to excel and to win at all costs, and an obsessive striving for power and prestige of the various stakeholders.

As a way out of the problems we have suggested developing an Integrity Management Policy including good governance, fairness, and CSR to defend sports' basic features against any attempt to weaken them, similar to the strategies that have been developed in the trade and the environmental protection sector. A policy including these themes involves breaking with dominant tendencies and must eventually lead to a New Sports Model.

However, we are realistic enough to grasp that the implementation of a New Sports Model will depend on "a pressure of necessity," i.e. a financial crisis with bankruptcies of high-profile clubs, the accumulation of incidents and scandals, and a related common outrage in our societies, going together with a worldwide pressing need to recognize sport as a right and to use sport for health and developmental purposes.

Note

1 This chapter draws on Vanden Auweele (2010).

References

Allison, L. (2005). Citius, altius, fortius ad absurdum: Biology, performance and sportsmanship in the 21st century. In C. Tamburrini & T. Tännsjö (Eds.), *Genetic technology and sport* (pp.149–157). London: Routledge.

Arnaut, J.L. (2006). *Independent sport review: final report October 2006 (UK presidency of the EU, 2005)*. Retrieved January 20, 2007 from www.independentsportreview.com.

Biddle, S. (2006). Defining and measuring indicators of psycho-social well-being in youth sport and physical activity. In Y. Vanden Auweele, C. Malcolm, & B. Meulders (Eds.), *Sport and development* (pp. 163–184). Tielt (Belgium): LannooCampus.

Brackenridge, C. (2006). Women and children first? Child abuse and child protection in sport. In R. Giulianotti & D. McArdle (Eds.), *Sport, civil liberties and human rights* (pp. 30–45). London: Routledge.

Bredemeier, B.J., & Shields, D.L. (1986). Athletic aggression: An issue of contextual morality. *Sociology of Sport Journal, 3* (1), 15–28.

Coakley, J.J. (1998). *Sport in society: Issues and controversies.* New York: McGraw Hill.

Cornelissen, S., & Swart, K. (2006). The 2010 Football World Cup as a political construct: The challenge of making good on an African promise. *Sociological Review, 54* (2), 108–123.

De Wachter, F. (1980). Is sport een vredesfactor? (Is sport a peace factor?). *Hermes, 14,* 5–20.

Dixon, N. (2007). The ethics of supporting sport teams. In W. Morgan (Ed.), *Ethics in sport* (pp. 441–449). Champaign, IL: Human Kinetics.

Donnelly, P., & Petherick, L. (2006). Worker's playtime? Child labor at the extremes of the sporting spectrum. In R. Giulianotti & D. McArdle (Eds.), *Sport, civil liberties and human rights* (pp. 9–29). London: Routledge.

Eitzen, D.S. (1988). Ethical problems in American sport. *Journal of Sport and Social Issues, 12* (1), 17–20.

Forster, J. & Pope, K. (2004). *The political economy of global sporting organizations.* London: Routledge.

Giulianotti, R. (2006). Human rights, globalization and sentimental education: The case of sport. In R. Giulianotti & D. McArdle (Eds.), *Sport, civil liberties and human rights* (pp. 63–77). London: Routledge.

Hong, F. (2006). Innocence lost: Child athletes in China. In R. Giulianotti & D. McArdle (Eds.), *Sport, civil liberties and human rights* (pp. 46–62). London: Routledge.

Kesenne, S. (2005). Do we need an economic impact study or a cost–benefit analysis of a sport event? *European Sport Management Quarterly, 5* (2), 133–142.

Lenskyj, H.J. (2006). The Olympic industry and civil liberties: The threat to free speech and freedom of assembly. In R. Giulianotti & D. McArdle (Eds.), *Sport, civil liberties and human rights* (pp. 78–92). London: Routledge.

Maesschalck, J. & Vanden Auweele, Y. (2010). Integrity management in sport. *Journal of Community and Health Sciences, 5* (1), 1–9.

Maesschalck, J. & Vanden Auweele, Y. (2013). Managing ethics in youth sport: An application of the integrity management framework. In S. Harvey & R.L. Light (Eds.), *Ethics in youth sport: Policy and pedagogical applications* (pp. 9–24). London: Routledge.

McNamee, M. (2008). *Sports, virtues and vices.* London: Routledge.

McNamee, M. & Fleming, S. (2007). Ethics audits and corporate governance: The case of public sector sports organizations. *Journal of Business Ethics, 73* (4), 425–437.

Mivelaz, N. & Cahn, C. (Eds.) (2007). *Fair play for housing rights: Mega-events, Olympic Games and housing rights opportunities for the Olympic movement and others.* Geneva (Switzerland): Centre on Housing Rights and Evictions (COHRE).

Morgan, W.J. (2006). *Why sports morally matters.* London: Routledge.

Oxford Research A/S (2010). *Examination of threats to the integrity of sports.* EurActiv. Retrieved May 3, 2010 from www.euractiv.com.

Parry, J. (2004). Children in sport: Ethical issues. In Y. Vanden Auweele (Ed.), *Ethics in youth sport* (pp. 103–116). Leuven: LannooCampus.

Pillay, U., Tomlinson, R., & Bass, O. (Eds.) (2009). *Development and dreams: The urban legacy of the 2010 Football World Cup.* Cape Town: HSRC Press.

Roberts, G. (2004). Cheating in sport: Why do we do it? What can we do about it? In Y. Vanden Auweele (Ed.), *Ethics in youth sport* (pp. 77–90). Leuven: LannooCampus.

Seifart, H. (1984). Sport and economy: The commercialization of Olympic sport by the media. *International Review for the Sociology of Sport, 19,* 305–316.

Tamburrini, C. (2005). *Genetic technology and sport-ethical questions,* London: Routledge.

UNICEF (2010). *Protecting children from violence in sport: A review with a focus on industrialized countries.* Florence (Italy): UNICEF Innocenti Research Centre.

Vanden Auweele, Y. (Ed.) (2004). *Ethics in youth sport.* Leuven: LannooCampus.

Vanden Auweele, Y. (2010). Challenging modern sports' moral deficit: Towards fair trade, corporate social responsibility and good governance in sport. *Journal of Community and Health Sciences, 5* (2), 45–53.

Walsh, A.J. & Giulianotti, R. (2001). This sporting mammon: A normative critique of the commodification of sport. *Journal of the Philosophy of Sport, 28* (1), 53–77.

3 Olympism for the twenty-first century

Jim Parry

Olympism

For most people, I suppose, the word "Olympic" will conjure up images of the Olympic Games, either ancient or modern. The focus of their interest will be a two-week festival of sport held once every four years between elite athletes representing their countries or city-states in inter-communal competition.

Fewer, however, will have heard of "Olympism," the philosophy developed by the founder of the modern Olympic Movement, Baron Pierre de Coubertin, a French aristocrat who had been much influenced by the British Public School tradition of sport in education. This philosophy has as its focus of interest not just the elite athlete, but everyone; not just a short truce period, but the whole of life; not just competition and winning, but also the values of participation and cooperation; not just sport as an activity, but also as a formative and developmental influence contributing to desirable characteristics of individual personality and social life.

Olympism: a universal social philosophy

Olympism is a social philosophy which emphasizes the role of sport in world development, international understanding, peaceful co-existence, and social and moral education. De Coubertin understood, toward the end of the nineteenth century, that sport was about to become a major growth point in popular culture, and that, as physical activity, it was apparently universalizable, providing a means of contact and communication across cultures.

A universal philosophy by definition sees itself as relevant to everyone, regardless of nation, race, gender, social class, religion, or ideology, and so the Olympic Movement has worked for a coherent universal representation of itself, a concept of Olympism which identifies a range of values to which each nation can sincerely commit itself while at the same time finding for the general idea a form of expression which is unique to itself, generated by its own culture, location, history, tradition, and projected future.

De Coubertin, being a product of late nineteenth-century liberalism, emphasized the values of equality, fairness, justice, respect for persons, rationality and understanding, autonomy, and excellence (De Coubertin, 1934). These are values which span nearly 3,000 years of Olympic history, although some of them may be differently interpreted at different times. They are, basically, the main values of liberal humanism – or perhaps we should say simply humanism, since socialist societies have found little difficulty in including Olympic ideals into their overall ideological stance toward sport.

The contemporary task for the Olympic Movement is to further this project: *to try to see more clearly what its Games (and sport in wider society) might come to mean.* This task will be both at the level of ideas and of action. If the practice of sport is to be pursued and developed according to Olympic values, the theory must strive for a conception of Olympism which will support that practice. The ideal should seek both to sustain sports practice and to lead sport toward a vision of Olympism which will help to deal with the challenges that are bound to emerge.

A philosophical anthropology of Olympism

Based on its heritage and traditions, each society (and each ideology) has a political and philosophical anthropology – an idealized conception of the kind of person that that society (or ideology) values and tries to produce and reproduce through its formal and informal institutions. Olympism is such a "philosophical anthropology," including a theory of physical education (Parry, 1998a, 1998b). The Olympic Idea translates into a few simple phrases which capture the essence of what an ideal human being ought to be and to aspire to. It promotes the ideals of:

- individual all-round harmonious human development;
- excellence and achievement;
- effort in competitive sporting activity;
- conditions of mutual respect, fairness, justice, and equality;
- view to creating lasting personal human relationships of friendship;
- international relationships of peace, toleration, and understanding; and
- cultural alliances with the arts.

Sport and universalism

However, Olympism achieves its ends through the medium of sport, and so it cannot escape the requirement to provide an account of sport which reveals both its nature and its ethical potential. Let me briefly suggest a set of criteria which might begin to indicate the fundamentally ethical nature of sport:

- *human* (while animals may play, sport is uniquely *human*);
- *physical* (*effort* is required);

- *skill* (effort is not enough, we have to *develop capacities*);
- *contest* (*contract to contest, competition*, and *excellence*);
- *rule-governed* (*obligation* to abide by the rules, *fair play, equality*, and *justice*);
- *institutionalized* (*lawful authority*);
- *shared values and commitments* (*due respect* is owed to opponents as co-facilitators).

It is difficult even to state the characteristics of sport without relying on terms that carry ethical import, and such meanings must apply across the world of sports participation. Without agreement on rule-adherence, the authority of the referee and the central shared values of the activity, there could be no sport. The first task of an International Federation is to clarify rules and harmonize understandings so as to facilitate the universal practice of its sport.

Olympism: immutable values?

The principles of Olympism, to be universal, must be unchanging, and yet they must apparently be everywhere different. They must not change over time, but at all times we see rule changes reflecting social changes. How are these paradoxes to be resolved?

Such differences are inevitable, over time and space. Social ideas, or ideas inscribed in social practices, depend upon a specific social order or a particular set of social relationships for their full meaning to be exemplified. This seems to suggest that such meanings are culturally relative and that, therefore, there could be no such thing as a universal idea of Olympism. But are we doomed to relativism?

Rawls' (1993) distinction between concepts and conceptions is useful here. The *concept* of Olympism, being an abstraction, will be at a high level of generality, although this does not mean it will be unclear. What it means is that the general ideas which comprise its meaning will admit of possibly contesting interpretations. Thus, naturally, the concept of Olympism will find different expressions in time and place, history and geography – just as the concepts of democracy, art, and religion do. There will be differing *conceptions* of Olympism, which will interpret the general concept in such a way as to bring it to real life in a particular context.

Taken together, the promotion of these values will be seen to be the educative task, and sport will be seen as a means. Each one of these values, being articulated at a high level of generality, will admit of a wide range of interpretation. But they nevertheless provide a framework which can be agreed upon by social groups with very differing commitments. This raises the questions of the relationships between such differing cultural formations, and of our own attitudes toward cultural difference. One way of addressing these questions is via a consideration of the very important notion of multiculturalism.

Liberalism and multiculturalism

In an earlier paper (Parry, 2006) I looked at the contemporary importance for liberalism of the idea of multiculturalism. The liberal state sees itself as deliberately not choosing any particular conception of the Good Life for its citizens to follow. Rather, it sees itself as neutral between the alternative conceptions of the Good to be found in most modern liberal democracies. In this it sharply distinguishes itself from "illiberal" states, which embody and enforce one view of the Good Life. Rather than promoting one culture over another, it sees itself as multicultural. Citizens can choose their own version of the Good and pursue their own aims and values, independently of the state. In such a state, attention to multicultural ideals such as recognition, respect, and equal status for all cultures will become increasingly important.

Multiculturalism is a fact nowadays for most Western societies, and it requires a political society to recognize the equal standing of all stable and viable communities existing in a society. It outlaws discrimination against groups and individuals on the grounds of ethnicity, race, nationality, religion, class, gender, or sexual preference. However, some of these communities may be authoritarian, illiberal, and oppressive – so does "multiculturalism" apply equally to all communities, or only to liberal ones?

Rawls (1993) attempts to draw guidelines for a Law of Peoples acceptable to members of both liberal and illiberal cultures, by introducing the notion of "reasonable societies." These societies, though illiberal, follow certain core principles:

- peace (pursuing their ends through diplomacy and trade);
- common good (a conception of justice);
- consultation (a reasonable hierarchy thereof);
- responsibility (citizens recognize their obligations and play a part in social life);
- freedom (some freedom of conscience/thought).

"Reasonable societies," even illiberal ones, could agree to a Law of Peoples based on such a "thin liberalism" as this, and this could be seen very positively: "as offering learning experiences both ways, as each culture learns from the other." But multiculturalism has its limits, and those limits are drawn by the universalistic claims of thin liberalism, supported by some form of Human Rights theory. As Hollis says (1999, 42), liberal societies

> must fight for at least a minimalist, procedural thesis about freedom, justice, equality and individual rights.

In the short term, in the interests of peace and development (or of political or economic gain), such basic moral commitments may be temporarily diluted or shelved, but they are the inalienable bedrock of the possibility of a global multiculturalism. There are limits to toleration. Liberal democracy is (still) an exclusionary system; some cultures are beyond the pale.

Why should we be multiculturalists? Because we want to honor and respect the widest variety of human culture. Why? Because it enriches us all. We value diversity because every culture expresses a form of human life and helps us to appreciate the full range of difference and choice. It is the same reason that we value knowledge of the history of human social evolution: To help us to understand more fully our identity as humans.

But this means that we have to tolerate difference, and we have to accept that sometimes other people's views will hold sway over our own. The liberal citizen permits democracy – people can see the reason for (and therefore accept) decisions even if they do not agree with them. Such a "rational pluralism" is characteristic of liberalism, but "unreasonable" doctrines will not accept such pluralism. Liberals see the problem as resting with those who object to the valuing of anything other than their own culture.

So what do we do? Internally, we seek to liberalize those cultures, at least to some small extent, e.g., to enforce basic liberal rights within the liberal states. So, in minority cultures, we permit no slaves, no mutilation, no forced marriage, no child prostitution, etc., or we permit individuals to escape from those circumstances if they want to; to deny others the right to "harness" individuals to their ends. Externally, we pursue foreign policies that seek to contain hostile illiberal societies in ways that minimize their threat to liberal ones.

Is universalism ethnocentric?

Critics of the liberal project put forward the objection that the idea of liberal democracy is a historical product, a kind of Western ethnocentrism, a kind of post-colonial imperialism, foisting local Western values on the rest of the world. The kind of "universalism" to which both liberalism and Olympism pretend is just an ethnocentric smokescreen. There is no basis for such a universalism of values, because all values arise within cultures, and therefore do not apply across cultural boundaries – they are culturally relative.

We may call this thesis *"the Anthropologist's Heresy"*: *liberalism for the liberals! cannibalism for the cannibals!* (Lukes, 2002; Hollis, 1999, 36). It holds that all cultures are equally valid because they can only be judged on their own *internal* terms, norms, and principles, which apply only to themselves.

Objections to relativism

1 This thesis cannot account for moral criticism across cultures, for how can we criticize unjust practices if that is all they are – the practices of others?
2 Is relativism itself a kind of concealed ethnocentrism? Is it true that to respect other cultures is to abstain from criticizing them? Or is this a kind of disrespect, failing to apply to others (denying to others) the standards of justification and argument we apply to ourselves?

3   Relativism is self-refuting. It is a theory that claims that there are no cross-cultural truths. Well, then: does relativism apply to itself? If so, relativism is not true (because it says that there are no cross-cultural truths; so relativism is just a cultural practice of anthropologists, with no claim to truth, and therefore nothing to say to outsiders like me). So: even if relativism could be true, it would make itself false. But relativism can't be "true" since it claims that there is no such thing as "truth."

4   The concept of *culture* is a tricky one here, too. Relativism, says Lukes (2002), trades on "poor man's sociology," according to which cultures are homogeneous, coherent wholes. But cultures are not "windowless boxes." Conflicts arise within cultures as well as between them, but relativism gives us no way of making progress.

5   Finally, adherence to the Anthropologist's Heresy means a rejection of all those organizations that pretend to universalist values, including the United Nations, the World Health Organization, and Amnesty International. It means that there is no such thing as human rights, an idea which, of course, is rooted in notions of our universally common humanity.

So Lukes (2002) and Hollis (1999) dismiss relativism as a sensible response to diversity. Of course, there is considerable diversity, and the job of the anthropologist is to seek it out and describe it for us. But the anthropologist exceeds his occupational remit when he seeks to convert his experiences into an ethical theory. The importance of such research cannot be overestimated. It continually reminds us that we should recognize the value of modesty or restraint in moral judgment and criticism, and avoid the dangers of abstract moralizing. But anthropological experience is not a sufficient basis for ethical theory. The facts of diversity require theoretical explanation – but the facts alone do not explain it.

Liberal democracy: a historical product?

So I must ask myself: do I accept liberalism just because it's the view of my tribe? I don't think so, because any political view requires a justification, and we offer arguments for and against particular systems.

"Liberal democracy is a historical product." Well, it is true that the benefits of liberal societies flow from a series of European inventions:

- the constitution of the individual as a legal subject;
- skepticism as to the truth;
- self-criticism;
- separation of Church and politics (and the emergence of the secular state);
- separation of Church and knowledge (and the development of the scientific worldview).

However, the fact that liberalism happened first in the West does not bestow a greater virtue upon us. Maybe it just "happened" here, as it were, contingently.

In Europe, historically, people just became exhausted from religious wars, and pluralism emerged as a pragmatic way of carrying on with life without the debilitating and destructive background of constant war. And look how long and painful was this development in the West, through religious and social persecution (there were witchcraft trials all over Europe; Catholics in England were still denied political rights in the mid-nineteenth century, women until after World War I, African-Americans until after World War II, etc.). It took hundreds of years of development, and we are still not satisfied with our political systems. It is a long and painful struggle to achieve stability with freedom and development, and maybe the preconditions do not yet exist everywhere.

"Liberal democracy is a historical product." This makes it sound as though there is no justificatory argument for liberalism, although a very important element of liberal thinking, part of the liberal project, is the claim that liberalism expresses a kind of "truth" about human beings and the human condition; that it is the best mode of social organization for the benefit of all citizens of the world. The arguments we advance for liberalism claim that it is the system within which individuals can find maximal freedom for self-development and maximal choice of lifestyle, and through which communities can progress along their own chosen path of development in peace and fruitful concord with other communities. It is a salient fact that no liberal democracy has ever declared war on another.

But we have to remain self-aware and self-critical. Just because some community claims the status of a liberal democracy does not automatically mean that they are the good guys. So we hope to see critical liberal democracies, striving toward ideals expressed in terms of human rights and peaceful co-existence. Since they are human creations, they will be imperfect and they will make mistakes. It is often said that democracy is not a very good system of government – it is inefficient, cumbersome, ridden with untidy and unsatisfactory compromises, and with many other faults and disadvantages – but every other system of government thought up by mankind is worse!

Olympism again

Above, I outlined the distinction between concepts and conceptions, and argued that the concept of Olympism will be at a high level of generality. In fact, it sets out a range of "thin" liberal values, allied to the thin values underlying the concept of sport. However, the values which comprise its meaning will admit of contesting interpretations, exhibiting a range of "thick" values as the concept of Olympism finds different expressions in time and place, history and geography.

In terms of promoting its aims of international understanding and multiculturalism, it is most important that the Olympic Movement continues to work for a coherent universal representation of itself, a concept of Olympism to which each nation can sincerely commit itself while at the same time finding for the general idea a form of expression (a conception) which is unique to itself, generated by its own culture, location, history, tradition, and projected future.

I believe that providing multicultural education in and for modern democracies is a new and urgent task, and one that must be made to work if we are to secure a workable political heritage for future generations. In the present global political context, this means promoting international understanding and mutual respect; and a commitment to the peaceful resolution of conflict.

In the case of Olympism, I think that the "thin" values underpinning the rule structures of sport, acceptance of which by all participants is a pre-condition of the continuing existence of sporting competition, support at the educational and cultural levels such political efforts. Children who are brought into sporting practices, and who are aware of international competitions such as the Olympic Games and the World Cup, are thereby becoming aware of the possibilities of international cooperation, mutual respect, and mutual valuing.

Nowadays the very idea of a "closed society" is under threat everywhere; the people are no longer reliant on restricted and controlled forms of information. The internet, satellite television, and global forms of communication are all contributing to a democratization of information, and the extensive migration of people across continents is producing a new cosmopolitanism.

It will require increasingly high levels of dogmatism, authoritarianism, isolationism, and extremism to sustain closed, exclusivist societies. Their life is limited. This, at any rate, has to be our hope, and the hope of any kind of peaceful internationalism based on the ideas of individual freedom and human rights.

References

De Coubertin, P. (1934). Forty years of Olympism. In Carl-Diem-Institut (1966). *The Olympic Idea: Pierre de Coubertin – discourses and essays* (pp. 126–130). Stuttgart: Olympischer Sportverlag.

Hollis, M. (1999). Is universalism ethnocentric? In C. Joppke & S. Lukes (Eds.), *Multicultural questions* (pp. 27–43). Oxford: Oxford University Press.

Lukes, S. (2002). *Liberals and cannibals*. London: Verso.

Parry, J. (1998a). Physical education as Olympic education. *European Physical Education Review, 4* (2), 153–167.

Parry, J. (1998b). The justification of physical education. In K. Green & K Hardman (Eds.), *Physical education: A reader* (pp. 36–68). Aachen: Meyer & Meyer.

Parry, J. (2006). Sport and Olympism: Universals and multiculturalism. *Journal of the Philosophy of Sport, 33*, 188–204.

Rawls, J. (1993). The law of peoples. In S. Shute & S. Hurley (Eds.), *On human rights* (pp. 41–82). New York: Basic Books.

4 The "fast track" as a future strategy for achieving gender equality and democracy in sport organizations

Jorid Hovden

Introduction

Nowadays sport organizations represent powerful symbolic institutions and thus central arenas in which dominant societal values, norms, and power structures are reflected, celebrated, and contested (e.g. Burstyn, 1999). How sport organizations frame gender therefore plays a crucial role for the advancement of gender equality in the society at large (e.g. Birell & Theberge, 1994; Hovden, 2000). Analyses of media sports narratives (e.g. Whannel, 2007) illustrate the direct or indirect ways in which gender is discussed, and mirrors dominant notions of gender as well as transgressions that reproduce, challenge, and blur dominant understandings.

Globally, the research on sport organization and gender (e.g. Bruce, Hovden, & Markula, 2010) documents how organizational practices are shaped by male dominance and accordingly a substantial democratic deficit regarding women. In other words, we face organizational cultures in which it is widely accepted that almost half of the population is excluded from leadership and management positions of their sports (Coakley & Pike, 2009). Feminist studies (e.g. Claringbould & Knoppers, 2008; Hovden, 2000) show how gender is an organizing principle in sport organizations and how access to influence and power are critical factors in becoming change agents of organizational sport practices.

From this point of departure this chapter will illustrate how gender equality as a future policy issue must be framed within so-called "fast track" discourses (Dahlerup & Freidenvall, 2005). These discourses define gender inequalities in sport organizations as an organizational power problem. Today, the most dominant gender political measures applied by sport organizations are embedded in "incremental" discourses (Adriaanse, 2013; Hovden, 2012), which most often define male dominance and women's democratic deficit as caused by a lack of competence and dedication among women as a gender category.

This chapter will argue for a future necessity of political strategies embedded in fast track discourses to ensure a future development toward advancing gender equality and democracy in sport. More concretely, I will discuss how gender quotas as a fast track measure can be seen as one of the most adequate and efficient strategies to challenge and change institutional gendered power structures (Borchorst & Dahlerup, 2003). When referring to sport organizations, I will mainly refer to voluntary and democratic sport organizations – organizations where gender equality and democracy are stated as central aim and values. For context, I will provide a brief background, describing some characteristics of the current gender structure of sport organization.

The gendering of power in sport organizations

During recent decades we can, in most countries, discern a substantial increase in women's possibilities to participate in sports (e.g. Adriaanse, 2013; Bruce *et al.*, 2010). For example, at the Olympic Games in London in 2012, for the first time in Olympic history, all sports were open for women (Pfister, 2013). On the other hand, in the top leading positions in sport organizations, women account for only 10–15 percent of the positions (e.g. Coakley & Pike, 2009; Bruce *et al.*, 2010). Globally, women are thus grossly underrepresented in the management of sport, including positions as top leaders, executive board members, and officers, as well as referees and coaches (Hartmann-Tews & Pfister, 2003; Pfister, 2013). Apart from some exceptions, this gender gap has not changed much during recent decades and thus is considered to be evident more of the status quo than progress (Hovden, 2010; Pfister, 2013).

In some countries, however, we find that the gender disparities in executive boards have been substantially lowered during recent years, and women possess up to 40 percent of the seats (International Working Group on Women and Sport, 2012). Looking behind these numbers, it is obvious that this progress is caused by use of gender quotas, often formed as legal rules, with a requirement of a minimum proportion of both sexes in all elected and appointed organizational boards and committees (e.g. Bruce *et al.*, 2010; Hartmann-Tews & Pfister, 2003). Among the top four are Norway (39.4 percent) and Sweden (32.1 percent), which have adopted gender quotas securing at least 33 per cent representation of each sex (Dahlerup & Freidenvall, 2008; Hovden, 2000). Thus gender quotas as a central "fast track" strategy indicate their potentials to undo democracy deficits by use of legal requirements. Quota regulations are, however, not a specific gender political measure, but an old democratic strategy used to balance political power among different population groups.

I will briefly describe and discuss the two main (ideal type) discourses mentioned – namely, the "incremental" and "fast track" discourses, and demonstrate how the fast track discourse can be seen as a necessary and adequate platform to fulfill future visions of gender balanced and democratic sport practices.

The future relevance of fast track versus incremental track discourses

The incremental and fast track discourses have quite similar aims regarding discrimination and underrepresentation of women in male-dominated institutions

(Dahlerup & Freidenvall, 2005). On the other hand, they differ substantially in their understanding of gender inequalities and male dominance as a political problem. This difference in framing has consequences for the solutions and strategies of adequate, reasonable and legitimate means to bring about targeted changes (Bacchi, 1999). I will provide a brief overview of some essential differences between incremental track discourses and fast track discourses. The proposal is based upon an ideal model type developed by Dahlerup & Freidenvall[1] (2005).

The two discursive tracks to equal gender representation illustrate two quite different future pictures on how to obtain gender equality and democracy in sport organizations. The incremental track justifies women's underrepresentation as caused by individual deficiencies in women. Women as a gender category are thus seen as lacking sufficient relevant competences to compete for positions with men on equal terms. The problem is, for example, identified as lack of experience, self-confidence, role models, mentors, etc. (Hovden, 2013). The incremental track is hence targeted toward individual support programs, suggesting that women simply need to acknowledge the level of competence and resources required by sport organizations. This understanding assumes that equality in competence based on a male standard is a prerequisite for equal share and fair

Table 4.1 Characteristics of the incremental versus the fast track discourse

	Incremental track	*Fast track*
Perceptions of the problem	• Gender equalization takes time, but will be achieved in due course as the organization develops (naturalized perception).	• Gender inequalities and lack of democracy are organizational (socially constructed) problems and must be framed as such. • Backlash is as possible as advancement.
Diagnosis	• Women lack resources and commitment to compete with men on equal terms. • Hard-coded prejudices limit women's opportunities.	• Informal and formal discrimination and processes of exclusion in sport organizations limit women's advancement
Policy aim	• More women.	• Gender balance. • Gender justice.
Strategy	• More active recruitment of women. • Increase women's commitment, resources, and capacity-building to fit the requirements of leading positions in sport organizations through measures like education, mentor programs and provisions programs.	• Implement active measures, such as quota provisions and structural reforms, which will "force" sport organizations to work actively to recruit women to leading positions. • Quotas seen as a compensation for structural organizational barriers.

Source: based on Dahlerup and Freidenvall's ideal type model (2005, 21).

treatment. Women acquire equal access to influence and power when they have obtained similar capacities as their male counterparts. This way of thinking includes an understanding of gender equality and democratization as a question of competence and time (Hovden, 2006).

Gender political measures and strategies implemented in sport organizations have mostly been underpinned by incremental track discourses (Hartmann-Tews & Pfister, 2003; Hovden, 2012). The policies have, for example, initiated projects for women and other types of gender-segregated interventions, in order to qualify more women for different types of influential organizational positions (e.g. Coakley & Pike, 2009; Hovden, 2012). Most of these projects indicate some progress for women, but after some years back-sliding is found as often as progress. Coakley and Pike (2009) have noted that the increasing status of women's sport has moved more men into management and coaching of women's sports.

The fast track discourse represents another identification of the problem. Lack of gender equality and democracy are identified as a power problem; a problem mostly related to male hegemony and dominance (Dahlerup & Freidenvall, 2005). The problem is therefore understood as an organizational and socially constructed problem, which only the sport organizations themselves can solve. The fast track discourse accentuates the organizational practices and processes that are shaped by informal and formal gender discrimination as well as mechanisms of gendered exclusion and marginalization. In this situation, legal quota provisions are seen as one the most adequate and efficient measures for change, because legal quota regulations are "forcing" organizations to actively give women a strong power base (Dahlerup & Freidenvall, 2008). Hence the fast track identification of the problem considers radical measures, such as quotas, as necessary measures to redistribute power and create gender-balanced power structures. Very seldom in history have power positions been redistributed voluntarily, and gender quotas are seen as a measure to enable change in hard-coded power structures and generate historical leaps in women's participation. Quota provisions prove to be most efficient when they have status as legal requirements (Dahlerup & Freidenvall, 2008).

As mentioned earlier, gender quotas as fast track measures are based on a different understanding of gender and gender inequalities than incremental track measures. While the incremental track understanding is based on the classic liberal notion of equality – equality of competence and competition – legal quota provisions are based on a radical notion, *equality of result* or *equality of outcome* (Dahlerup & Freidenvall, 2005; 2008). Because of the slow development of women's representation in most powerful societal institutions, the notion of equality of outcome has gained increasing political relevance and support. This is, for example, often the case among women in leading positions in sport organizations where quotas are adopted (e.g. Hovden, 2013). The diagnoses of the gendered political situation in male-dominated organizations reveal that new conceptualizations of equality are needed to fulfill the future visions of a gender-balanced power share (Dahlerup & Freidenvall, 2008). Equality of outcomes is thus the only equalizing principle that has redistribution of power and resources as its starting point (Hernes, 1976). However, the current power structures in sport organizations do not seem to be ready for more radical conceptualizations of equality. For example, none of the quota provisions adopted by sport organizations are provisions that regulate the distributions of the top positions on boards and committees, such as the presidency of sport clubs and sport federations. As a consequence, women still appear as spectacular exceptions in the most influential organizational power positions (Hovden, 2013).

Studies of implementation processes of gender policies in sport organizations (e.g. Adriaanse, 2013, Claringbould & Knoppers, 2008) indicate that these are both complex and contested, shaped by controversies, resistance, and power play. No route or political strategy represents a "quick fix," including the implementation of gender quotas (Hovden, 2012). Gender quotas are threatening the power and privileges of hegemonic organizational groups, and the implementation phase is thus most often shaped by strong resistance. In the following section I will shed light on a few prerequisites in the implementation process necessary to make quotas work.

Challenges to make gender quotas work

According to Dahlerup and Freidenvall (2005), some factors are important for a successful implementation of quota provisions. It is stated that passing quota provisions may just become a symbolic gesture if the specification of the system is not regulated according to institutional conditions and, further, if there are no sanctions for non-compliance.

Gender quotas, as they are currently practiced in sport organizations, do not require equality for men and women in decision-making roles, but aim to ensure that women and men represent at least a required minimum of 30 percent. This is, for example, the case in Norway and Sweden, the countries with the highest representation of women in political decision-making roles (Adriaanse, 2013). Additionally, the legal rules are formulated in a gender-neutral way. This ensures less resistance and a required minimum of men's representation. Male political allies have been a crucial prerequisite for approving gender quotas as well as ensuring efficient implementation processes (Hovden, 2000). Dahlerup and Freidenvall (2005) argue for the importance of 50:50 quotas, because this regulation is by nature gender neutral. A 50:50 structure will allow women and men to act as two separate categories and may contribute to less heated selection processes among the genders. Furthermore, studies of implementation processes (e.g. Borchorst Dahlerup, 2003; Dahlerup & Freidenvall, 2005) maintain that in the case of legal quotas, sanctions for non-compliance are crucial, assuming that the suggested sanctions are taken seriously. Studies of Norwegian sport organizations (e.g. Hovden, 2000) indicate that the sanctions for non-compliance were often not followed up by the electoral authorities and thus many of the boards of Norwegian sport federations do not fulfill the legal gender quota regulation. Regarding sport organizations, I will guess, based on the experiences of sanctions for non-compliance in the boards of Norwegian business organizations (Teigen & Wägnerud, 2009), that if financial sanctions were introduced and followed up, the adopted gender provisions would be fulfilled according to their intentions. More comparative studies are, however, needed to gain more knowledge about the efficacy of different types of sanctions (Dahlerup & Freidenvall, 2008). Also, further knowledge and assessments of the gender political effects of gender quota provisions in sport organizations seem to be crucial to make quotas work according to their objectives.

Fast track routes toward future feminist visions

The adoption of fast track measures to promote gender equality can, among other things, be interpreted as both a growing political recognition of the use of gender quotas, as well as an expression of impatience for advancing gender equality in sport organizations as a whole. Male and female quota advocates maintain that women cannot wait another 50 years to achieve a fair share of their power base in sport (Hovden, 2006; 2013). Today both the UN and EU recognize gender quotas as important institutional measures to open up systems of male-dominated and closed recruitment patterns, and give way to women (Dahlerup & Freidenvall, 2008; Teigen, 2011). The international adherence to gender quota regulations, particularly in political institutions, has become a significant marker of democracy, anti-discrimination, and justice. But can we expect a similar breakthrough for gender quotas in sport organizations in the future?

Sport organizations are today shaped by increasing commercialization and neoliberal mindsets. The latter seeks to turn back the clock on gender equality and democracy rather than the opposite (Coakley & Pike, 2009; Hovden, 2012). A crucial question, given these conditions, is whether "forced emancipation" or a "gender shock," such as the adoption of 50:50 quota provisions, can be seen as a realistic future vision. Is it possible for sport organizations characterized by a persistent male hegemony to expect a future breakthrough for fast track approaches, which will include a formidable reduction of male power and privileges? I will in my concluding remarks present some arguments that indicate favorable conditions for optimism and changes in the near future.

Fast track advocates in sport policy emphasize that quotas must be seen as compensation for the structural and cultural barriers that women are facing in sport (Hovden, 2006; 2013). Among these advocates are both women and men. And men, as the majority in organizational decision-making, are thus the most important group responsible for substantial future changes. My studies of Norwegian sport organizations (Hovden, 2000; 2006) indicate that most of the male advocates for gender quotas support either a political party that has adopted quotas, or are among the youngest male representatives in the decision-making bodies. These men emphasize how the use of gender quotas created more gender-balanced decision-making in sports politics, and further brought about changes in the political climate in favor of both men and women. Their views were, for example, that gender quota provisions, properly implemented, do obstruct male succession patterns, and thus are crucial in the forming of future sport policies. Because quotas "force" sport organizations to scrutinize and change their male-dominated gender profile, they were seen as necessary measures to make a difference. Most of the advocates supported the use of radical legal quota regulations, because they had experienced how such provisions had been the most efficient way to advance gender balance in Norwegian politics (Hovden, 2006). But why do such perceptions provide optimistic future visions for achieving more gender-equalized and democratic sport organizations?

Piketty's (2013) analyses of the development of Western democratic capitalistic societies state how the best countries to live in today are those characterized by the smallest social inequalities in the population. Welfare states like Norway and Sweden are among these, and they are also characterized by the world's smallest gender gap (Hausmann *et al.*, 2012). Nordic feminist studies (e.g. Bjørk Eydal and Rostgaard, 2014; Brandth and Kvande, 2014) indicate that men, especially younger men, support gender political measures like quotas, because they have experienced how these have been beneficial for their own life situation as well as contributing to substantial changes toward more gender-balanced social institutions. If sport mirrors society it is fair to expect that the group of men and women who acknowledge the benefits of more democratic, fair, and gender-balanced sport practices represents an organizational majority. My future feminist imaginations are therefore devoted to a future mobilization of men and women advocating fast track routes like quotas to fulfill our visions of democratic and gender-equalized sport organizations.

Notes

1 The presentation is a rewritten version of Dahlerup and Freidenvall's (2005, 29) version, which has the underrepresentation of women in politics as the point of departure. My rewriting comprises, among other things, an adaptation to my subject – gender policy in sport organizations.

References

Adriaanse, J. (2013). The role of men in advancing gender equality in sport governance. In G. Pfister and M.K. Sisjord (Eds.), *Gender and sport: Changes and challenges* (pp. 50–71). Münster: Waxmann.

Bacchi, C.L. (1999). *Women, policy and politics*. London: Sage.

Birell, S., & Theberge, N. (1994). Feminist resistance and transformations in sport. In M.D. Costa and S.R. Guthrie (Eds.), *Women and sport interdisciplinary perspectives*. Champaign, IL: Human Kinetics.

Bjørk Eydal, E. and Rostgaard, T. (2014). *Fatherhood in the Nordic welfare states*. Bristol: Polity Press.

Borchorst, A., & Dahlerup, D. (2003) *Likestillingspolitikk som diskurs og praksis* [Gender equality policy as discourse and practice]. Fredriksberg: Samfunnslitteratur.

Brandth, B. & Kvande, E. (2014). *Ferdrekvoten og den farsvennlige velferdsstaten* [The father quota and the father-friendly welfare state]. Oslo: Universitetsforlaget.

Bruce, T., Hovden, J., and Markula, P. (2010). *Sportswomen at the Olympics: A global content analyses of newspaper coverage*. Rotterdam/Boston/Tapei: Sense Publications.

Byrstyn, V. (1999). *The rites of men: Manhood, politics and the culture of sport*. Toronto: University of Toronto Press.

Claringbould, I., & Knoppers, A. (2008). Doing and undoing gender in sport governance. *Sex Roles*, *58*: 81–92.

Coakley, J., & Pike, E. (2009). *Sports in society: Issues and controversies*. London: McGraw Hill Education.

Dahlerup, D. & Freidenvall, L. (2005). Quotas as "fast track" to equal representation for women. *International Feminist Journal of Politics*, *7*: 26–48.

Dahlerup, D., & Freidenvall, L. (2008). *Kvotering* [Quotas]. Stockholm: Pocketbiblioteket nr 32.

Hartmenn-Tews, I., & Pfister, G. (2003). *Sport and women: Social issues in international perspective*. London: Routledge.

Hausmann, R., Tyson, L.D., & Zahidi, S. (2012). *The global gender gap report*. Geneva: The World Economic Forum.

Hernes, G. (1976). Om ulikhetens reproduksjon [About reproduction of inequalities], *Forskningens lys*. Oslo: Norges almennvitenskaplige forskningsråd.

Hovden, J. (2000). *Makt, motstand og ambivalens. Betydningar av kjønn i idretten*. [Power, resistance and ambivalence. Meanings of gender in sport]. Unpublished doctoral dissertation at University of Tromsö.

Hovden, J. (2006). The gender order as a policy issue in sport: A study of Norwegian sports organizations. *NORA (Nordic Journal of Women's Studies)*, *14*, 41–53.

Hovden, J. (2010). Female top leaders – prisoners of gender? The gendering of leadership discourses in Norwegian sports organizations. *International Journal of Sport Politics*, *2*, 198–203.

Hovden, J. (2012). Discourses and strategies for the inclusion of women in sport: The case of Norway. *Sport in Society*, *15*, 287–302.

Hovden, J. (2013). Women as agents of change in male dominated sports cultures. In G. Pfister & M.K. Sisjord (Eds.), *Gender and sport: Changes and challenges* (pp. 33–50). Münster: Waxmann.

International Working Group on Women and Sport (2012). *Sydney scoreboard*. Retrieved from www.sydneyscoreboard.com.

Pfister, G. (2013). Outsiders: Female coaches intruding upon a male domain? In G. Pfister & M.K. Sisjord (Eds.), *Gender and sport: Changes and challenges* (pp. 50–71). Münster: Waxmann.

Piketty, T. (2013). *Kapitalen i det 21århundre* [The capital of the 21st century]. Oslo: Cappelen Forlag.

Teigen, M. (2011). Kvoteringstradisjon og styringsekspensjon [Quotas traditions and management to expend it's operation]. *Tidsskrift for kjønnsforskning*, *35*, 84–102.

Teigen, M., & Wägnerud, L. (2009). Tracing gender equality: Elite perceptions of gender equality in Norway and Sweden. *Politics & Gender*, *5*, 21–44.

Whannel, G. (2007). Mediating masculinities: The production of media representations in sport. In C.C. Aitchison (Ed.), *Sport and gender identities* (pp.7–21). London: Routledge.

5 Shifting the focus from reducing emotional harm to optimizing growth

The role of athlete-centered coaching

Elaine Cook and Gretchen Kerr

Sport as innately good

Every year in Westernized countries, millions of parents enroll their children, usually at their own personal cost, in organized, outside-of-school sport programs. Organized sport programs have such popularity because of a set of beliefs associated with youth sport participation. Generally accepted assumptions of youth participation in sport include benefits for physical, psychological, and social health. More specifically, engaging in organized sport is thought to enhance children's self-esteem, perseverance, physical strength and endurance, leadership, teamwork, and other prosocial skills, and some evidence supports these claims (Fraser-Thomas, Côté, & Deakin, 2005). And yet, substantial evidence also exists that challenges these beliefs of sport being "innately good" (Giulianotti, 2004).

Challenges to these claims of sport as innately good

Despite the benefits assumed to result from sport participation for young people, the significant drop-out rates from sport serve as compelling evidence that sport is not a positive experience for all. In fact, sport participation in Canada declines dramatically after the ages of 10–13 years (Hunter, Grenier, & Brink, 2002). Furthermore, there has been nearly a 25 percent decline over the past 18 years, with only 54 percent of young Canadians aged 15–19 participating in sports in 2010, compared to 77 percent in 1992 (Canadian-Heritage, 2013; Ifedi, 2008). Previous research indicates that young people leave sport because of negative experiences such as "lack of fun" and "coach conflicts" (Weiss & Williams, 2004), although the precursors to these reasons have not been fully explored.

In addition to high drop-out rates, the scholarly literature and media are replete with examples of young athletes experiencing harm as a result of their sport experience, including, for example, sexual and emotional abuse, long-term physical injuries, and social isolation (David, 2005). Until recently, research has emphasized sexual abuse (Kerr & Stirling, 2008) and the abuse of elite athletes specifically (Brackenridge & Rhind, 2010). Yet evidence suggests that the occurrence of such harmful experiences is not unique to elite athletes and that sexual abuse is perhaps a small concern proportionately (Brackenridge, 2010).

With respect to experiences of maltreatment within the coach–athlete relationship, a number of researchers have reported that emotionally harmful experiences tend to be the most common experience. Myers *et al.* (2002; as cited in Wolfe & McIsaac, 2011, 804) define psychological and emotional maltreatment as "a repeated pattern of caregiver behavior or a serious incident, that transmits to the child that s/he is worthless, flawed, unloved, unwanted, endangered, or only of value in meeting another's needs." Within the sport context, emotional abuse is defined as "a pattern of deliberate non-contact behaviors by a person within a critical relationship role that has the potential to be harmful" (Stirling & Kerr, 2008, 178). It refers to a persistent pattern of behavior and most often one in which the coach lacks malicious intent and may not fully appreciate the harmful effects of emotionally harmful coaching behaviors. Emotional abuse is non-contact in nature, and occurs within a relationship in which the athlete depends on the coach for his/her sense of safety, trust, and fulfillment of needs. This type of relationship is often viewed as analogous to that of a parent–child relationship in order to capture the dependence and significant influence therein.

In one of the earliest studies on emotional abuse, Gervis and Dunn (2004) interviewed 12 former elite athletes and reported that shouting, belittling, threats, and humiliation were the most commonly reported forms of athlete emotional abuse, with more abusive behaviors reported as the competitive level increased. Subsequent studies (Stirling & Kerr, 2007; 2008) confirmed reports of emotional abuse within the coach–athlete relationship, and noted that such experiences are often normalized by athletes as a required part of the training process. Given this presumed normalization and the power disparity between the coach and athlete, athletes may be reluctant to question and/or report their coaches' harmful behaviors (Stirling & Kerr, 2009). In a recent online survey of more than 6,000 university students who retrospectively reported childhood experiences of harm in sport (Alexander *et al.*, 2011), emotional harm was most frequently reported and occurred as a result of their coaches' behaviors. This finding was consistent for both male (29 percent, $n = 328$) and female (36 percent, $n = 1,056$) athletes. Interestingly, a greater percentage of athletes from individual sports (e.g. dance, swimming, athletics) reported emotionally harmful coaching experiences compared with athletes from team sports (e.g. netball, football, hockey, rugby).

In all of the existing studies of young athletes across a number of countries and sports, emotional abuse is the most commonly reported form of maltreatment within the athlete–coach relationship. The behaviors that characterize emotionally abusive coaching practices include verbal comments (e.g. yelling, belittlement, degrading comments), physical behaviors (e.g. throwing objects with the purpose of intimidating the athlete), and the denial of attention (Stirling & Kerr, 2008).

Most of the research on emotionally harmful experiences has involved older athletes recalling earlier experiences. An exception to this is the work of Raakman and colleagues. Results from the categorization of over 700 coaching behaviors across youth hockey, football, soccer, baseball, and basketball indicate that approximately 80 percent of all classified behaviors could be classified as potentially harmful (Cook & Dorsch, 2014; Raakman, Dorsch, & Rhind, 2010). The same research revealed that the most prevalent type of harmful coaching behavior was psychological or emotional harm, which accounted for approximately 48 percent of all classified behaviors (Cook & Dorsch, 2014). In addition to contributing information on youth sport participants' experiences to the existing literature, this work also highlights the frequency with which young athletes are exposed to violence indirectly through the observation or witnessing of adults in conflictual interactions. In fact, 80 percent of the problematic behaviors reported by Cook and Dorsch (2014) involved youth athletes witnessing others' conduct. Based upon the extant research on partner violence (Slep, Heyman, & Snarr, 2011), which suggests that child emotional abuse is incurred when a child witnesses severe partner violence, it is reasonable to propose that emotionally harmful experiences occur when a young athlete witnesses a coach or parent threatening or intimidating other players and/or adults with whom the athlete also has important relationships.

Although evidence of the outcomes incurred by athletes as a result of emotionally harmful experiences in sport is lacking, evidence from community and school violence studies suggests that exposure to violence *or* witnessed violence has serious long-term effects, including: aggressive behaviors (Janosz, Archambault, Pagani, Pascal, Morin, & Bowen, 2008); mal-adjustment and diminished well-being (Janosz *et al.*, 2008); PTSD symptoms (Mathews, Dempey, & Overstreet, 2009); and emotional and behavioral problems (Aisenberg & Herrenkohl, 2008). Given the seriousness of these outcomes, investigation of long-term consequences of athletes' emotionally harmful experiences deserves future attention.

Substantial effort has been devoted to understanding risk factors for the maltreatment of youth in sport, including environmental, demographic, and personal characteristics, and the absence of policies (Beyer, Higgins, & Bromfield, 2005). Of all potential risk factors, the power differential between coaches and athletes has received particular attention in this body of literature; in fact, power is fundamental to understanding any form of maltreatment (Fasting & Brackenridge, 2009). More specifically, youth have low social power (Beyer, Higgins, & Bromfield, 2005), limited autonomy, and an inability to protect themselves (Finkelhor, 1995); in fact, children's dependency on their caregivers – including coaches – is cited as a major factor of vulnerability (Finkelhor, 1995). Similarly, coaches, by virtue of their age, size, expertise, access to resources, and ascribed authority, hold positions of greater power over young athletes (Burke, 2001). Several authors have cited examples of athletes referring to their coaches as "god-like" figures, surrogate parents, and "masters" (Brackenridge, 2001; Stirling & Kerr, 2009), which highlights coaches' positions of power.

In response to evidence of harm caused to young sport participants, significant attention has been devoted by sport organizations (in Canada) to addressing ways to prevent such incidences of harm. Responses have included policy development in the form of Coaches' Codes of Conduct and various Harassment and Abuse Policies (Donnelly, Kerr, Heron, & DiCarlo, 2014). Moreover, a number of educational programs have also been initiated to help athletes, coaches, and parents learn more about harmful coaching practices and ways to prevent these experiences. It should be noted, however, that none of these policies or educational initiatives have been evaluated empirically for their effectiveness (Kerr, Stirling, & MacPherson, 2014).

Shifting the approach from reducing harm to optimizing the experience

While recognizing the benefits of efforts to reduce harmful experiences for youth participants, we suggest that much more could be gained from considering ways in which sport experiences might be optimized for youth participants. Academics generally like to begin the research process by defining a problem. This problem-solving approach is considered foundational to science-based practice (Tilly, 2008) and is often referred to as the hypothetico-deductive model of problem-solving (Hardin, 2003), or more commonly as the medical model of problem-solving (Tilly, 2008). In its simplest form, this process involves four phases: (1) Is there a problem? If so, what is it?; (2) Why is the problem happening?; (3) What can be done about the problem?; (4) Did the intervention work? (Tilly, 2008, 18). We suggest that this process characterizes the extant literature on the harm experienced by youth in sport. It is our supposition, however, that further benefits may be reaped through a different approach and perspective, to be described in the following section.

In recent years the "positive psychology" movement has demonstrated that it is equally important – if not more important – to build what is right, as it is to fix what is wrong (Seligman, 2002). Moreover, evidence suggests that by amplifying and concentrating on the strengths of people at risk, we are doing preventative work (Seligman, 2002). This concept is particularly relevant when considering the issue of sport participation as a growth-enhancing experience for young participants. With such a positive approach, the question changes from "How can we prevent harm to young people in sport?" or "How might we better safeguard young people from harm in sport?" to "How can we ensure youth experience positive growth and development from their sport participation?" This approach will be detailed in the following section.

Ensuring growth: an athlete-centered approach to sport

Imagine a sport system in which young people experience a sense of belonging, a growth in self-esteem, physical enhancement, joy, creativity, and playfulness. Athlete-centered sport, which is often considered a philosophy as well as an approach to sport program delivery, may be a vehicle by which such benefits accrue (Kerr & Stirling, 2008). Essentially, it is considered a value-based approach, in which the health and wellness of the "whole" person is prioritized

(Kidman & Lombardo, 2010). The tenets of an athlete-centered approach suggest that coaches: (1) foster the holistic development of the athlete; (2) implement a collaborative relationship with the athlete; (3) lead from behind; (4) establish a democratic team environment; and (5) cultivate awareness (Jenny, 2013).

The tenets of an athlete-centered coaching approach are rooted in humanistic psychology and self-determination theory. Proponents of humanistic psychology (Maslow, 1943) focus on each individual's potential and emphasize growth and self-actualization; they also suggest that individuals have agency over their lives and are motivated to use this agency to grow, to learn, and to fulfill their full potential. When applied to sport, a humanistic approach suggests a focus on the holistic growth and development of the individual, including and extending beyond athletic development.

Deci and Ryan's Self-Determination Theory (Deci & Ryan, 2008), which stems from humanistic psychology, also informs an athlete-centered approach. Proponents of Self-Determination Theory (SDT) emphasize the belief that human nature is characterized by the positive features of effort, agency, and commitment, otherwise known as "inherent growth tendencies." According to SDT, and similar to humanistic psychology, individuals have an innate tendency to grow and fulfill their potentials. Deci and Ryan focus specifically on psychological needs for autonomy, competence, and relatedness that form the basis for one's motivation. Research on SDT has highlighted the associations between development of these needs with enhanced psychological well-being, increased persistence and performance in experiential types of activities (Deci & Ryan, 2008).

Within the sport-related literature, Lyle (2002) recommends that coaches adopt an athlete-centered coaching approach because it fosters the coach–athlete relationship, thus increasing coaching effectiveness, athletes' motivation and satisfaction, and team performance. Researchers have also proposed that an athlete-centered coaching approach diminishes the "win-at-all-costs" approach that so often characterizes sport. It is well known that the primary concerns of many coaches and sporting organizations typically revolve around winning games, making money, and being champions (Kidman & Lombardo, 2010). Further, these desires for performance excellence can eclipse coaches' focus on athletes' personal well-being (Miller & Kerr, 2002). In fact, Kerr and Stirling (2008) recommend that an athlete-centered philosophy may be the most effective way to diminish the "win-at-all-costs" approach which has been associated with occurrences of athlete maltreatment, thus enhancing athlete protection. And when the athlete's needs and rights are prioritized, and when they are encouraged to share power and control of their sporting environment, their safety is much more assured. In fact, Jenny (2013) posits that a humanistic approach *is* an athlete-welfare approach.

The future imagined

Table 5.1 summarizes tenets of an athlete-centered approach and offers concrete coaching behaviors that operationalize these principles.

Table 5.1 Examples of athlete-centered coaching behaviors

Tenet: holistic development of the athlete
- Ask one-self, "How can I use this sport experience to enhance the young person's sense of self-esteem and competency?"
- Use teachable moments in sport to enhance responsibility, autonomy, and decision-making skills
- Redefine success in order to support the athlete's long-term well-being
- Communicate that sport is an important, but only one, aspect of life

Tenet: create a collaborative athlete–coach relationship
- Facilitate the empowerment of athletes
- Encourage athletes to question and even challenge authority
- Encourage athletes to establish personal and team goals
- Provide opportunities for athletes to take responsibility
- Provide opportunities for athletes to discuss and evaluate their sport experience

Tenet: lead from behind
- Assume that the athlete is the expert of her or his own experience
- Ask questions first and avoid prescribing
- Invite feedback
- Provide opportunities for the athlete to strategize and make valuable choices
- Encourage athletes to make mistakes and fail

Tenet: democratic team culture
- Ensure that athletes contribute to the development of team strategies, goals, and culture with minimal interference
- Provide athletes with the frequent opportunities to make decisions regarding performance, training, and resources
- Reinforce the contribution and value of each athlete as a member of the larger team
- Establish a team environment that values respect, trust, and supporting one another

Tenet: cultivate awareness (of athlete and self)
- Commit to knowing and understanding each athlete as a person, rather than only as an athlete
- Commit to the process of personal development rather than "winning"
- Commit to establishing important, valuable, healthy relationships with each athlete
- Commit to the assumption that every athlete is inherently competent
- Remain engaged in ongoing professional development
- Engage in self-reflective practice

Conclusion

The future of athlete well-being rests in the hands of those responsible for coach education, coach learning, and, most significantly, in the hands of coaches. Fortunately, some organizations have taken a proactive approach – the Child Protection in Sport Unit (UK), for example, contributed to the drafting of International Standards for Safeguarding and Protecting Children in Sport (Ruuska, 2013), which includes a section devoted to coaching standards. We argue, however, that the Standards do not go far enough in specifying the tenets of athlete-centered coaching and the behaviors required to support them. One suggestion would be that principles of athlete-centered coaching must be emphasized as *minimum* standards for coach accreditation, even at the most basic level.

Research supports this suggestion, as technical instruction for coaches has been shown to be far less important with regard to athlete satisfaction and well-being than instruction for supportive behaviors (Smith, Shoda, Cumming, & Smoll, 2009). If the growth-enhancing potential of sport for young people is to be actualized, national governing bodies must acknowledge the evidence indicating the necessity of coaching programs that support the holistic development of athletes.

References

Aisenberg, E., & Herrenkohl, T. (2008). Community violence in context: Risk and resilience in children and families. *Journal of Interpersonal Violence, 23* (3), 296–315.

Alexander, K., Stafford, A., & Lewis, R. (2011). *The experiences of children participating in organised sport in the UK*. Edinburgh: University of Edinburgh, Child Protection Research Centre. Retrieved January 2015, from www.nspcc.org.uk/globalassets/documents/research-reports/experiences-children-participating-organised-sport-uk-main-report.pdf.

Beyer, L.R., Higgins, D.J., & Bromfield, L.M. (2005). *Understanding organisational risk factors for child maltreatment: A review of literature*. Australia: National Child Protection Clearinghouse Australian Institute of Family Studies. Retrieved January 2015 from www3.aifs.gov.au/cfca/publications/understanding-organisational-risk-factors-child-maltreat

Brackenridge, C. (2001). *Spoilsports: Understanding and preventing sexual exploitation in sport*. London: Routledge.

Brackenridge, C. (2010, February). Myths and evidence; learning from our journey. Keynote address, Coventry Sports Foundation and the NSPCC Child Protection in Sport Unit.

Brackenridge, C. & Rhind, D. (2010). *Elite child athlete welfare: International perspectives*. London: Brunel University Press.

Burke, M. (2001). Obeying until it hurts: Coach–athlete relationships. *Journal of the Philosophy of Sport, 28* (2), 227–240.

Canadian Heritage. (2013). Sport Participation 2010 research paper. Government of Canada. Retrieved January 6, 2015 from http://publications.gc.ca/collections/collection_2013/pc-ch/CH24-1-2012-eng.pdf

Cook, E., & Dorsch, K.D. (2014). Monitoring in youth sport: A paradigm shift. *Surveillance and Society, 11* (4), 508–520.

David, P. (2005). *Human rights in youth sports: A critical review of children's rights in competitive sports*. London: Routledge.

Deci, E., & Ryan, R. (2008). Self-determination theory: A macro theory of human motivation, development, and health. *Canadian Psychology, 49* (3), 182–185.

Donnelly, P., Kerr, G., Heron, A., & DiCarlo, D. (2014). Protecting youth in sport: An examination of harassment policies. *International Journal of Sport Policy and Politics, 6* (3), 1–18.

Fasting, K., & Brackenridge, C. (2009). Coaches, sexual harassment and education. *Sport, Education and Society, 14* (1), 21–35.

Finkelhor, D. (1995). The victimization of children: A developmental perspective. *American Journal of Orthopsychiatry, 65* (2), 177–193.

Fraser-Thomas, J.L., Côté, J., & Deakin, J. (2005). Youth sport programs: An avenue to foster positive youth development. *Physical Education & Sport Pedagogy, 10* (1), 19–40.

Gervis, M., & Dunn, N. (2004). The emotional abuse of elite child athletes by their coaches. *Child Abuse Review, 13*, 215–223.

Giulianotti, R. (2004). Human rights, globalization and sentimental education: The case of sport. *Sport in Society*, *7* (3), 355–369.

Hardin, L.E. (2003). Research in medical problem solving: A review. *Journal of Veterinary Medical Education*, *30* (3), 230–235.

Hunter, L., Grenier, S., & Brink, S. (2002). Statistics Canada: National longitudinal survey of children and youth: Participation in activities. Government of Canada.

Ifedi, F. (2008). Sport participation in Canada, 2005. Statistics Canada, Government of Canada.

Janosz, M., Archambault, I., Pagani, L.S., Pascal, S., Morin, A.J.S., & Bowen, F. (2008). Are there detrimental effects of witnessing school violence in early adolescence? *The Journal of Adolescent Health: Official Publication of the Society for Adolescent Medicine*, *43* (6), 600–608.

Jenny, S.E. (2013). A case study of the coaching philosophy of men's NCAA distance running coach: To what extent is it humanistic? Unpublished doctoral dissertation at University of New Mexico.

Kerr, G., & Stirling, A.E. (2008). Child protection in sport: Implications of an athlete-centered philosophy. *Quest*, *60* (2), 307–323.

Kerr, G., Stirling, A.E., & MacPherson, E. (2014). A critical examination of child protection initiatives in sport contexts. Special Issue: Contemporary Developments in Child Protection. *Social Sciences*, 3 (4), 742–757.

Kidman, L., & Lombardo, B. (2010). *Athlete-centered coaching: Developing decision makers* (2nd ed.). Worcester: Innovative Print Communications Ltd.

Lyle, J. (2002). *Sports coaching concepts: A framework for coaching*. London: Routledge.

Maslow, A.H. (1943). A theory of human motivation. *Psychological Review*, *50* (4), 370–396.

Mathews, T., Dempsey, M., & Overstreet, S. (2009). Effects of exposure to community violence on school functioning: the mediating role of posttraumatic stress symptoms. *Behavior Research and Therapy*, *47* (7), 586–591.

Miller, P., & Kerr, G. (2002). Conceptualizing excellence: Past, present and future. *Journal of Applied Sport Psychology*, *14*, 140–153.

Raakman, E., Dorsch, K., & Rhind, D. (2010). The development of a typology of abusive coaching behaviors within youth sport. *International Journal of Sport Science and Coaching*, *5* (4), 503–515.

Ruuska, M. (2013). Move to protect children in sport. Retrieved from Retrieved January 6, 2015 from www.sportanddev.org/en/newsnviews/news/?5705/1/Move-to-protect-children-in-sport

Seligman, M.E.P. (2002). Positive psychology, positive prevention, and positive therapy. In C.R. Snyder & S. Lopez (Eds.), *Handbook of positive psychology* (pp. 3–9). New York: Oxford University Press.

Slep, A.M.S., Heyman, R.E., & Snarr, J.D. (2011). Child emotional aggression and abuse: Definitions and prevalence. *Child Abuse and Neglect*, *35* (10), 783–796.

Smith, R., Shoda, Y., Cumming, S., & Smoll, F. (2009). Behavioral signatures at the ballpark: Intraindividual consistency of adults' situation-behaviour patterns and their interpersonal consequences. *Journal of Research in Personality*, *43* (2), 187–195.

Stirling, A.E., & Kerr, G.A. (2007). Elite female swimmers' experiences of emotional abuse across time. *Journal of Emotional Abuse*, *7* (4), 89–113.

Stirling, A.E., & Kerr, G.A. (2008). Defining and categorizing emotional abuse in sport. *European Journal of Sport Science*, *8* (4), 173–181.

Stirling, A.E., & Kerr, G.A. (2009). Abused athletes' perceptions of the coach–athlete relationship. *Sport in Society, 12* (2), 227–239.

Tilly, D.I. (2008). Psychology to science-based practice: Problem solving and the three-tiered model. In A. Thomas & J. Grimes (Eds.), *Best practices in school psychology V* (5th ed.; pp. 17–36). Bethesda, MD: National Association of School Psychologists.

Weiss, M., & Williams, L. (2004). The why of youth sport involvement: A developmental perspective on motivational processes. In M.R. Weiss (Ed.), *Developmental sport and exercise psychology: A lifespan perspective* (pp. 223–268). Morgantown, WV: Fitness Information Technology.

Wolfe, D., & McIsaac, C. (2011). Distinguishing between poor/dysfunctional parenting and child emotional maltreatment. *Child Abuse & Neglect, 35,* 802–813.

6 Ludo-diversity

An argument for a pluralistic movement culture

Roland Renson

Introduction: the concepts of movement culture and ludo-diversity

Movement culture

The term *movement culture* is proposed here as a more universal concept than the term *sport*. Sport refers to a rather recent modern and typically Western cultural product, which has been exported and imported worldwide. Imposing this concept of sport on periods of the past or on other non-Western cultures can be seen as a form of anachronism on the one hand, and of cultural imperialism on the other. Several sport historians and sport sociologists who are aware of this conceptual problem have therefore carefully pointed out that they use *sport* as an umbrella concept for a great variety of playful and competitive physical activities. Some postmodernists promote the term and concept of body culture, but in our opinion *movement culture* is a more adequate denominator.

This concept of movement culture encompasses four spheres of activities, which are historical and cultural universals, elements shared by all groups of people throughout time. Physical exercises such as gymnastics, fitness exercises, tai chi, etc. are part of the "instrumental" physical culture sphere of *Homo exercens*. Physical contests such as track and field athletics, boxing, wushu, judo, taekwondo, etc. are part of the "competitive" sphere of *Homo agonizens*. Movement games such as ball games, bowls games, throwing games such as darts, etc. belong to the "ludic" play sphere of *Homo ludens*. Acrobatics such as juggling, tightrope walking, etc. and all sorts of dances are part of the "expressive" performance sphere of *Homo exhibens*. These four spheres are all intertwined and sport appears as a central overlapping element (Renson, 2000).

This search for a new model was instigated by cross-cultural comparisons of traditional games and movement activities between Europe (De Vroede & Renson, 1991) and Africa (Scheerder & Renson, 1998), China (Damman, 1994; 1995), and South America (Van Mele & Renson, 1992).

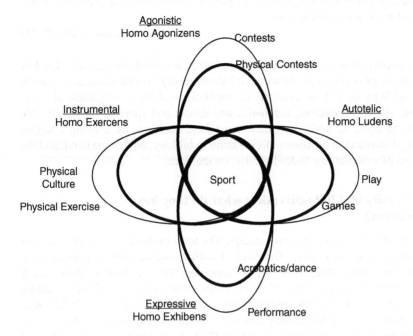

Figure 6.1 The concept of movement culture (Renson, 2000; 2007)

The term *body culture* seems too broad as it includes also non-motor aspects such as body painting, piercing, tattooing, hair styling, etc. Moreover, in our model movement culture is restricted to movement forms of play, contests, exercise, and performance, excluding other passive or non-motor forms such as card playing, song contests, body decoration, or theater performances, etc.

Ludo-diversity

Many expressions of traditional movement culture can be considered as endangered species, which are seriously threatened by modernization (Guttmann 1978; 1994), (neo-)colonization (Eichberg, 1984), and now by globalization (Bale, 1991; Bale & Maguire, 1994; Maguire, 1999; Guttmann, 2004). Innumerable forms of traditional games, physical contests, physical exercises, or dances already belong to the "living dead" and their number is still shrinking. There are some signs of hope, however. Globalization seems to go hand-in-hand with localization: as a reaction against the global sport monoculture, a new awareness is growing to preserve the cultural heritage and variety of our movement cultures (Renson, 1984; Maguire, 1999). Therefore I introduced the concept of *ludo-diversity*:

> Ludo-diversity means the variation among all movement cultures, encompassing the domains of play, physical culture and movement expression and

their respective subfields such as: games, sports, physical exercises, dance and acrobatic performances.

(Renson, 2004, 10–11)

The concept was further elaborated in another article (Renson, 2013). The key question is, of course, why do we need ludo-diversity? Is extinction not a natural process? Why should the diversity of our traditional forms of games, physical contest, physical exercises, acrobatics and dance, and sport be preserved? We will try to come up with some answers to these questions by drawing a further analogy between the processes of extinction in biology, on the one hand, and the problem of safeguarding ludo-diversity, on the other.

Biodiversity and ludo-diversity: what do they have in common?

Biodiversity is a relatively new concept. The term *biological diversity* was first used in this sense in 1980 by Thomas E. Lovejoy, and was further elaborated by Elliott Norse and colleagues (Norse, Rosenbaum, Wilcove, Romme, Johnston, & Stout, 1986). The contraction *biodiversity* appeared as a keyword for a meeting in Washington, DC in 1986, entitled "National Forum on Biodiversity" (Wilson & Peter, 1988). Wilson has contributed much to the dissemination of the concept with his publication, *The Diversity of Life* (1992). In the Convention on Biological Diversity, a result of the UN Conference on Environment and Development in Rio de Janeiro in 1992, biodiversity was defined as follows:

> Biological diversity means the variability among living organisms from all sources including, inter alia, terrestrial, marine and other aquatic ecosystems and the ecological complexes of which they are part; this includes diversity within species, between species and of ecosystems.
>
> (Glowka, Burhenne-Guilmin, & Synge, 1994, 16)

Although biodiversity and ludo-diversity originate from the different spheres of biology on the one hand and culture on the other, they both have certain ecological processes and concerns in common.

Just as there is a "red list" of endangered animal and plant species, an equivalent list can be drawn of endangered forms of movement culture. Let us therefore first examine how the mechanisms of extinction function in biology and see if we can find some comparisons with the mechanisms of ludic extinction in our cultural history.

Biodiversity, ludo-diversity, and four mechanisms of extinction

Animal physiologist Diamond (1992) had pointed out that virtually all animal extinctions were caused in one way or another by humans. Diamond describes four main mechanisms by which our growing population exterminates species: overhunting, species introduction, habitat destruction, and ripple effect. Can parallels be drawn between these mechanisms by which we exterminate species and the mechanisms by which we endanger our ludo-diversity?

Overhunting

> Killing animals faster than they can breed is the main mechanism by which we've exterminated big animals, from mammoths to Californian grizzly bears.
> (Diamond 1992, 358)

Diamond warns that at the current rate of change, not just elephants and rhinos but most populations of other large mammals of Africa and Southeast Asia will be extinct outside game parks and zoos in a decade or two.

If we replace the term *hunting* by *forbidding* then we see how in the past a hegemonic principle was applied whereby – in the name of civilization, Christianization, colonization, or modernization – certain play, dance, or other physical activities were forbidden, prosecuted, and finally abolished. Brailsford (1969) has poignantly analyzed how traditional English pastimes were degraded by the Puritans to "unlawful activities." Dancing was attacked for its carnality, folk football for its violence, maypoles for their paganism, and sports in general for their despoliation of the Sabbath. However, Brailsford has also remarked that any government [or other authority] which seeks to destroy a country's recreational life is faced with a virtually impossible task, and that – despite their restrictions – "old rural sports often persisted with a remarkable stubbornness, even in the most unpromising environments" (Brailsford 1969, 156). Similar conclusions on the Puritans' ambiguous attitudes toward pleasure and recreation in the New World were explored by Daniels (1995) and Struna (1996).

Holt (1981) has also shown how, in modern France, bullfighting in the South and cockfighting in the North formed part of the general fabric of popular regional culture and proved remarkably resilient to the attacks of reformers. Although cockfighting became illegal in the North through a "humanitarian" prefectural law in 1852, it remained virtually unaffected and the number of *gallodromes* (cockpits) continued to grow. The success of cockfighting in the North was mirrored by a growing enthusiasm for the bullfight in the South during the same period.

When traditional games are "hunted" by social or moral reformers and become "forbidden games," they often seem to provoke a spontaneous reaction and even a "regional" revival of the endangered ludic activities.

Introduction of other species

The second mechanism by which species are exterminated is through intentionally or unintentionally introducing certain species to parts of the world where they did not previously occur.

> When species are introduced from one region to another, they often proceed to exterminate some of the native species they encounter, by eating them or

causing diseases. The victims evolved in the absence of the introduced pests and never developed defenses against them.

(Diamond, 1992, 358)

A classic study concerning the introduction of a competitive sport in a non-competitive culture is the anthropological case study of Fox (1961) on *Pueblo Baseball: A New Use for Old Witchcraft.* What Fox's analysis of Cochiti Pueblo in New Mexico has shown is that social conflicts are engendered when there are changes in the social structure (two rival baseball teams) without corresponding changes in the cultural structural ideals of harmony and cooperation of the social system. Originally Cochiti Pueblo had one baseball team, tragic-comically called the "Redskins" [sic], which played in the Pueblo Baseball League. But with the return of servicemen to Cochiti after World War II, a second team was formed, first called the "Silversmiths" but later the "Braves." Through this baseball split, old latent hostilities erupted, which never before had a basis to come out in opposition:

> Baseball in the pueblos was a competitive intrusion into an essentially non-competitive social system.

(Fox, 1975, 172)

My own short visits to Cochiti Pueblo in 1996 and 1999, completed by the field observations by De Ceuster (2000), have shown that the construction of an 18-hole golf course in 1981, which is mostly frequented by retired Anglo senior citizens, has drastically changed the landscape and the nature of Cochiti.

Contrary to the unintentional introduction of other games species, as in the Cochiti example, the mechanism of intentionally introducing other species is often linked with the first-mentioned mechanism of overhunting or "forbidding" endemic games. Some Christian missionaries have played the role of proselytizing champions by first abolishing indigenous forms of movement culture, then propagating modern sports as a "civilizing" alternative:

> The Christian missionaries symbolized God in action. Their skills were practical as well as spiritual.

(Mangan, 1986, 169)

The Belgian Catholic missionary Raphaël de la Kethulle de Ryhove (1890–1956), who became the sports apostle of the Belgian Congo, was such a proselyte. He was convinced that the young Congolese had to be kept away from their "immoral dances, obscene songs and orgies" and he propagated sport – especially football – as an ideal alternative (Renson & Peeters, 2004).

Several outstanding publications have been dedicated to this "non-silent entente" between sport, on the one hand, and imperialism, colonization, and proselytism, on the other by sport history scholars such as Arbena (1990), Baker and Mangan (1987), Bale and Maguire (1993; 2002), Eichberg (1998), Guttmann (1994), Mangan (1986; 1988), Stoddart (1997), Van Bottenburg (1994), Combeau-Mari (2004), and several others.

Finally, the topic of *globalization* must also be seen in the post-colonial – or neo-colonial – perspective of distributing – or rather marketing – Western sport forms throughout the "global village." This new worldwide process is, however, like most cultural processes, characterized by dialectic tendencies. Joseph Maguire has articulated this paradox as:

> a balance and blend between diminishing contrasts and increasing varieties ... in the late twentieth century we are witnessing the globalization of sports and the increasing diversification of sport cultures.
>
> (Maguire, 1999, 213)

Habitat destruction

Habitat destruction is the third means by which we exterminate species. Most species occur in just a certain type of habitat:

> If one drains marshes or cuts forests, one eliminates the species dependent on those habitats just as certainly as if one were to shoot every individual of the species.
>
> (Diamond, 1992, 359)

Diamond warns us that, in the case of habitat destruction, the worst is still to come, because we are just starting in earnest to destroy tropical rain forests, which cover only 6 percent of the Earth's surface but harbor about half of its species.

The results of the research project of the Flemish Folk Games Files (Renson & Smulders, 1981), which was started in 1973, have shown that traditional games are often thriving in a specific habitat and risk vanishing when this familiar habitat is changed. In Flanders (the Dutch-speaking part of Belgium), for instance, the pubs have been the traditional havens where folk games felt at home. Traditional bowling, nine-pins, horizontal and vertical popinjay shooting, and the traditional pelote ball game seem to be doomed when they are artificially transplanted from the cozy cafés in the village or city center to modern sport halls or sterile playing fields. Here, we also notice a negative interplay with the second mechanism of introducing other species. Indeed, the "good old games" don't like to be replanted or repotted. On the other hand, some recently imported "globalized" games, such as British flat green bowls or curve bowls, (American) ten pin bowling, (Olympic) target archery, and (British) squash rackets or (American) racket ball, are resistant to these new "sporting" habitats and can become a threat to the indigenous movement culture.

Ripple effect

> Every species depends on other species for food and for providing its habitat. Thus, species are connected to each other like branching rows of dominoes.
>
> (Diamond 1992, 359)

Just as the toppling of one domino will topple the others in a row, so the extermination of one species may lead to the extermination of others. This fourth mechanism is therefore described as the ripple or domino effect.

Looking for examples to illustrate the domino effect in the disappearance of play and game forms, we thought of the eradication of many traditional children's games in streets and playgrounds in urbanized Europe in the second half of the twentieth century. This mass extinction was caused by a combined effect of all three mentioned mechanisms: overhunting, introduction of other species, and habitat destruction. It was indeed remarkable that most of the European children's games which were inventoried by the first wave of sixteenth-century play scholars were still observed "alive and kicking" by the second wave of play folklorists at the end of the nineteenth century.

Even 50 years later, in the 1950s, many games from the encyclopedic inventory of François Rabelais' *Gargantua* of 1535 and most of the games of Pieter Bruegel's 1560 painting *The Children's Games* were still played by youngsters in the first half of the twentieth century, at least in the rural parts of Europe (Hills, 1957; Renson & De Vroede, 2012). Several of these games perished through *overhunting*, that is to say they were forbidden for being either too violent, too dirty, too indecent, or too dangerous, or simply for being no longer part of the unrestrained "progress" of the post-war (re)construction mania. But, an even more lethal factor in the killing off of these game species was probably the introduction of some new sport species: football, volleyball, basketball, tennis, etc. These were often propagated by teachers as welcome "civilizing" replacements of the children's own "wild" play culture.

On top of these two factors came the massive habitat destruction of the natural *ludotopes*. School playgrounds were paved; games in mud, snow, or water were no longer tolerated. Sometimes recess or recreation time was considered as "wasted time" by school authorities and simply scrapped (Sutton-Smith, 1990). Streets and squares became banned for children after they had been invaded by herds of automobiles. No wonder these conspiring factors decimated the ludodiversity of the children's play lore.

Sutton-Smith (1990) has held an apology in praise of the school playground. The reason for his protest were some current attempts in the United States either to abolish "recess" and to replace it with physical education, or to reduce it by allowing only children of the same age at the same time on the playground. He argued that the school playground is a child cultural event with "festival" characteristics and that "Its preservation deserves support on the basis of children's rights."

On the other hand, Sutton-Smith has warned against the idealization of play and recreation by the early Romanticists, nineteenth-century folklorists, or present day nostalgists:

> traditions are the reflexive selections and transformations of those aspects of past customs which create identity and value for those engaged in this preservation. Tradition is the reflection of how we think about ourselves and to be accepted by others. Tradition is a rhetoric of our identity.
>
> (Sutton-Smith, 1991, 26)

Discussion: why are biodiversity and ludo-diversity important?

One can, of course, ask the question of whether extinction, both in the biosphere and in the ludo-sphere, isn't a natural process anyway. Diamond's answer to this is that the current human-caused extinction rate of plants and animals is far higher than the natural rate.

Dismissing the extinction crisis on the grounds that extinction is natural "would be just like dismissing genocide on the grounds that death is the natural fate of all humans" (Diamond, 1992, 36). Neither can we just preserve those particular species that we need and let other species go extinct because the species we need also depend on other species.

Worldwide some 300 million people, roughly 5 percent of the global population, still retain a strong identity as members of an indigenous culture, rooted in history and attached by language, myth, and collective memory to a particular area. But their unique visions of life are increasingly lost by a globally blowing wind of change. Can they adopt some of the beneficial aspects of the modern world while rejecting at the same time those intrusions which can harm their way of life and heritage? (Davis, 1999).

Should we share the same pessimism where ludo-diversity is concerned? Worldwide traditional movement culture is confronted with the rapidly spreading export–import of modern sports, which has been described as "sportification" "sportization" (Eichberg, 1991; 1995; Renson, 1997; Van Bottenburg, 1994).

Very much in the same line of thought, but now applied to modern sports versus traditional games, I have already referred to the tandem operation of globalization–localization, which can therefore be contracted to "glocalization." Indeed, at the height of the global sportization wave alternative attempts to preserve and revivify the diversity of the ludic cultural heritage are seen both at a local and international scale (Jarvie, 1991; Renson, 1984; 1997).

Games have a much higher regenerative potential than animal species. Compared to the dinosaur, the moa, the dodo, and other extinguished species, games and other forms of movement culture can be invented or reinvented, revived or revivified, adopted or adapted in order to meet our ludic, competitive, physical, and expressive movement needs.

Conclusions: the dialectic and dialects of modern sport

UN Secretary-General Kofi Anan declared in 2004 that sport is a universal language (UN press release, 2004). Both IOC President Rogge (2007) and Pope Francis (2013) have repeated this *unisono*. This is a rather simplistic contention, a "rhetoric" which should be seriously questioned by a "dialectic," a discourse between the *sport universalists* on the one hand and the *movement culture pluralists* on the other.

As already mentioned in this contribution, (modern) sport has frequently been examined as a principal front of globalization, one of the most universal features of popular culture, which crosses language barriers and national boundaries (Maguire, 1999; Bairner, 2001; Miller, Lawrence, Mckay, & Rowe, 2001; Van Bottenburg, 2001; Giulianotti & Robertson, 2009). Maguire (1999, 213) characterized globalization as "a balance and blend between diminishing contrasts and increasing varieties," which – in the case of sport – might lead to the increasing diversification of sport cultures. Maguire admitted, however, that "aspects of globalization are powered by Western notions of 'civilization'." Indeed, sportization appears more as a universal hegemonic trend of standardization and globalization of sport practices, thus affecting and repressing the regional differentiation, and threatening the ludo-diversity of still-existing or vanishing traditional forms of movement culture (Renson, 2004).

"If the IOC promotes sport as a universal language, then what is your concern about the dialects?" was the question I addressed to IOC President Rogge after a presentation he gave at the University of Louvain-la-Neuve in Belgium (Rogge, 2012). Rogge admitted that these "dialects" – or local traditional games – had never been a priority in his nor his predecessors' Olympic policy.

Davis warned in 1999 that languages, like cultures and species, have always evolved, but that today languages are being lost at an alarming rate within a generation or two. Traditional forms of movement culture can also be seen as such endangered languages or dialects. Without a local language, cultural identity loses its roots and quickly disappears. Without local forms of traditional games, physical contests, physical exercises, dances, and acrobatics, our movement cultural heritage becomes more and more "McDonaldized," as Ritzer (1993) has described this process, which is characterized by standardizing products by efficiency, predictability, calculability, and control.

Recent initiatives give evidence of a growing concern to save and preserve the ludic heritage, both on a local and global level. UNESCO selected in 2011 the "Program of cultivating ludo-diversity: safeguarding traditional games in Flanders" of the Sportimonium as a project, best reflecting the principles and objectives of the Convention for the Safeguarding of Intangible Cultural Heritage (Van Den Broucke & Thys, 2012). Both the International Traditional Sports and Games Association (ITSGA) and The Association for International Sport for All (TAFISA) aim to preserve and promote the rich heritage of traditional forms of movement culture and, thus, they try to counteract the monomaniac tendency of sportization, which risks reducing the existing ludo-diversity of the world to a movement monoculture.

References

Annan, K. (2004). *Universal language of sport brings people together, teaches teamwork, tolerance*, New York: UN.

Arbena, J.L. (1990). The diffusion of modern European sport in Latin America: A case study of cultural imperialism? *South Eastern Latin Americanist, 33* (3), 1–8.

Bairner, A. (2001). *Sport, nationalism and globalization: European and North American perspectives*. Albany, NY: State University of New York Press.

Baker, W.J., & Mangan, J.A. (1987). *Sport in Africa*. New York: Africana.

Bale, J. (1991). *The brawn drain*. Urbana, IL: University of Illinois Press.

Bale, J. (2002). *Imagined Olympians: Body culture and colonial representation in Rwanda*. Minneapolis, MN: University of Minnesota Press.

Bale, J. & Maguire, J. (Eds.) (1993). *The global sports arena*. London: Cass.

Brailsford, D. (1969). *Sport and society: Elisabeth to Anne*. London: Routledge & Kegan Paul.

Combeau-Mari, E. (Ed.) (2004). *Sports et loisirs dans les colonies: XIXe–XXe siècles* [*Sports and leisure in the colonies: XIXth–XXth centuries*]. Paris: Le Publieur.

Damman, I. (1994). *Geschiedenis van de traditionele lichaamscultuur in China* [History of traditional physical culture in China]. Leuven (Belgium): Licentiate thesis Faculty of Physical Education, KU Leuven.

Damman, I. (1995). *Sport in China: Een verkennend onderzoek in de provincie Sichuan* [*Sport in China: An exploratory investigation in the Province of Sichuan*]. Leuven: Sock.

Daniels, B.C. (1995). *Puritans at play: Leisure and recreation in colonial New England*. New York: St. Martin's Griffin.

Davis, W. (1999). Vanishing cultures. *National Geographic, 196* (2), 62–89.

De Ceuster, A. (2000). *Acculturatie en assimilatie in de bewegingscultuur van de Pueblo-Indianen: Case study van Cochiti Pueblo, New Mexico* [*Acculturation and assimilation in the movement culture of Pueblo Indians: Case study of Cochiti Pueblo, New Mexico*]. Leuven (Belgium): Licentiate thesis Faculty of Physical Education, KU Leuven.

De Vroede, E., & Renson, R. (Eds.) (1991). *Proceedings of the Second European Seminar on Traditional Games* (Leuven 1990). Leuven: Vlaamse Volkssport Centrale.

Diamond, J. (1992). *The third chimpanzee: The evolution and future of the human animal*. New York: HarperPerennial.

Eichberg, H. (1984). Olympic sport: Neo-colonization and alternatives. *International Review for the Sociology of Sport, 19*, 97–105.

Eichberg, H. (1991). A revolution of body culture: Traditional games on the way from modernisation to "postmodernity." In J.J. Barreau & G. Jaouen (Eds.), *Eclipses et renaissances des jeux populaires* [*Eclipse and renascence of traditional games*] (pp. 101–129). Rennes: Falsab.

Eichberg, H. (1995). Vom Fest zur Fachligkeit: Über die Sportifizierung des Spiels [From festival to professionality: The sportification of play]. *Ludica, 1*, 183–200.

Eichberg, H. (1998). *Body cultures: Essays on sport, space and identity* (Edited by J. Bale & C. Philo). London: Routledge.

Fox, J.R. (1961). Pueblo baseball: A new use for old witchcraft. *Journal of American folklore, 74*, 9–16.

Fox, J.R. (1975). *Encounters with anthropology*. Harmondsworth: Peregrine.

Giulianotti, R. & Robertson, R. (2009). *Globalization and football*, London: Sage.

Glowka, L., Burhenne-Guilmin, F., & Synge, H. (1994). *A guide to the Convention on Biological Diversity*. Gland: IUCN.

Guttmann, A. (1978). *From ritual to record: the nature of modern sports*. New York: Columbia University Press.

Guttmann, A. (1994). *Games & empires: Modern sports and cultural imperialism*. New York: Columbia University Press.

Guttmann, A. (2004). Modern sports as a global phenomenon. In: A. Guttmann, *Sports: The first five millennia* (pp. 307–321). Amherst, MA: University of Massachusetts Press.

Hills, J. (1957). *Das Kinderspielbild von Pieter Bruegel d. Ä (1560): Eine volkskundliche Untersuchung [The children's games painting by Pieter Bruegel the Elder (1560): An ethnological study]*. Wien: Österreichisches Museum für Volkskunde.

Holt, R. (1981). *Sport and society in modern France*. London: Macmillan.

Jarvie, G. (1991). *Highland games: The making of the myth*. Edinburgh: Edinburgh University Press.

Maguire, J. (1999). *Global sport: Identities, societies, civilizations*. Cambridge: Polity Press.

Mangan, J.A. (1986). *The games ethic and imperialism*. London: Frank Cass.

Mangan, J.A. (Ed.) (1988). *Pleasure, profit, proselytism: British culture and sport at home and abroad 1700–1914*. London: Frank Cass.

Miller, T., Lawrence, G., Mckay, J., & Rowe, D. (Eds.) (2001). *Globalization and sport*. London: Sage.

Norse, E.A., Rosenbaum, K., Wilcove, D., Romme, W., Johnston, D., & Stout, M. (1986). *Conserving biological diversity in our national forests*. Washington, DC: Wilderness Society.

Pope Francis (2013). Address to the members of the European Olympic Committee, 23 November, Vatican.

Renson, R. (1984). The "traditionalist" renascence: the revival of sports, games, dance and recreation around the world. In: U. Simri, D. Eldar, & S. Lieberman (Eds.), *Health, physical education, recreation and dance education in perspective* (Proceedings of the 26th ICHPER World Congress Netanya 1983) (pp. 149–159). Netanya: Wingate Institute.

Renson, R. (1995). Games of science: The science of games. In: G. Pfister, T. Niewerth, & G. Steins (Eds.), *Games of the world between tradition and modernity* (Proceedings 2nd ISHPES Congress Berlin 1993) (pp. 17–22). Sankt Augustin: Academia.

Renson, R. (1997). The reinvention of tradition in sports and games. *Journal of Comparative Physical Education and Sport, 19*, 46–52.

Renson, R. (2000). Sport for all: New and old forms of movement culture. In: VII World Congress Sport for All Barcelona 1998 (Ed.), *Final report* (pp. 196–200). Barcelona: Ajuntament de Barcelona (CD Rom).

Renson, R. (2004). Ludo-diversity: Extinction, survival and invention of movement culture. In: G. Pfister (Ed.), *Games of the past: Sports of the future?* (pp. 205–218). Sankt Augustin: Academia.

Renson, R. (2013). Safeguarding ludo-diversity: Chances and challenges in the promotion and protection of traditional movement culture. *East Asian Sports Thoughts, 3*, 139–158.

Renson, R. & De Vroede, E. (2012). De boog mag niet altijd gespannen staan: Sport en ontspanning [The bow cannot always stand bent: Sport and recreation]. In: S. Luyten & Y. Segers (Eds.), *Het Vlaamse platteland in de fifties [The Flemish country-side in the fifties]* (pp. 84–131). Leuven: Davidsfonds.

Renson, R. & Peeters, C. (2004). Sport et mission au Congo belge: "Tata" Raphaël de la Kethulle 1890–1956 [Sport and mission in Belgian Congo : "Tata" Raphaël de la Kethulle 1890–1956]. In: E. Combeau-Mari (Ed.), *Sports et loisirs dans les colonies: XIXe–XXe siècles [Sports and leisure in the colonies : XIXth–XXth centuries]* (pp. 239–253). Paris: Le Publieur.

Renson, R., & Smulders, H. (1981). Research methods and development of the Flemish Folk Games File. *International Review of Sport Sociology, 16*, 97–107.

Ritzer, G. (1993). *The McDonaldization of society: An investigation into the changing character of contemporary social life*. Los Angeles, CA: Pine Forge Press.

Rogge, J. (2007). *Sport for peace: The winning difference* (Remarks to the United Nations 31 October), Lausanne, IOC.

Rogge, J. (2012). *Sport et diplomatie* [*Sport and diplomacy*] (Olympic Chair Lecture Henri de Baillet-Latour & Jacques Rogge, 5 November), Louvan-la-Neuve (Belgium), Université Catholique de Louvain.

Scheerder, J. & Renson, R. (1998). *Annotated bibliography of traditional play and games in Africa.* Berlin: ICSSPE.

Stoddart, B. (1997). A transnational view. In: IOC (Ed.), *Report on the sport-culture forum* (pp. 69–82). Lausanne: IOC.

Struna, N.L. (1996). *People of prowess: Sport, leisure and labor in early Anglo-America.* Urbana, IL: University of Illinois Press.

Sutton-Smith, B. (1990). School playground as festival. *Children's Environments Quarterly, 7* (2), 3–7.

Sutton-Smith, B. (1991). Tradition from the perspective of children's games. In: E. De Vroede & R. Renson (Eds.), *Proceedings of the Second European Seminar on Traditional Games (Leuven 1990)* (pp. 15–27). Leuven: Vlaamse Volkssport Centrale.

Van Bottenburg, M. (1994). *Verborgen competitie* [*Hidden competition*]. Amsterdam: Arko Sports Media.

Van Bottenburg, M. & Jacksonn, B. (2001). *Global games.* Urbana, IL: University of Illinois Press.

Van Den Broucke, D. & Thys, A. (Eds.) (2012). A programme of cultivating ludo-diversity: Safeguarding traditional games in Flanders – ludo-diversity in Flanders and elsewhere. In: J. Van Rillaar (Ed.), *The government of Flanders's policy on safeguarding intangible cultural heritage* (pp. 197–201), Brussels: Arts and Heritage.

Van Mele, V. & Renson, R. (1992). *Traditional games in South America.* Schorndorf: ICSSPE.

Wilson, E.O. & Peter, F.M. (Eds.) (1988). *Biodiversity (National Forum on Biodiversity)*, Washington, DC: National Academy Press.

Wilson, E.O. (1992). *The diversity of life.* Cambridge, MA: Harvard University Press.

PART II

Good governance in a globalized sports world

Introduction

Bart Vanreusel

The lack of good governance in globalizing international sport is the common starting point of observations in the chapters of this second part. Together the chapters clearly point to a need for good governance in future sport and they all present ideas on how to move forward in this matter.

Hilary Findlay (Canada) addresses the question of regulation in globalizing sport. The debate on accountability and control of key international sport bodies such as the IOC, WADA, and CAS is a crucial issue for future developments in globalizing sport. Starting from Agamben's concept of "the state of exception," the author proposes a grass-roots "social contract" approach to accountability in the relationship between global sport organizations and civil society.

On the same topic, **Sandro Arcioni** (Switzerland) presents a different perspective. The author also argues that there is a need for more regulation in the world of sport, but he advocates an independent body of control, a World Sport Governance Agency (WSGA), defending the Olympic Charter and principles of good governance and ethics in sport organizations.

Global sport increasingly presents itself as an event-based culture with mega sport events in the focus of world attention. **Marijke Taks** (Canada) takes a different perspective and calls for a "game change," a shift of attention toward non-mega sport events. She argues that the sustainable social impact and durable social legacies of small- and middle-scale sport events have much more potential. Future sport governance should develop the potential benefits of such local events.

The chapter by **Arnout Geeraert** (Belgium) starts from the observation of governance failures in international sport with a negative impact on wider society. He advocates the concept of normative power in order to enhance good governance in sport. The author explores how the European Union has the potential to be a normative power in international sport.

The quest for shared ownership and control over sport by players and fans is gaining momentum in various world sports, from European soccer to American football. **Peter Donnelly** (Canada) takes the case of a players' strike and its consequences in American football in his study on (the lack of) athletes' rights in games and teams from a human rights and labor rights perspective. The author calls for a future of sport where these athletes' rights are realized.

Many of the changes and processes needed to reach good governance in sport are already taking place at different levels of governance of sport. The chapters in this part contribute to these emerging changes in world sport

7 Accountability in the global regulation of sport

What does the future hold?

Hilary A. Findlay

Are the current regulations capable of ensuring that the globalized sport bodies are accountable?

The globalization of sport has shifted the legal regulation of the international sport system increasingly towards the private authority of international sport bodies, such as the International Olympic Committee (IOC), the World Anti-Doping Agency (WADA), the Court of Arbitration for Sport (CAS), and international sport federations (IFs) (Foster, 2003).

Nation states have accepted this regulatory autonomy by either refraining from enacting legislation governing national sport bodies, or (and this seems to have been the trend) adopting legislation that actually recognizes the exclusive authority of such bodies over national sport organizations (NFs), which in some instances trumps existing regulatory provisions (Findlay, 2013).[1] Similarly, with respect to dispute resolution, the emergence of mandatory sport arbitration has seriously limited the ability of national courts to intervene in sporting disputes. The effect of these developments has been to shield the autonomy of the global sport system from regulation by national legal systems. From a legal accountability perspective, this self-regulation has significant implications where the rules and regulations of these global bodies contravene fundamental principles of equity, fairness, and respect for human rights typically enshrined in and protected by national law (Mazzucco & Findlay, 2010a; 2010b).

The concerns associated with the globalization of the Olympic sport system, in particular, in many ways mirror those that exist in other fields similarly affected by globalization, including security, environmental protection, banking and financial regulation, and internet regulation. Indeed, as Kingsbury and Stewart (2008, 3, 5) point out, the "phenomena of globalization can no longer be effectively managed by separate national regulatory or administrative measures." As a consequence, "global regulatory bodies are either not subject to domestic political and legal accountability mechanisms at all or only to a very limited degree." This raises questions around the nature of the relationship between these bodies and those subject to them and, more specifically, as to whether the current regulation of the international sport system is capable of ensuring that these globalized sport bodies are accountable to those affected by their decisions, in particular, athletes.

Agamben's construct "state of exception" applied to the governance of globalized sport

Questions of globalization and control can be explored through the lens of Agamben's (2005) concept of "the state of exception." A state of exception exists where the ordinary judicial order is suspended. It depends upon a declaration of exceptional or dire necessity for its legitimacy. It does not create a juridical void; indeed, it creates the necessity to implement additional regulations and exert authority in response to the "dire necessity." Thus, the power, or sovereign, which declares (even creates) the state of exception fills the juridical space through the exercise of authority and the creation of rules to deal with this state of exception.

In Agamben's (1998) theory, the state of exception is linked to the concept of the "camp" or a "space" that is opened when the state of exception begins to become the rule. The camp thus becomes a permanent state of exception, almost a lacuna, where the "old rules of law and justice no longer seem to apply" (Hardie, 2009, 5) and the intervening authority, and its rules, become permanent. Agamben's construct of the state of exception is based on state or governmental power; however, others have extended the concept beyond governmental operations. It has also been used to describe the operation of elements within sport, including the regulatory environment of anti-doping (Hardie, 2011; 2014; Kreft, 2011), mega-event securitization (Hassan, 2013; Graham, 2012; Fussey & Coaffee, 2011), the operation of the Olympic Games (Marrero-Guillamón, 2012), the cultural and legal operation of various sports, including hockey (Fogel, 2013) and football (McLeod, Lovich, Newman, & Shields, 2014), and the world inhabited by the elite athlete (Kreft, 2009).[2]

Marrero-Guillamón (2012), for example, argues that the operation of the Olympic Games requires a state of exception regulated by exceptional laws (relating, for example, to security, ambush marketing, and infrastructure creation) and protected by extraordinary measures, particularly the surveillance of the public and private space. Hardie (2014, 87, 89) speaks to the inconsistency of anti-doping measures with respect to "traditional notions of the rule of law and the separation of powers." Indeed, he argues that the law has been "transformed" through the operation of anti-doping measures, including both the "whereabouts system" and the "biological passport," both of which he suggests have been allowed to infiltrate the mainstream of anti-doping, with little or no opposition, through the creation of a state of exception (a state described as one of moral crisis or panic [Ritchie & Jackson, 2011] and upon which anti-doping measures have been promulgated, legitimized, and generally accepted with little question, particularly around issues of efficacy and individual human rights).

Examples are most evident within the operation of the key international sport bodies, particularly the IOC, WADA, and CAS; however, Agamben's construct can also be applied to the governance of these globalized sport bodies and to the very process of their globalization, not just to their *modus operandi*. Indeed, it is argued that the IOC has engaged in a strategy of so-called creeping, or "trickle-down" state of exception so as to increasingly consolidate an "empire" of broad control and economic largesse, in part through the creation of other global sport institutions and events. However, this empire may not be a stable state. Though Hardie (2009, 5) argues that "we cannot return to a time of governance and judicial order existent before the 'state of exception'," this trickle-down state of exception created within the Olympic Movement by the IOC, and other global players, may not be sustainable. People cannot live in an unquestioning state of exception forever. At some point people become ready to engage, to become advocates for their interests, and those of their "community," and to hold parties to account.[3]

What does the future hold?

Kingsbury and Stewart (2008) propose a global system of administrative law to legitimate and ensure the accountability of these global institutions. Within the sport domain, Sandro Arcioni (in this volume) similarly advocates for a "World Sport Governance Agency" (WSGA). This chapter proposes a more grass-roots, bottom-up approach to accountability and raises the concept of *social license* as a potentially meaningful way of thinking about the relationships between these global organizations and civil society. It is a relatively new concept, though it has been linked to a much older idea – that of the *social contract* – which speaks to the legitimacy of the authority of the state over the individual. The term *social license* arose from the mining industry in Canada and Australia in the mid-1990s and has transformed management practices there and in a number of other resource extraction sectors. *Social license* does not refer to any regulatory or legal requirements. To the contrary, it considers how certain activities of an organization or business may gain or lose legitimacy in the eyes of a community, however *community* might be defined (Morrison, 2014).

Brown (2012) describes social license to be that which makes the use of power legitimate for a desired outcome. With reference to political power, he writes, "Power used without social license is just blunt force; the power to act with authority is only as good as the social license that supports it" (np).

Morrison (2014, 14) defines social license as describing "the sum of expectations between an organization and relevant social groups (usually represented by other organizations) in relation to a specific activity or set of related activities" and identifies three preconditions for a social license to exist: first, the particular activity, and those responsible for it, must be perceived to have sufficient "legitimacy"; second, there is sufficient "trust" between parties; and third, there is "consent" from those affected. Legitimacy is based on the established and accepted norms pertinent to the context. They may be formal rules or laws, they may be cultural, social, or legal, they may be written or unwritten and they may be local or universal, or all of the above. According to Morrison (2014), the critical issue of concern is the organization's basis for legitimacy. For example, we can ask: Is it supposed to be from the democratic representation of a particular community or interest group, from the internationally recognized norms it espouses, or both? What policies does the organization have, and do they reflect acceptable normative standards? And how, and with what, does the organization align itself? With legitimacy, an organization or project has a basic or "acceptance" level of social license, a willingness on the part of stakeholders to let a particular project proceed. With trust, social license rises to a level of "approval" and general support for a project. Trust is largely created by consistently providing true and clear information, by listening, by promise-keeping, and by fair dealing (Morrison, 2014). Finally, if an organization manages to earn the consent of stakeholders, the project's social license can rise to the level of psychological identification, wherein stakeholders see their future inextricably tied to the future of the project and consider themselves fully vested in the project. This level of social license comes from creating opportunities to work together and collaborate, and generates the shared experiences within which trust can evolve to consent. In sum, social license is strongest, or weakest, when the interests of the various stakeholder groups are aligned in favor of or against an activity.

The construction of social license is multifaceted and complex. Indeed, a creeping criticism of the concept is that it is increasingly being overly simplified (Gerson, 2014). Nonetheless, there are valuable lessons to be drawn from other sectors, especially those organizations whose prospects of acquiring and sustaining legitimacy in the absence of social license are remote, and where the likelihood of an increasingly distrustful and disillusioned stakeholder community is significantly enhanced. Applied research into social license in the resource sector has progressed to the point where it now provides companies with a validated and measurable roadmap toward stable access to resources, while at the same time ensuring stakeholder support. Evidence from Ponsford and Williams (2010) suggests the same could be true for the sport sector, specifically the importance of social license to the construction of an Olympic venue.

Similarly, anecdotal findings of Kidd (2011) with respect to the 2010 Winter Olympic and Paralympic Games in Vancouver, Canada, alludes to a number of positive outcomes where social license may have been present and negative outcomes suggesting an absence or loss of social license.[4]

To be sure, these are merely speculative conclusions based on post-hoc anecdotal observations. Much work would have to be done exploring social license in the context of sport-specific programs and events, investigating ways of calculating the value such initiatives bring to community stakeholders and, most particularly, identifying strategies and tools for building and maintaining social license (such as pre-planning consultation and consensus building, contractually based promises, and mechanisms of independent overview, to name a few such strategies). Nonetheless, as a concept, social license brings a stronger emphasis to the interests of society. It raises interesting ideas and questions for all types of organizations and stakeholder groups when they claim to be acting in the public interest.

Conclusion

Reflecting on outcomes of the 2010 Vancouver Winter Olympic Games, Kidd (2011, 12) wrote: "There needs to [be] a better way to ensure that the promised democratization of sport and physical activity through the hosting of major games is effectively realized." The issue this chapter started with was the creeping devolution of power and authority into the hands of private sport organizations and, along with it, increasingly minimal standards of accountability. The recognition of social license at both the global and local levels may be a way of bringing the reins of accountability back into the hands of those affected by the decisions of such bodies.

Notes

1 For example, in preparation for an Olympic Games, host committees are required to amend existing national trademark legislation, security legislation, and municipal by-laws, among others.
2 According to Kreft (2009, 7) "non-governmental bodies such as civil society's autonomous sport associations produce legal systems that promote a state of exception without constitutional or international law legal restraints."
3 For example, only two contenders remain in the bid to host the 2022 Winter Olympic Games – Beijing and Almaty, the capital of Kazakhstan, after public opposition to hosting an Olympic Games forced four others to withdraw.
4 Positive examples: a community plebiscite ensuring majority support for the submission of a bid for the Games; measures toward environmental sustainability; and an independent monitoring and review process, among others. Negative examples: tensions involving relations between Games organizers and First Nations groups; the reinstatement of gender verification testing for selected women; opposition to the granting of event status to female ski jumping; and struggles over the legacy program of the Games. Brown (2012) provides a direct example, where the British Columbia provincial government lost its social license through its unilateral diversion of ongoing community cultural funds to one-time Olympic cultural initiatives during the 2010 Vancouver Winter Olympic and Paralympic Games.

References

Agamben, G. (1998). *Homo sacer: Sovereign power and bare life.* Stanford, CA: Stanford University Press.

Agamben, G. (2005). *The state of exception.* Chicago, IL: University of Chicago Press.

Brown, M. (2012). *Towards a new government in British Columbia.* [Online Kindle Edition, Amazon Digital Services, Inc.] D01-4760516-3965121.

Findlay, H. (2013). *Sagen v VANCO* [2009] BCCA 522. In J. Anderson (Ed.), *Landmark cases in sports law* (pp. 53–67). The Hague: TMC Asser Institute Press.

Fogel, C. (2013). On-ice assault: Difficulties in discerning assault in Canadian ice hockey. *International Law Research, 2* (1), 96–101.

Foster, K. (2003). Is there a global sports law? *Entertainment and Sports Law Journal, 2* (1), 1–18.

Fussey, P., & Coaffee, J. (2011). Olympic rings of steel: Constructing security for 2012 and beyond. In Bennett, C.J. & Haggerty, K.D. (Eds.), *Security games: Surveillance and control at mega-events* (pp. 36–54). London: Routledge.

Gerson, J. (2014, October 17). Rise of "social licence": Claiming they speak for their community, protest groups are undermining the law. *National Post*. Retrieved December 16, 2014, from: http://news.nationalpost.com/2014/10/17/rise-of-social-licence-believing-they-speak-for-their-community-protest-groups-are-undermining-the-law/

Graham, S. (2012). Olympic 2012 security: Welcome to lockdown London. *CITY: Analysis of urban trends, culture, theory, policy, action*, *16* (4), 446–451.

Hardie, M. (2009). From Barthes to Foucault and beyond: Cycling in the age of empire. A paper delivered at *Foucault: 25 Years On*. Centre for Postcolonial Studies and Globalisation, University of South Africa, Adelaide, SA, June 25.

Hardie, M. (2011). It's not about the blood! Operacion Puerto and the end of modernity. In M. McNamee & V. Moller (Eds.), *Doping and anti-doping policy in sport: Ethical, legal and social perspectives* (pp. 160–182). London: Routledge.

Hardie, M. (2014). Making visible the invisible act of doping. *International Journal of Semiotics of Law*, *27*, 85–119.

Hassan, D. (2013). Securing the Olympics: at what cost? *Sport in society: Cultures, commerce, media, politics*, *17* (5), 628–639.

Kidd, B. (2011). The legacies of the 2010 Winter Olympic and Paralympic Games in Vancouver. Retrieved January 22, 2015, from: https://doc.rero.ch/record/22123/files/2010_-_Kidd.pdf.

Kingsbury, B., & Stewart, R.B. (2008). Legitimacy and accountability in global regulatory governance: The emerging global administrative law and the design and operation of administrative tribunals of international organizations. In S. Flogaitis (Ed.), *International administrative tribunals in a changing world*. London, England: Esperia Publications Ltd. Retrieved February 26, 2014, from: www.iilj.org/aboutus/documents/LegitimacyAccountabilityandGAL.UNATvolumefinalAug82008.pdf.

Kreft, L. (2009). The elite athlete: In a state of exception. *Sport, Ethics and Philosophy*, *3* (1), 3–18.

Kreft, L. (2011). Elite sportspersons and commodity control: Anti-doping as quality assurance. *International Journal of Sport Policy and Politics*, *3* (2), 151–161.

Marrero-Guillamón, I. (2012). Olympic state of exception. *Games Monitor*. Retrieved May 3, 2014, from www.gamesmonitor.org.uk/node/1780.

Mazzucco, M., & Findlay, H. (2010a). Re-thinking the legal regulation of the Olympic Movement: Envisioning a broader role for the Court of Arbitration for Sport. In R. Barney, J. Forsyth, & M.K. Heine (Eds.), *Rethinking matters Olympic: Investigations into the socio-cultural study of the modern Olympic Movement* (pp. 363–375). Proceedings of the 10th Olympic Symposium, University of Western Ontario, Ontario, October 28–30.

Mazzucco, M., & Findlay, H. (2010b). The supervisory role of CAS in regulating the international sport system. *Sport and Society*, *1* (2), 131–144.

McLeod, C., Lovich, J., Newman, J.I., & Shields, R. (2014). The training camp: American football and/as spectacle of exception. *Journal of Sport and Social Issues*, *38* (3), 222–244.

Morrison, J. (2014). *The social license: How to keep your organization legitimate*. New York: Palgrave MacMillan.

Ponsford, I.F., & Williams, P.W. (2010). Crafting a social license to operate: A case study of Vancouver 2010's Cypress Olympic Venue. *Event Management*, *14* (1), 17–36.

Ritchie, I., & Jackson, G. (2011). Moral panic and Canadian anti-doping rules: Anti-doping – rational policy or moral panic. International Conference at Aarhus University, Denmark, August 18–19.

8 The creation of an independent body for the control of governance in sport worldwide

Sandro Arcioni

How can the world of sport regulate itself and improve its governance?

Over the last 15 years, sport associations and organizations have encountered profound changes in their operating conditions and funding, thanks to the considerable increase in revenues from television rights, sponsorship from local events such as lucrative cups or world championships, and the organization of international circuits.[1] They had to combine in a hybrid way the logic of associations and the logic of business to ensure their development at the cost of a compromise of identity management (Bayle, 2007). These non-governmental organizations (NGOs), which historically obtained a quasi-monopoly position, are not directly subject to a regulatory or public stock market (except for the financial review system of organizations). The situation of the international sport federations (IFs) is not unique; NGOs have the same type of structure (Futurible, 2001; Queinnec & Igallens, 2004), such as the Comité International de la Croix-Rouge (CICR).[2]

Although an NGO is non-profit and of "public interest," its functioning is totally private and derives from a democratic system. Contrary to a company, where the financial result is essential and where the interests of shareholders play a major role, non-profit international organizations such as sport organizations are not primarily designed for profit-making. This does not rule out the need for resource development, for a balanced budget, and for the development of media coverage of a sport event, or its expansion into new countries or continents. Moreover, these organizations must strive to avoid dishonest dealings (personal enrichment, secret funding, etc.) that strongly contradict the humanistic values they seek to promote.

The governance of the IOC, the National Olympic Committees (NOCs), and the national and international federations is nevertheless often at fault, though in this matter, not different from other large organizations. The doubts which arose at the beginning of the twenty-first century concerning the functioning of the IOC, the Fédération Internationale de Volley-Ball, FIFA, and other IFs, illustrates this fact. However, since 2000, major changes in governance methods have occasionally been adopted or envisaged – e.g. at the IOC (Chappelet, 2007).

Currently, except for the Olympic Charter, the 2000 IOC report, the IOC document "Basic universal principles of good governance in the sports Olympic Movement," and Resolutions 41 and 42 in the 2009 Copenhagen IOC (2009b) report, "The Olympic Movement in society," there is no recommendation, no law, nor regulatory body (control) that has been applied to the domain of sport. Except for the Court of Arbitration (CAS) created in 1983 and the Anti-Doping Agency (WADA), there is in sport no law or regulation body similar to the Sarbanes-Oxley Act controlling economic companies or UN-Watch controlling NGOs. So the question remains: How can the sports world regulate itself – i.e. control and improve its governance?

Needs for regulating the world of sport

What are the needs for regulating the world of sport despite the actions of the IOC concerning governance?

Under the leadership of former President Juan Antonio Samaranch, the major international sports associations have followed some regulatory recommendations. Following the IOC 2000 report and through the actions of Dr. Jacques Rogge (Samaranch's successor) some improvements continue, although they remain marginal. Only two recommendations (41 and 42) concerning good governance in the world of sport were produced at the IOC Congress in Copenhagen on October 5, 2009.

Recommendation 41 states:

> The legitimacy and autonomy of the Olympic Movement depend on the abiding of the highest standards of ethical behavior and good governance. All members of the Olympic Movement should adopt (as a minimum standard) the basic universal principles of good governance of the Olympic Movement, as proposed by the IOC. All members of the Olympic Movement must at all times demonstrate integrity, accountability and transparency, as well as strong management skills, and ensure that under all circumstances, their legal status is fully compatible with their activities and responsibilities and in full conformity with the laws of the country (applicable laws).

Recommendation 42 was equally clear, stating:

> All members of the Olympic Movement should keep proper accounts respecting the accounting standards; ensure they are reviewed or audited independently, adopt rules, standards and practices whereby those who do not respect the principles of good governance could lose their funding or be punished, adopt and implement a code of ethics founded on the principles and rules of the IOC code of ethics, and always strive to protect and promote the interests of the athletes they represent.

Unfortunately, the text of these recommendations includes only an *encourage-ment* to follow the process, similar to the "rules of conduct for IF" in the Code of Ethics (2009a) of the IOC. Several researchers (e.g. Chappelet, 1991; 2001; 2007; Arcioni, 2007a,b) have made proposals to the IOC that go beyond encouragement to target the "control structures of governance." For example, a proposal to establish the Lausanne Covenant by Chappelet was issued during his lecture to the Panathlon Club of Lausanne in 2010.

The IOC risks a lot when some issues are not addressed properly

A number of issues have to be addressed by the IOC, such as the procedures for selecting a host city for the Olympics (national policy) and their controls; the application of measurable criteria for maintaining a sport against the claims of another on the Olympic Program (conflict between a traditional sport and a "fun" sport or the "gigantism" of the Olympics); the necessity to set up a jurisdiction hierarchy within the IF and to have access to the CAS (e.g. FILA, Fédération Internationale de Lutte Amateur during the Olympic Games in 2008); the defini-tion of the rules applied for the redistribution of the Olympic revenues; controls in the implementation of development plans (e.g. in the International Judo Federation there are no controls); "competition" between the IOC and the IFs about the development of sport (recognition of states/countries for the creation of NOC and National Sporting Federations); the use of Olympic receipts (by IF or NOC) for diverted aims (even arms trade), etc.

Even more is at stake for the IOC if issues such as the following are not intro-duced, promoted, changed, or challenged:

* The promotion of an "anti-corruption" image creating a "World Anti-Corruption Agency" (WACA as Dick Pound, member of the IOC and first CEO of WADA, proposed in 2009). The risk of doing nothing could imply that sport management equals corruption!
* The creation of a supervisory body in the UN-Watch. UN-Watch is in charge of verifying systematically the implementation of the UN Charter for the UN system. In our case: to defend athletes' rights.
* The ownership of the control rights by another organization (financial interests).
* The pressure of the media (the same as in 1998–1999, before the IOC Report 2000).
* Consumers' rights.
* Contrary to WADA and to the CAS, a new controlling body without direct connection with the world of sport.

But the greatest risk for the IOC lies in its reluctance and slowness to change in general, let alone that the IOC should quickly create the suggested independent control body.

For example: if the Commissions responsible for legislation on sport in the European Union, spurred by the major European media, developed a law on TV rights, these Commissions might be able to operate before the world of sport. Such a law on TV rights could include a maximal cap, a distribution key with withheld tax accruing to the signing country – 30 percent to be distributed to aid projects for development and to sports projects in the developing countries; 40 percent to be returned to the organizing country (with a 10 percent tax); and only 30 percent remaining in the keeping of the IF.

Another example: if these Commissions asked the world of sports (IFs) to replace their customs by strict rules, then these rules must be enacted by the EU as the only alternative to the world of sport, but if an independent agency was created it would enact such rules and would help transform the IF customs into rules in agreement with all the world sports bodies.

Currently, unlike the business world, in sport there is a loophole in the field. No official authority exists to date. Moreover, since the disappearance of OATH (Olympic Advocates Together Honorability), there is no longer an athletes' union, and it is not in the competence of the CAS to address them. Conversely, UN-Watch is interested in an athlete's union (e.g. there were a few appearances of this organization during the Beijing Olympics in 2008).

On the other hand, the huge size of the sport system and the involvement of some governments from totalitarian or developing countries in national sports systems, the control of sport by some mafia organizations (e.g. NSF FILA from former USSR countries, money laundering, the organization of online betting, etc.) would need more governance control from the world of sport.

An independent body to monitor good functioning and governance of sport in a globalized world

What should be the function of this independent body?

In our opinion it should not be a supervisory body *per se*, but rather an independent organization working in sport and able to support all stakeholders in sport, especially the players involved in amateur and professional sport, at the national and international levels, in order to improve governance structures and move toward full transparency and harmonization. This body would have to establish a monitoring system of governance in order to reach a governance standard in sport.

This body could be named *World Sport Governance Agency* (WSGA). It would be an NGO defending the Olympic Charter, and the principles of good governance and ethics within the Olympic system and the world of professional and amateur sport. Its logo and slogans could be *Monitoring Sport* and *Promoting Ethics and Good Governance*.

This body should enjoy the full support of the IOC, just as CAS and WADA did at their inception, as well as the support of the IFs. This is in the interests of all, because it is a way for the IOC to have a compliance guarantee for the governance of the NOCs and IFs, and the same guarantee as for the national sporting federations (NFs). The pattern is identical for the organizers of major sporting events.

How could the work of the WSGA be developed?

The WSGA could become independent and neutral after a start-up period assisted by the IOC. It should become legally and financially independent, and be the recognized body for audit and certification of good governance (standards to be defined) in the world of sport. It should also offer support to all sports bodies wishing to improve their governance. It would have the following aims:

- To assist the members of the Olympic system to improve their structures (e.g. harmonizing the structures of different stakeholders in the sporting world, and striving for good governance).
- To dictate the rules regarding the good governance of sport and to remain the master of the destiny of global sport.
- In no way to be equated with corruption or money-laundering, for example.

Just as in the business world (e.g. the corporate governance rules dictated by the Sarbanes–Oxley Act in the USA), the WSGA should order one or two internal audits per year, depending on the size of sports organizations, as well as an external audit performed by certified auditors of the WSGA. The assessment system (audit or evaluation system) should focus on the "basic universal principles of good governance of the Olympic Movement," a draft document dated February 1, 2008, as well as on the assessment system of governance of sports organizations by Arcioni (2007a,b). The integration of the two systems, with additional indicators based on the size of organizations and the summer and winter sports, should take into account the autonomy of the members of the Olympic Movement.

Which evaluation methodology could be applied to the WSGA?

In order to improve, it is necessary to measure. That is why we created a measurement system. However, to improve the governance of an organization, it is not enough to measure it once and improve the governance system according to the comments reported. It will be necessary to establish a system of control (or a regulatory system) of governance that will serve as a method for measuring the governance of an organization.

This system can be modeled using the conventional graph of a control system as described below. Somehow, the indicators highlighted in the proposed tool will drive the good governance of an organization through constant regulation (or fine-tuning) of the governance of an organization.

The system of governance assessment will measure the five levels of organizational governance: (1) management: professional, independent financing and management; (2) governance: identity, values, flexibility, and internal configuration of power; (3) regulation: control, communication, and accountability; (4) harmonization: partnership relations, reputation, and jurisdiction; (5) meta-governance: meta-jurisdiction, social and economic development, conservation, and management of resources for development, strengthening of major groups and means of implementation.

To summarize, Henry's (2001) contribution, with organizational and systemic governance, is situated at level 5 in Pérez's (2003) framework. The interrelation between policy governance described by Carver (2001) and political governance demonstrated by Henry (2001) continues our quest to show sport governance theories in policy governance. This is the epitome of all sport governance models. Figure 8.1 shows the intricacies of meta-governance.

It is only thanks to the use of such a control system that we will be able to notice that (and how) governance changes over time. That is the reason why the measurement should be made at various times during the year. If, for example, we take the recommendations of the Sarbanes-Oxley Act as the operating reference, this measurement should be done four times per year internally and once externally in order to be fully comprehensive in measurement results. As to IFs, we propose to have two internal audits and one external audit per year.

The conceptual framework of audits is described in a narrative form by the principal dimensions studied and their relationships according to the levels of management in the framework proposed and tested by Pérez (2003).

There are 2 types of controls: (1) internal, by the auditor or the audit committee of the IF or the IOC; and (2) by the external auditor or the audit committee of the WSGA (World Sport Governance Agency).

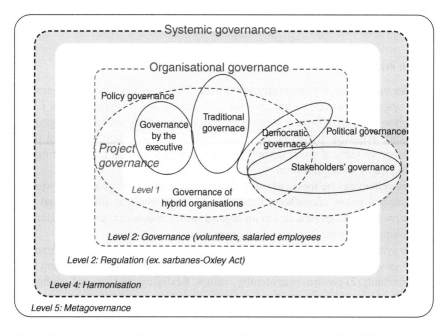

Figure 8.1 An overview of governance models (Arcioni & Vandewalle, 2008)

Indeed, on the basis of these two audits, we would have an internal measurement (e.g. two measurements per year) of the governance of an IF and an external measurement (unbiased) of the governance of an IF and the IOC. Then we would compare the two tests and measure the differences between them. This will not only provide an interesting complement to the transparency of an IF, but it will be the average of the two results which will give the final rating of the organization which is analyzed.

Perspectives: opportunities and impediments

The advantage of setting up a system with measurement tools for improving governance in sports organizations is somewhat obvious, allowing an organization to represent its governance visually and therefore to see the failures and to correct them each year in order to develop a virtuous learning process. Once these qualities are demonstrated, the IF could continue to express them using an independent label (annual certification). It may also be recommended to these IFs to create an internal commission to monitor the evolution of their governance and constantly seek to improve it.

To illustrate current shortcomings in governance at the level of harmonization (Level 4, Pérez, 2003), we can discuss the case of Lance Armstrong (seven-time winner of the Tour de France) related to doping to demonstrate that the rules of the world of sport, the laws and international agreements do not go far enough (AFLD, WADA, UCI rules, etc.). For example, France has all the elements to prove a doping case, yet France does not act! In June 2012 the USA's Anti-Doping Agency (USADA) banned Armstrong from competitive cycling for life for doping offences, and said he had been engaged in "the most sophisticated, professionalized and successful doping program that sport has ever seen." For the record, we recall also the case of Marion Jones, who went to prison and paid for her crimes (perjury), so Armstrong could also serve a prison sentence, let alone pay his debts. The harmonization of sanctions brings a new justification for the creation of an independent body for the control of governance in the world of sport.

However, it is clear that the organizations studied are also and sometimes essentially "political configurations" and even political arenas focused on power struggles, according to Mintzberg (2004), or a behaviorist perspective (Cyert & March, 1963). The preservation of power by the president and the managers in office appear to be the driving force behind the dynamics of governance and management.

The control of the Board of Directors of the IOC and of IFs, though not very frequently exercised, is professional. However, the question of whether their purpose and strategy (between the Board and the salaried senior management employees, between national and/or continental organizations and the IFs, and between the organization and its stakeholders) are beyond reproach and properly served by the leadership and management is not really addressed.

Another item of discussion concerns the other forms of rationality present in terms of governance and power. There are three spheres – the science of management, sociology, and political science – hence Ian Henry's model, stressing a transition from a centralized (vertical hierarchical structure) towards a horizontal regulation and coordination of the actions based on consensus, compromises and shared power. Today, organizations need such a structure to justify their legitimization in sport.

The financial responsibility for such NGOs is theoretically to ensure the optimization of its administration, to reduce the operating costs, and to direct maximum resources toward its social objective. Because these elements are difficult to measure and to control, neo-institutionalists like Berger and Luckmann (1966) suggest following the way in which all multinationals are now changing the institutionalization of their governance. This includes a development from a redistributive internal rationality based on a financial logic (i.e. to organize profitable competitions contributing to the image of the IF while organizing a financial redistribution to the most disadvantaged areas) toward a more global societal rationality based on citizens and society (i.e. "do good" using sport by disseminating the values of sport and Olympism for the benefit of society) in order to regain a challenged legitimacy. This trend seems similar to what we know as corporate social responsibility (CSR), which is in fact not new in a sports world driven by the Olympic values, i.e. aiming at a better and more peaceful world via sport. Trying to restore civic and societal rationality is therefore only new in terms of strategy, management, and especially communication. That is the reason why Levels 4 and 5 of governance are becoming more and more important to facilitate the implementation of these new challenges and help restore the legitimacy of NGOs.

However, unlike the business world, there is a legal vacuum in the world of sport. As already mentioned, no official authority currently exists in the sports world, whereas there are many reasons to call for control and regulation, given the gigantism of the sport system, the meddling of some totalitarian or Southern countries with their national sporting systems, and the control of sport by some mafia organizations. To fill this legal vacuum the creation of a World Sport Governance Agency (WSGA) would offer an interesting perspective and could even be used outside the sport world, i.e. in all international non-profit organizations. This agency could become a model for the control of the governance of NGOs. Based on the same model, the world of NGOs could create a similar agency and include a measurement tool for the standard corporate governance of large NGOs, adapting some indicators according to their specific purpose (e.g. humanitarian, charitable, climate change, etc.).

Notes

1 As an example, one of the most lucrative was the Football World Cup in 2006, which generated turnover of €557 million and a profit of €155 million. FIFA has the ownership rights for the organization of this event. FIFA has a turnover of €553 million and a profit of €184 million (FIFA Financial Report, 2008).
2 The credibility of the actions of the CICR and its legitimacy are regularly questioned: payment for rights of way in Africa, moral values of some members, functioning of the headquarters, etc.

References

Arcioni, S. (2007a). La gouvernance des fédérations sportives internationales: proposition d'un cadre d' analyse [Governance of international sport organizations, proposal of a analytical framework]. In E. Bayle & P. Chantelat, *Gouvernance des organisations sportives* (pp. 49–76). Paris: L'Harmatan.

Arcioni, S. (2007b). Les modalités de la gouvernance dans les organisations internationals à but non lucratif: le cas des Fédérations internationales sportives [Governance rules in international organizations without lucrative purpose: The case of international sport organizations]. Thèse de doctorat, Université Claude Bernard Lyon 1, France.

Arcioni, S., & Vandewalle, P. (2010, September). Creation of an independent body for the control of the governance of sporting organisations worldwide. Paper presented at the meeting of 18th Conference of the European Association for Sport Management, Prague, Czech Republic.

Bayle, E. (2007). La recherche en management des organisations sportives: Objet, champ, niveaux d'analyse et spécificités des pratiques de management [Research on management in sport organizations: Object, area, levels of analysis and specifics of management practices]. *Revue Internationale en Science du Sport et de l'Education Physique*, *75*, 59–81.

Berger, P., & Luckmann, T. (1996). *La construction sociale de la réalité* [Social construction of reality]. Paris: Armand Colin.

Carver, J. (2001). Carver's policy governance model in nonprofit organizations. *The Canadian Journal of Governance: Revue Internationale*, *2* (1), 30–48.

Chappelet, J.-L. (1991). *Le système olympique*, Grenoble: Presses Universitaires.

Chappelet, J.-L. (2001). Le système olympique et les pouvoirs publics face au dopage et à la corruption. In *Sport et ordre public*, Paris: La Documentation Française.

Chappelet, J.-L. (2007). La gouvernance du Comité International Olympique [Governance of the IOC]. In E. Bayle & P. Chantelat, *Gouvernance des organisations sportives* (pp. 29–48). Paris: L'Harmatan.

Chappelet, J.-L. (2010). Vers une solution globale pour lutter contre les dérives du sport, [Towards a comprehensive solution to fight against the excesses of sport]. Paper presented at the meeting of Panathlon Club Lausanne, Lausanne.

Cyert, R., & March, J.G. (1963). *Behavioral theory of the firm*. Engelwood Cliffs, NJ: Prentice Hall.

Futurible (2001). Le défi de la gouvernance [The challenge of governance], *Etudes prospectives*, *265*, n.p.

Henry, I.P. (2001). *The politics of leisure policy*. London: Palgrave.

IOC (2000). *Réformes* [Reforms]. Lausanne: IOC.

IOC (2004). *Charte Olympique* [Olympic Charter]. Lausanne: IOC.

IOC (2008). *Principes universels de base de bonne gouvernance du Mouvement Olympique et Sportif* [Universal principles of good governance in the Olympic Sportive Movement]. Lausanne: IOC.

IOC (2009a). *Code éthique* [Code of Ethics]. Lausanne: IOC.

IOC (2009b). *Le Mouvement Olympique dans la société* [The Olympic Movement in society]. Copenhagen: IOC.

Mintzberg, H. (2004). *Pouvoir et gouvernement d'entreprise* [Power and governance in companies]. Paris: Editions d'organisation.

Pérez, R. (2003). *La gouvernance de l'entreprise* [Company governance]. Paris: La écouverte.

Queinnec, E., & Igalens, J. (2004). *Les organisations non gouvernementales et le management* [NGOs and management]. Paris: Vuibert.

9 The rise and fall of mega sport events

The future is in non-mega sport events

Marijke Taks

Introduction

Most research on the impacts of events has focused on mega-events, such as the Olympic Games (OG) and the FIFA World Cup, and the outcomes are not always positive. The OG and the FIFA World Cup are the largest sporting events, with a tremendous global reach, and they have a remarkably high positive image and a passionate audience. The Olympic rings are one of the strongest global brands (Barney, Wenn, & Martyn, 2004), and corporate partners are granted exclusive rights to this symbol. As such, the OG offer a dazzling global platform for transnational corporations to expose their brands, create awareness, inform the world, and stimulate consumption, all with the assistance of the efforts of elite athletes. These athletes are frequently positioned as *role models*, inspiring others to participate in sport, and thereby promoting a so-called *trickle-down* effect, a claim which is poorly substantiated (Weed, Coren, & Fiore, 2009). The "feel-good factor" that this type of event generates is temporary (Kavetsos & Szymanski, 2010), and the lasting effects for host communities can be negative, both socially (Horne & Manzenreiter, 2006) and economically (Kesenne, 2012). Thus, mega-events have a tremendous global exposure and global power, but their sustainable impact is questionable.

Smaller-sized non-mega sport events (NMSEs) have been under-researched when it comes to sustainable legacies. However, NMSEs are more ubiquitous, and require tight local partnerships to stage the events. As such they have the potential and the power to reach out to people in local communities in a more profound way compared to mega sport events (MSEs). Therefore, NMSEs may be more relevant in creating durable benefits for host communities, as opposed to MSEs; and at the aggregate level, NMSEs provide more lasting global benefits. The key question in this chapter is: What makes NMSEs different from and more suitable than MSEs for developing positive outcomes for host communities?

Events are known to have a variety of impacts including economic, tourism, social, and sport participation impacts.[1] In what follows, examples of impacts, outcomes, and legacies of NMSEs and MSEs are provided to demonstrate how NMSEs (may) lead to more positive and sustainable outcomes for people living in the host communities, whose quality of life is directly impacted by those events.

Conceptual framework

Definitions of NMSE and MSE events

There are no universal definitions or typologies of events. For the purpose of this contribution we define an MSE as an event that generates "very high levels of tourism, media coverage, prestige or economic impact for their host community" (Getz, 2012, 45), although their impact and meaning reaches far beyond the event and the host city. An NMSE is also a "major" event, but it is generally smaller in size, scale, scope, and reach than its mega counterpart. For the purpose of this contribution, we define NMSE as a smaller version of MSE, being significant, one-off sport events, of short duration and out of the ordinary. Examples of NMSE are the Pan American Junior Athletic Championships, the European Junior Boxing Championships, or the World Badminton Championships (Gratton & Taylor, 2000).

Impacts, outcomes, legacies, and sustainability

The MSE and NMSE discussed in this contribution are temporal and trigger short- or long-term impacts (positive or negative) which lead to outcomes (positive or negative). When these outcomes are sustained, they become legacies. Preuss (2007, 86) defines a legacy as "all planned and unplanned positive and negative, intangible and tangible structures created by and for a sport event that remains for a longer time than the event itself." *Tangible* legacies are, for example, economic and infrastructure; *intangible* legacies are, for example, transfer of knowledge, image, and reputation. Sport governing bodies responsible for staging mega-events have recognized the importance of long-term legacy planning, in the hope of changing the lives of host residents for the better.

In the last two decades there has been a call to shift the focus from merely *impacts* to producing *sustainable outcomes* (e.g. Chalip, 2006). Sustainable development refers to the needs of the present, without compromising the needs and wants of future generations. Thus, we focus on outcomes that are: (1) created through the event; and (2) maintained for a longer period of time after the event in the host communities.

Economic perspective

The overestimation of the benefits and underestimation of the costs of hosting an MSE, particularly during the bidding phase, has been well documented in the literature. The IOC and FIFA (Fédération Internationale de Football Association) have both followed a strategy of commercializing their assets, exploiting media rights, and sponsoring partnerships to generate significant revenues for the organization (Foley, McGillivray, & McPherson, 2012), while leaving the host communities with significant debts. Driven by a neoliberal ideology, bidding for an MSE is often part of a city's pro-growth strategy based on the notion that they drive investments (public and private), jobs, and tourism (e.g. Misener & Mason, 2006). One-off sport events create a typical temporary "shock" in the economy, since the demand for a range of products, services, and facilities rises dramatically for a very short period of time. Economic-impact analyses (EIAs) try to capture the extent of this increased demand, but fail to mention the opportunity cost (e.g. diverting investments from other projects, crowding out regular tourists, etc.). This is the reason why standard EIAs overestimate the so-called *economic benefits*, since they only account for the positive impacts while ignoring the negative ones (Kesenne, 2012). Several sport economists have therefore proposed alternative methods of capturing the economic impact of events, such as cost-benefit analyses or computable general equilibrium models. These methods reveal more realistic (and often negative) outcomes (e.g. Taks, Kesenne, Chalip, Green, & Martyn, 2011). The next section highlights why and how the outcomes of economic impacts are different for MSEs compared to NMSEs, and in favor of the latter.

Both types of events create (some) winners (e.g. usually the organizing committee, the hospitality industry, some businesses). However, negative economic impacts of MSEs (e.g. tax payers' debt) are dramatically higher for MSEs compared to NMSEs. To this day, Australia claims that its industry still benefits from hosting the OG in 2000 (Toohey, 2008). The global audience of MSE brings in large income through TV broadcasting, sponsorships, and other types of revenues (merchandising, tickets, etc.). It is the so-called *ménage a trois* (Thibault, 2009) – the sport-media-business alliance, also called the global sport media complex – that reap the major benefits of the MSE, leaving tax payers with significant debt (Kesenne, 2012).

Agha and Taks (2015) assessed economic impact using a cost-benefit approach (including five benefit and five cost drivers) and redefined event size and city size as continuums of resources allowing for a joint analysis of supply and demand. Using the concept of *resource deficiency* and bringing local economic conditions into the analysis, it was demonstrated that: (1) no city has the resources required to host a mega-event and will therefore never achieve the optimal economic impact; (2) smaller events have a higher potential for maximum optimal economic impact compared to larger events; and (3) smaller events have positive impacts in many more cities than larger events. Thus, evidence is beginning to show that NMSEs may be more successful in generating positive economic impacts compared to MSEs.

Tourism perspective

In addition to stimulating economic development, cities hosting events are particularly keen about branding their city as a tourism destination. Two types of tourism should be distinguished: flow-on (i.e. at the time of the events) and future (i.e. sustainable) tourism. Both MSE and NMSE events attract visitors at the time of the event, thereby creating opportunities for flow-on tourism. However, the drastic difference in number of visitors may have reverse effects on flow-on tourism. For MSE, the enormous influx of tourists may crowd out regular tourists (Preuss, 2005), thereby negatively impacting the number of tourists engaging in classic tourism activities (e.g. visiting museums, sight-seeing tours). Alternatively, large crowds and long waiting lines may hinder participating in certain tourism activities. NMSEs also create opportunities for flow-on tourism activities (e.g. Gibson, Kaplanidou, & Kang, 2012; Taks, Challip, Green, Kesenne & Martyn, 2009), but the tourism industry has yet to learn how to capitalize on this opportunity and leverage NMSEs to enhance tourism in the host community (Weed, 2003).

Because MSEs attract global media attention, they are expected to brand their city as an *international* tourist destination, with the intention of generating future tourism (e.g. Ritchie, 1984). Except for the summer OG in Barcelona, which saw the number of tourists grow post-OG, there is no evidence that MSEs have created sustainable tourism outcomes (Solberg & Preuss, 2007). Follow-up studies to actually measure these outcomes are usually missing, because outcomes are extremely difficult to measure, since multiple externalities can affect tourism behavior. Australia, for example, had great expectations of boosting future tourism through the hosting of the OG, but this strategy was counteracted by both the September 11 attacks in 2001 and SARS in 2003 (Toohey, 2008), making it impossible to attribute any tourism gains or losses to the OG.

In summary, the tourism industry can potentially benefit from hosting events. However, the likelihood that NMSEs create sustained future tourism is slim. This is particularly true if the event is not part of a larger event portfolio (Ziakas & Costa, 2011). NMSEs have the potential to create new tourism opportunities, particularly for small- and medium-sized cities, which are likely not at full capacity, have room for growth, and can take advantage of these events to showcase unique features of the city or region.

Social impact perspective[2]

Social impact of events refers to "changes in the collective and individual value systems, behavior patterns, community structures, lifestyle and quality of life" (adapted from Hall as cited in Balduck, Maes, & Buelens, 2011, 94). However, accurate social impact assessments of events are missing. The well-intended rhetoric indicates that social outcomes are generally hoped for and desired, as opposed to being planned for (Chalip, 2006). Much of the evidence of the capacity of sport events to enhance social unity is on MSE and emphasizes feelings of euphoria, enhanced national pride, and unity. However, much of this evidence is anecdotal (e.g. Smith, 2009), and accurately measuring the social impacts of events is extremely complex. Taks (2013) contrasted and compared social impacts and outcomes of MSEs and NMSEs using four different perspectives: power relations, urban regeneration, socialization, and human capital. Overall,

NMSEs appeared to provide more positive social impact and outcome opportunities for local residents compared to MSEs. This is based on the premise that NMSEs create tighter social networks and connectedness of the local population with the event. For instance, the nature of MSE planning does not start at the community level. The community reacts to plans presented to them (top-down strategy), rather than being involved in creating them and taking part in each step of the process (bottom-up strategy). This bottom-up strategy installs a sense of ownership (Hiller, 2000), a solid foundation for carrying positive outcomes. Starting to understand how social impacts vary according to the size of event, and the type of community that hosts them, is a first step in increasing an understanding of what events actually mean for the residents who are directly affected by these events.

The concept of *social capital* may help explain why NMSEs may have a more positive social impact on the quality of life of the residents in the host community. Community networks, relationships of trust and reciprocity, and social inclusion are central to social capital (Onyx & Bullen, 2000). NMSEs seem to have a higher potential for the creation or reinforcing of horizontal social capital (i.e. horizontal ties among members of the community, stimulating civic participation and high levels of social trust), and ownership. In contrast, MSEs reinforce vertical social capital (i.e. vertical ties between community members and elites), which represents a form of inequality between citizens. According to Misener and Mason (2006), events can offer meaningful sources of social capital if: (1) community values are central to all decision-making processes; (2) various stakeholders, particularly community interest groups, are involved in strategic activities related to events; (3) collaborative actions empower local communities to become agents of change; and (4) open communication and mutual learning throughout strategic activities related to events is maintained to minimize power brokering. All four conditions have a better chance to succeed for NMSEs because of the tighter social networks and the greater likelihood that the local population is connected with the event (Taks, 2013). Creating coherent networks within communities seems more plausible for NMSEs, which are by default embedded in local communities. While bids for MSEs, such as the OG or the World Cup, are required to demonstrate some kind of meaningful social outcomes, their relative value in terms of social *capital* remains uncertain, and they clearly employ a top-down strategy, *enforcing* change in communities, including displacement of less powerful groups, forced evictions, and loss of affordable housing (e.g. Smith, 2012).

MSEs are primarily externally focused and commercially oriented, trying to gain a better market position in this global world. Their primary concern is not the people in the host community. However, MSEs can contribute to creating *connectedness* at the local level. Activities such as Olympic Torch relays, for example, boost pride and identity (Chalip, 2006); but note that these events again are much smaller in scale than the actual MSE. Examples of sustainable, tangible social outcomes of MSE are Olympic parks, where people can gather and socialize many years after the OG (e.g. Atlanta 1996 OG; Kaplanidou, 2012).

Events allow local communities to create meaningful partnerships, which have the potential to remain in existence long after the event is gone. However, long-term sustainability requires meaningful involvement of citizens at every stage. Again, this seems more plausible to succeed in the context of smaller events because of the bottom-up strategy. What is important here is that the structures created for a one-off event do not evaporate once the event is over, but rather that lines of communication and collaboration are sustained and may even be strengthened after the event. In order for sport events to fulfill a local communi-ty's needs, these needs will first have to be identified, and such information is easier to gather in the context of NMSEs. Subsequently, specific tactics and strategies can be put into place to create desired outcomes.

Sport participation and development

Sport participation and development can be considered as a component of social impact. Since *sport* is the core of sport events, stimulating sport participating is a plausible outcome. Claims that sport events will foster sport participation are found in bid documents of both types of events, and are based on the notion of the so called *trickle-down, demonstration,* or *inspiration* effects, which suggest that the successes of elite-level athletes will inspire others to become more active and get involved, resulting in increased levels of sport participation and physical activity. Evidence supporting this *trickle-down effect* is mixed, and is mainly focused on major sporting events (Weed *et al.*, 2009).

The OG, like no other event, attracts unparalleled interest from people around the world, but also from people within the host country with no interest in sport or the Olympics. So, the OG can be considered a powerful tool to create aware-ness, especially for its core product, *sport*. However, the most substantial sport-related impact is an increase in passive involvement such as live and television spectating (Toohey, 2008). Further, it seems that (1) those people who already do a little sport can be inspired to do a little more; (2) those people who have played sport before can be inspired to play again; and (3) some people might give up one sport to try another (Weed *et al.*, 2009). Thus, large-scale events seem-ingly have the capacity to enhance sport participation, but the effects are limited at best and are more likely to retain existing participants than to recruit new participants into sport.

Opportunities for personal growth and skill development related to sport participation and development of local residents (e.g. through volunteering, offi-ciating, organizing) are expected to be higher in the context of NMSE, since the chances that locals will take part in the planning and management of NMSE is far greater than for MSE. We found evidence for this in the case of the 2005 Pan American Junior Athletic Championships (PanAmJacs; Taks, Green, Misener, & Chalip, 2014), but not for the 2005 Canadian Figure Skating Championships (Misener, Taks, Chalip, & Green, 2015). The PanAmJacs enhanced the experi-ence of local coaches and positively affected the number and development of local officials. These two outcomes have played a major role in the development of athletics in the region. In the case of the Figure Skating Championships, the national governing body (Skate Canada) brought in their own experts to execute more complex tasks instead of drawing from the local people. This is also common practice for MSEs, which recruit experts from far-away regions, thereby limiting opportunities for local people to execute meaningful roles, and assigning residents to lower-end volunteering tasks that do not necessarily contribute to the development of the sport.

MSEs systematically require either the upgrading of existing sport facilities or the construction of new ones, while this may or may not be the case for NMSEs. Sport facilities for MSEs are high-end, which seldom meet the sport participation needs of local residents. "White elephants" are detrimental outcomes of MSEs. These are facilities which cost fortunes to build (see: https://podio.com/site/budget-busters), but remain unused post-event because they do not meet the needs and wants of the local community. They carry extravagant maintenance costs and end up being closed (e.g. most Olympic facilities in Athens following the 2004 OG, see: http://darkroom.baltimoresun.com/2014/08/athens-olympic-venues-in-ruins-ten-years-after-the-games/#1). In the sporadic cases that facilities are being upgraded or built for NMSEs, community needs are of utmost importance. This assures long-term use by residents, which is central for sustainable community development. Examples are a stadium built for the hosting of the 2005 PanAmJacs, which has played a major role in the development of local track-and-field athletes and programs, and also contributed to the development of other sports such as American football and soccer (Taks *et al.*, 2014). Thus, residents' needs are central in the case of building or upgrading sport facilities for NMSEs, and MSEs could learn from this practice.

Besides adequate sport facilities, other advantages of hosting of NMSEs is that sport equipment, related items, and financial surpluses are more likely to be donated locally (e.g. to sport organizations or schools) after the event (Koemig & Leopkey, in Taks *et al.*, 2014). The potential for creating partnerships between businesses and local sport organizations to enhance the sport experience for the local people is, again, more likely in the context of an NMSE because of the tighter social connectedness. Business partnerships with MSEs are clearly at the global level, thereby circumventing the local level, unless other local initiatives are taken alongside the MSE (Chalip 2006). Overall, there is little evidence for sport participation outcomes from hosting events, and leveraging is essential (Taks *et al.*, 2014).

Conclusion

Events are being organized regardless, so how can they be used to actually *serve* the local community? In fact, we have so far been looking at examples of event outcomes, whether they were positive or negative, sustainable or not. It must be acknowledged that most examples in this contribution are taken from MSEs, and that many outcomes of NMSEs are theorized or assumed. The reason is that, so far, little research attention has been given to NMSEs, and so we are lacking empirical evidence to substantiate these claims. This contribution calls for a shift in research attention from MSEs to NMSEs to start exploring the power of NMSEs for host communities (e.g. Taks, Chalip, & Green, 2015). Positive outcomes of NMSEs for host communities are more noticeable than for MSEs, particularly economic and social outcomes. This makes NMSEs more relevant as a means to creating durable benefits for host communities. In addition, there are many more NMSEs organized worldwide compared to MSEs and, thus, at the aggregate level, their impact may provide more lasting global benefits, as opposed to MSEs. Based on the above, they have the capacity to be "big fish in small ponds," while MSEs are rather "small fish in a big pond" when it comes to their potential or capacity to leave a positive and sustainable legacy in the global world.

Notes

1 Note that "environmental impact" is not included here. While the 1994 Olympic Winter Games in Lillehammer were the pioneers of the "Green Games" (Chappelet, 2008), Atlanta 1996 followed suit, but in 2000 Sydney was the first Olympics to include a section on environmental protection in their bid document (Toohey, 2008). While this is an important component with regard to impact and sustainability, and some progress has been made on environmental impact assessment (e.g. footprints) (Horne & Manzenreiter, 2006), it will not be addressed here.
2 Parts of this section are retrieved from a previously published paper by Taks (2013).

References

Agha, N., & Taks, M. (2015). A theoretical comparison of the economic impact of large and small events. *International Journal of Sport Finance*.

Balduck, A., Maes, M., & Buelens, M. (2011). The social impact of the tour de France: Comparisons of residents' pre- and post-event perceptions. *European Sport Management Quarterly*, *11* (2), 91–113.

Barney, R.K., Wenn, S.R., & Martyn, S. (2004). *Selling the five rings*. Salt Lake City, UT: University of Utah Press.

Chalip, L. (2006). Towards social leverage of sport events. *Journal of Sport Tourism*, *11* (2), 109–127.

Chappelet, J.I. (2008). Olympic environmental concerns as a legacy of the Winter Games. *The International Journal of the History of Sport*, *25* (14), 1884–1902.

Foley, M., McGillivray, D., & McPherson, G. (2012). *Event policy: From theory to strategy*. London: Routledge.

Getz, D. (2012). *Event studies: Theory, research and policy for planned events*. London: Routledge.

Gibson, H.J., Kaplanidou, K., & Kang, S.J. (2012). Small-scale event sport tourism: A case study in sustainable tourism. *Sport Management Review*, *15* (2), 160–170.

Gratton, C., & Taylor, P. (2000). *Economics of sport and recreation*. London: Spon.

Hiller, H.H. (2000). Mega-events, urban boosterism and growth strategies: An analysis of the objectives and legitimations of the Cape Town 2004 Olympic bid. *International Journal of Urban and Regional Research*, *24* (2), 439–458.

Horne, J., & Manzenreiter, W. (2006). *Sports mega-events: Social scientific analyses of a global phenomenon*. Oxford: Blackwell Publishing.

Kaplanidou, K. (2012). The importance of legacy outcomes for Olympic Games: Four summer host cities residents' quality of life: 1996–2008. *European Sport Management Quarterly, 12* (4), 397–433.

Kavetsos, G. & Szymanski, S. (2010). National well-being and international sports events. *Journal of Economic Psychology, 31* (2), 158–171.

Kesenne, S. (2012). The economic impact, costs and benefits of the FIFA World Cup and the Olympic Games: Who wins, who loses? In W. Maennig & A. Zimbalist (Eds.), *International handbook on the economics of mega sporting events* (pp. 270–278). Cheltenham: Edward Elgar.

Misener, L., & Mason, D.S. (2006). Creating community networks: Can sporting events offer meaningful sources of social capital? *Managing Leisure, 11* (1), 39–56.

Misener, L., Taks, M., Chalip, L., & Green, C. (2015). The elusive "trickle down effect" of sport events: Assumptions and missed opportunities. *Managing Leisure, 20* (2), 135–156.

Onyx, J. & Bullen, P. (2000). Measuring social capital in five communities. *The Journal of Applied Behavioural Science, 36* (1), 23–41.

Preuss, H. (2005). The economic impact of visitors at major multi-sport events. *European Sport Management Quarterly, 5* (3), 281–301.

Preuss, H. (2007). FIFA World Cup 2006 and its legacy on tourism. In R. Conrady & M. Buck (Eds.), *Trends and issues in global tourism 2007* (pp. 83–102). Berlin/ Heidelberg: Springer.

Ritchie, B.J.R. (1984). Assessing the impact of hallmark events: Conceptual and research issues. *Journal of Travel Research, 23* (1), 2–11.

Smith, A. (2009). Theorising the relationship between major sport events and social sustainability. *Journal of Sport Tourism, 14* (2/3), 109–120.

Smith, A. (2012). *Events and urban regeneration: The strategic use of events to revitalize cities*. Oxon: Routledge.

Solberg, H., & Preuss, H. (2007). Major sport events and long-term tourism impacts. *Journal of Sport Management, 21* (2), 213–234.

Taks, M. (2013). Social sustainability of non-mega sport events in a global world. *European Journal for Sport and Society, 10* (2), 121–141.

Taks, M., Chalip, L., & Green, B.C. (2015). Impacts and strategic outcomes from non-mega sport events for local communities (introduction to the special issue). *European Sport Management Quarterly, 15* (1), 1–6.

Taks, M., Chalip, L., Green, B.C., Kesenne, S., & Martyn, S. (2009). Factors affecting repeat visitation and flow-on tourism as sources of event strategy sustainability. *Journal of Sport and Tourism, 14* (2/3), 121–142.

Taks, M., Kesenne, S., Chalip, L., Green, B.C., & Martyn, S. (2011). Economic impact study versus cost–benefit analysis: An empirical example of a medium sized international sporting event. *International Journal of Sport Finances, 6* (3), 187–203.

Taks, M., Green, B.C., Misener, L., & Chalip, L. (2014). Evaluating sport development outcomes: The case of a medium sized international sport event. *European Sport Management Quarterly, 14* (3), 213–237.

Thibault, L. (2009). Globalization of sport: An inconvenient truth. *Journal of Sport Management, 23*, 1–20.

Toohey, K. (2008). The Sydney Olympics: Striving for legacies – Overcoming short-term disappointments and long-term deficiencies. *The International Journal of the History of Sport, 25* (14), 1953–1971.

Weed, M. (2003). Why the two won't tango! Explaining the lack of integrated policies for sport and tourism in the UK. *Journal of Sport Management, 17* (3), 258–283.

Weed, M., Coren, E., & Fiore, J. (2009). *A systematic review of the evidence base for developing a physical activity and health legacy from the London 2012 Olympic and Paralympic Games.* Canterbury: Canterbury Christ Church University.

Ziakas, V., & Costa, C.A. (2011). Event portfolio and multi-purpose development: Establishing the conceptual grounds. *Sport Management Review, 14* (4), 409–423.

10 The European Union as a normative power in international sport

Arnout Geeraert

Introduction

Imagine a world in which international sports governance reflects the values that the grandiose opening ceremonies of major sports events laud. Sports governance would be characterized by ethical principles such as respect, equality, respect for human rights, solidarity, and so on. While this may seem like a distant dream, the European Union (EU), in fact, holds the potential to see that this increasingly becomes a reality.

Governance failures in international sport often point to a lack of respect for fundamental values (Henry and Lee, 2004). For a large part, these failures are induced by the absence of robust, democratic, and transparent decision-making in international sport organizations (ISOs) (Geeraert, Alm &, Groll, 2014). These organizations thus fail to ensure that international sports governance is fully characterized by adherence to universal principles such as democracy, the rule of law, respect for human rights, good governance, and sustainable development.

At the same time, the idea that the EU acts normatively in its external policy, dispersing (universal) values and ideas into the international system, has gained considerable ground in EU studies. The concept of "Normative Power Europe (NPE)" emerged to describe the EU's unique international identity as a force for good in the world (Manners, 2002). Normative power is an identity attributed to a political entity that diffuses its universal norms in the international system. More so than other political entities, the EU "comes some way towards approximating" this ideal type (Forsberg, 2011, 1199). Since the EU is increasingly playing a role in international sport (Geeraert, 2014), questions arise of how the EU can contribute to the dispersion of universal norms in international sports governance.

The aim of this chapter is to demonstrate how the EU can be an NPE in international sport by building upon insights from normative political theory. Only when the EU comes closer to this ideal type will it maximize its positive influence and contribute to more ethical international sports governance. The chapter proceeds as follows. The next section addresses the need for controlling ISOs.

The third section discusses the EU's potential to control ISOs. The fourth section lists a number of criteria the EU must meet in order to be a normative power in international sport. The final section formulates policy advice by drawing from the analysis.

The need for controlling international sport organizations

Autonomy from political institutions is a deeply ingrained principle in the sports world; it has even become an obsession for ISOs (Geeraert, Mrkonjic, & Chappelet, 2014). These organizations were able to consolidate their monopoly as global regulating bodies for their respective sports without being subject to external interference. But the almost complete autonomy they have enjoyed for nearly a century has undermined their efforts to be executors of good governance. Geeraert, Alm, and Groll (2014) present empirical evidence for the lack of generally accepted elements of good governance in sport governing bodies, such as internal accountability mechanisms and term limits for elected officials. The "status quo" constitutes a breeding ground for corruption and the concentration of power and it influences the organizations' overall performance.

The lack of good governance in ISOs has a potentially negative impact on wider society (Geeraert, 2015). States have implicitly delegated certain tasks to these organizations, since they demonstrate "a tacit or explicit tolerance" of sport organizations' regulatory activities on states' behalf (Héritier and Lehmkuhl, 2008, 5). Such tasks include, for instance, the selection procedures for host countries of major sport events, in which national governments rather than national sport federations de facto compete against each other, as well as the organization and regulation of sport competition in general (Geeraert & Drieskens, 2015). Via their governance activities, ISOs de facto govern substantial areas of social life. This highlights the importance of having efficient, effective, and innovative global regulators of sport. However, the fact that senior sport officials hold their office for many years combined with the lack of state-of-the-art internal accountability mechanisms, complicate a continuous reflection on governance failures (Geeraert et al., 2014a). Put simply, change toward better governance within sports governance bodies is very difficult. In order to uphold the values international sports vow to project, external control is necessary to ensure these values translate.

The reality, however, is that many ISOs remain largely unconstrained. In fact, the external context predicates ISOs' sweeping autonomy. Analogous to multinational corporations operating on a global playing field, in principle ISOs can pick a favorable regulatory environment as the home base for their international activities. The majority of ISOs opt for Switzerland, where they benefit from a quasi-unregulated system. The Swiss Civil Code lists minimum requirements for associations, while the overall Swiss legal framework allows for large degrees of both fiscal and organizational autonomy and limited prosecution of private corruption.[1] While Switzerland thus exercises only very limited control of ISOs, other actors are generally unable or unwilling to hold them to account (Geeraert, 2015). Importantly, ISOs are generally outside the scope of national-level laws

and policies, meaning they are outside national jurisdiction and the national regulatory system. On the contrary, certain powerful ISOs have been able to exercise
control on governments (Garcia & Meier, 2013). This illustrates that international
sport governance often operates in a topsy-turvy world. States have implicitly
delegated certain regulatory tasks to ISOs, and in order to fully reap the benefits
of this delegation, a substantial degree of organizational autonomy is indeed
desirable. However, political autonomy should not imply immunity from
accountability processes. Public authorities have every right to exercise pressure
for efficient, effective, accountable, transparent, and innovative global regulators
of sport.

The EU's opportunities for controlling international sport organizations

It is generally acknowledged that the EU has been the only public actor to have
a significant impact on sports governance. The EU has two options for exerting
influence on ISOs: through the enforcement of EU law, which has (thus far) had
the greatest impact, and by creating sports policy (Geeraert & Drieskens, 2015).
Sports rules issued by these organizations often fall under the realm of the EU's
internal market competence and consequently come under the scope of EU freedom of movement and competition law (Parrish, 2003). The sports world realized
this belatedly, in 1995 to be precise, when the Court of Justice of the EU (CJEU)
infamously ruled in *Bosman* that both the system regulating the international
transfer of football players and a quota system restricting the number of foreign
players on a team violated the free movement of workers.[2] The CJEU's ruling in
Meca-Medina in 2006 further highlighted the large scope of sports rules potentially infringing EU (competition) law.[3]

In contrast to its strong means for enforcing internal market rules, the EU only
has a supporting sporting competence. This seems to limit its influence in international sport to those areas where sporting rules and measures potentially
infringe upon EU law. Yet since the signature and implementation of the Lisbon
Treaty, the EU inherited formal sports policy, and these measures increasingly
affect ISOs. Given the context of non-legislative decision-making, EU sports
policy is implemented by the European Commission (the executive branch of the
EU) through non-hierarchical modes of governance, such as bargaining and
persuasion, which may include arguing, sharing best practices, goal creation, and
providing (financial) incentives (Geeraert, 2014).

The question remains why ISOs would be willing to listen to the EU when it
has no options for enforcing sports policy measures. The governance literature
suggests that compliance with non-hierarchical instruments is only possible
when entities expect costs associated with non-compliant behavior (Sharpf,
1994). In this light, two of the most prominent ISOs – FIFA and UEFA – fear
that non-compliance with EU policy measures will decrease both the
Commission's goodwill in the application of EU law and the EU institutions'
respect for the autonomy of ISOs to regulate sport. Put simply, non-compliance

poses the potential to spark increased EU regulatory activity in sport-related areas (Geeraert & Drieskens, 2015). Since there is incentive for ISOs to comply with non-hierarchical measures, the EU seems to have a great potential to steer the behavior of ISOs.

Nonetheless, policy measures have had limited impact on ISOs. This is hardly surprising because dialogue is currently the Commission's main instrument for steering ISOs' behavior, while implementation of policy directed at these organizations does not include target setting and monitoring. Recently, however, the EU has opened the door to benchmarking and reputation mechanisms (naming and shaming). The new EU Work Plan for Sport (2014–2017) foresees the possible introduction of so-called "pledge boards," where sport organizations can voluntarily publicize their commitment to certain issues. Yet the question remains how the EU can effectively diffuse universal norms in international sports governance.

Criteria for a Normative Power Europe in international sport

How can the EU best disperse universal norms in international sport? A simple answer is that it must maximize the *normative impact* of its policy measures. But the projection of norms also needs to be normatively justified, which is more convincing and attractive when means involve a *normative intent* and a *normative process* (Manners, 2011). Importantly, these two components ensure that the EU's actions are not characterized by an instrumental use of power and that they have a positive impact on international sports governance. They require the EU to turn itself into a virtuous example that applies the same principles that it seeks to disperse.

Normative intent

It is important that the EU's engagement in international sport has a normative intent, meaning that the EU is motivated by normative interests rather than being means-ends oriented (Forsberg, 2011). Hence, the EU's engagement should not be rooted in the pursuit of power, differentiating it from the more instrumental use of power in international sport witnessed in the case of Russia (Persson & Petersson, 2014).

Normative process

Once the EU decides to initiate external action in international sport, it must promote universal norms. According to Manners, norms are universal when they "are generally acknowledged with the United Nations system to be universally applicable" (Manners, 2008, 46). Manners advocates that the EU's external practices are guided by five core norms (peace, liberty, democracy, the rule of law, and respect for human rights) and four minor norms (social solidarity, anti-discrimination, sustainable development, and good governance) (Manners, 2002). It must be stressed that these norms do not have to be made explicit. For instance, actions toward promoting social dialogue in sport can be regarded as promoting the universal principles of liberty and democracy (Parrish, 2011; Geeraert, 2014). Likewise, combating financial crime in sport can be conceived as promoting the rule of law. The dispersion of norms should take place through an accountable, inclusive, and reflexive process.

Within an EU context, accountability generally implies that EU actors are responsive to participatory input demands and can be held responsible for their output decisions. Policies are input-legitimate when they correspond with the popular will expressed by the political majority of the elected assemblies. It is therefore important that the European Parliament has the possibility to scrutinize policy processes (Lord, 2004), yet it is equally important to involve the public at large. Public accountability is crucial to prevent policy processes from operating in the dark. Narrative accounts should be published that seek to "justify decisions, actions and results in the eyes of the broader citizenry," and it is essential that the EU is responsive to constructive proposals raised in public debate (Torfing, Sørensen, & Fotel, 2009, 291).

Inclusiveness refers to granting a role for external actors affected by the policy process, which ensures that a normative power's actions "gain approval in a free and open debate in which all those affected are heard" (Sjursen, 2006, 243). This implies that all affected actors must be granted a say in the policy process (Young 2000). The degree of inclusion in the process should be "a function of the intensity of the actors' affectedness, and the included actors should be able to influence the decisions" (Torfing *et al.*, 2009, 294). The EU must also guarantee that members of representative organizations who participate in the policy process at the European level have access to information as well as the capacity to evaluate how their interests are represented (Torfing *et al.*, 2009).

Reflexivity includes the capacity of EU policy-makers to "critically analyze the EU's policy and adapt it according to the effects the policy is expected to have on the targeted area" (Bicchi, 2006, 288). Before implementing measures in international sport, the EU must make a deliberate effort to critically analyze the expected effects of proposed measures.

Normative impact

Finally, a normative power must have a normative impact – the normative power much transfer universal norms to external actors. The implementation reports of actions included in relevant policy documents demonstrate that, thus far, the normative impact of the EU in international sport has been rather limited (European Commission, 2012; 2014). The EU can maximize its normative impact in international sport by using non-hierarchical instruments to steer ISOs' and other relevant (sport) actors' behavior.

In order to effectively steer ISOs' behavior, the Commission should take into account the following four recommendations (Geeraert, 2014). First, it must proactively shape the interactions of relevant actors by framing issues that are discussed, allocating resources, including and excluding actors from discussions, and empowering weaker actors. Second, it must clearly formulate goals and objectives ISOs and other relevant actors should attain. Third, it should continuously monitor, evaluate, and report progress on the goals the EU sets for ISOs and other sport actors. Finally, it is important to involve the EU member states (united in the Sport Council of the EU) in the process. The member states' active support of the Commission's steering efforts increases the likelihood that ISOs' noncompliant behavior will spark increased regulatory activity (Geeraert & Drieskens, 2015). Fearing possible hierarchical measures, they will thus be more inclined to comply with steering efforts.

Conclusion: imagining the EU as a normative power in international sport

The aim of this chapter is to demonstrate how the EU can be a normative power in international sport while capitalizing on its potential to steer the behavior of ISOs. The analysis above prompts concrete policy recommendations in this respect. The EU can be a normative power in international sport by acting in accordance with the following sequential process. First, the Commission's decision to initiate action in international sport should be guided by the intent to disperse universal norms established via a clear mandate from the EU member states. Second, its actions should be directed toward dispersing universal norms. Third, the Commission should actively shape interactions between relevant actors and frame the issues that are being discussed. It should establish criteria for actors' inclusion in the policy process that take into account the intensity of their affectedness. Weak actors should be empowered, and representative organizations need to be encouraged to inform and involve their members. Fourth, the Commission should produce narrative accounts of negotiations and respond to constructive proposals in public debate. Fifth, once concrete measures are considered, their effects must be critically analyzed. Sixth, concrete goals and objectives must be formulated, and the implementation should be continuously monitored and evaluated against these targets. Seventh, the Commission should report on both the policy process and the implementation of measures to the Parliament and the Council. Eighth, in case of insufficient progress, the Council should call upon ISOs and relevant stakeholders to increase their efforts.

Although this process seems rather straightforward, implementing it would be a tall order. Indeed, this contribution does not take into account real-world constraints such as preference heterogeneity among EU member states on the appropriateness of EU interventions in international sport. Yet its aim is not to explore or critique the *status quo*. After all, EU sports policy is still in its infancy and it remains to be seen how it will crystallize. It is important, however, that the EU takes account of its potential to be a force for good in the sports world. International sports governance could benefit greatly from a proper interpretation of this function. Before the window of opportunity closes and the balance of power shifts more decisively toward countries like Russia, the EU should strengthen its position in international sports governance. In this light, this chapter aims to provoke thought on the EU's possible avenues for affecting more ethical sports governance in the twenty-first century.

Notes

1 Recently proposed amendments to the Swiss Unfair Competition Act and Criminal Code would make corruption in international sports organizations a criminal offence that is actively prosecuted by Swiss authorities.
2 Case C-415/93 [1995] ECR I-4921.
3 Case C-519/04 [2006] ECR II-3291.

References

Bicchi, F. (2006). Our size fits all: Normative Power Europe and the Mediterranean. *Journal of European Public Policy, 13* (2), 286–303.

European Commission (2012). *White Paper on Sport, Action Plan 'Pierre de Coubertin' Communication on 'Developing the European Dimension in Sport', EU Work Plan for Sport Implementation Report. Implementation period: July 2007–December 2014.* Retrieved June 16, 2010 from http://ec.europa.eu/sport/library/documents/eusf2012-pdc-comm-euwork-plan-implementation-rpt-july-2012.pdf.

European Commission (2014). *Report on the implementation of the European Union Work Plan for Sport 2011–2014.* Com (2014) 22, 24 January.

Forsberg, T. (2011). Normative Power Europe, once again: A conceptual analysis of an ideal type. *Journal of Common Market Studies, 49* (6), 1183–1204.

García, B., & Meier, H.E. (2013). Keeping private governance private: Is FIFA blackmailing national governments? Paper presented in the 13th EUSA Biennial Conference, Baltimore, MD, May 9–11.

Geeraert, A. (2014). New EU governance modes in professional sport: Enhancing throughput legitimacy. *Journal of Contemporary European Research, 10* (3), 302–321.

Geeraert, A. (2015). Football is war: The EU's limits and opportunities to control FIFA. *Global Affairs, 1* (2).

Geeraert, A., & Drieskens, E. (2015). The EU controls FIFA and UEFA: A principal–agent perspective. *Journal of European Public Policy*, published as IFirst.

Geeraert, A., Alm, J., & Groll, M. (2014a). Good governance in international sport organisations: an analysis of the 35 Olympic sport governing bodies. *International Journal of Sport Policy, 6* (3), 281–306.

Geeraert, A., Mrkonjic, M., & Chappelet, J. (2014b). A rationalist perspective on the autonomy of international sport governing bodies: Towards a pragmatic autonomy in the steering of sports. *International Journal of Sport Policy*, published as IFirst.

Henry, I., & Lee, P.C. (2004). Governance and ethics in sport. In S. Chadwick and J. Beech (Eds.), *The business of sport management* (pp. 25–42). Harlow: Pearson Education.

Héritier, A., & Lehmkuhl, D. (2008). The shadow of hierarchy and new modes of governance. *Journal of Public Policy, 28* (1), 1–17.

Lord, C. (2004). *A democratic audit of the European Union.* Basingstoke: Palgrave Macmillan.

Manners, I. (2002). Normative Power Europe: A contradiction in terms? *Journal of Common Market Studies, 40* (2), 235–258.

Manners, I. (2008). The Normative Ethics of the European Union. *International Affairs, 84* (1), 45–60.

Manners, I. (2011). The European Union's normative power. In Whitman, R. (Ed.), *Normative Power Europe: Empirical and Theoretical Perspectives* (pp. 226–277). Basingstoke: Palgrave.

Parrish, R. (2003). The politics of sports regulation in the European Union. *Journal of European Public Policy, 10* (2), 246–262.

Parrish, R. (2011). Social dialogue in European professional football. *European Law Journal, 17* (2), 213–229.

Persson, E. and Petersson, B. (2014). Political mythmaking and the 2014 Winter Olympics in Sochi: Olympism and the Russian Great Power myth. *East European Politics, 30* (2), 192–209.

Scharpf, F.W. (1994). Games real actors could play: Positive and negative coordination in embedded negotiations. *Journal of Theoretical Politics, 6* (1), 27–53.

Sjursen, H. (2006). The EU as a "Normative Power": How can this be? *Journal of European Public Policy, 13* (2), 235–251.

Torfing, J., Sørensen, E., & Fotel, T. (2009). Democratic anchorage of infrastructural governance networks: The case of the Femern Belt Forum. *Planning Theory, 8*, 282–308.

Young, I.M. (2000). *Inclusion and democracy.* Oxford: Oxford University Press.

11 We are the game?

Player democratization and the reform of sport governance

Peter Donnelly

> Q: Why a percentage of the gross [revenue]?
> A: Because We are the Game[1]
> > (NFLPA, 1981)

In 1982, in the USA, the National Football League Players' Association (NFLPA) called a strike. Their current contract had just expired, and the league (NFL) owners had just signed a new television contract worth $2 billion. The players' union, under the leadership of labor lawyer Ed Garvey and former player Gene Upshaw, demanded that a percentage (55 percent) of the league revenue be assigned to the salaries and benefits of players because, as they had argued in a pamphlet produced the previous year, without the players there would be no league and no games. In other words, "we are the game."

Before the strike began, "Upshaw declared that the NFLPA would not only put on exhibitions [games], it would create a league of several teams, owned and operated by the players themselves" (Ford, 2001, 3). Such a league was certain to fail. The players understood that they were engaged in a strike, so there was little reason to invest themselves in a player-owned league; if they played, the NFL informed them that they would be in breach of contract which could lead to their termination; many of the stadia where such teams could play were owned by the NFL owners, who would refuse player-owned teams the right to play in them; and the media contracts ensured that any players' league games would not be broadcast on the major networks.[2]

Despite these barriers, the players managed to organize and play two games before they were closed down by NFL legal sanctions. The strike was settled a month later and the players eventually received more than 55 percent of the revenues. The idea of player-owned teams has stayed with me for over 30 years now, especially as it relates to my interest in the democratization of sport. I would argue that the short-lived Players' All-Star Season (PASS, as the league was called) is much more than "an interesting footnote in professional football history" (Ford, 2001, 5); rather, it provides a model for a more democratized sport. The players are "the game," so why is it that they do not have more control over the form, circumstances, and meaning(s) of their participation?

This chapter attempts to answer the question and to imagine a future of sport by first considering the circumstances under which players lost control of their participation, then considering athletes' rights, and finally by imagining a future of sport where those rights are realized.

Sport before and after "the fall"

The fall is a term used in Christian theology to characterize the loss of innocence, a departure from an ideal state. It would be a mistake to idealize sport as it existed for approximately 100 years before the "nexus" of the 1970s and 1980s. On the one hand, there were exclusions from participation based on class, gender, and race; professional athletes were often poorly paid and had few benefits; and elite amateur athletes were drawn largely from the classes who could afford travel and training. As Donnelly and Kidd (in press) note, however, even though the base of the pyramid was quite narrow, "there was a relatively seamless transition from playgrounds and high schools to Olympic and professional sport." On the other hand, the amateur ethos generated the character of sportspersonship – competition was supposed to occur under conditions of collegiality and identities did not depend on the outcome; antagonisms were left on the field of play; and good fellowship between opponents was valued. The great monopolies and monopsonies of modern sport (professional leagues, international [sport] federations [IFs] and multi-sport organizations such as the International Olympic Committee [IOC]) had not fully developed, and the governance of sport, even professional sport, was often amateur and amateurish.

Those who governed sport, even professional sports, were often volunteer members of the boards of sports clubs; the larger governing organizations were run by (often paternalistic) individuals who saw themselves as the stewards of sport, but not the owners (Donnelly, 2014). In both amateur and professional sports, the board members often contributed to the costs of governing. For example, Avery Brundage, the independently wealthy president of the IOC from 1954 to 1974, used his own money to run the IOC ($75,000 per year) and did not take any expenses. Professional athletes were often "journeymen," traveling from team to team on the basis of how much they were paid and where they wanted to play rather than working under the modern system of drafts, contractual obligations, and reserve clauses (Wilson, 1994).[3]

By the 1930s, the signs of change were there; the popularity of sport made it an ideal cultural form to become a propaganda tool for competing political ideologies, and by the 1950s the Cold War was beginning to be fought at international sports competitions. However, it was the convergence of those ideologies with the interrelated processes of globalization, professionalization, mediatization (especially national and international television coverage), and commercialization that began to reveal the general "innocence" of the earlier period in sport. A number of commentators point to the Los Angeles 1984

Olympics as the culminating cultural moment, when professional athletes first participated in the Olympics, and where the media rights and the start of the TOP sponsorship program first made even a boycotted Olympics a profitable venture for the IOC. Gruneau (1984), perhaps in anticipation of Ritzer's subsequent thesis, used McDonald's sponsorship to refer to Los Angeles as the "Hamburger Olympics" (see also Gruneau & Neubauer, 2012); and Donnelly (1996) saw Los Angeles as the "Prolympic" moment, where amateurism and professionalism converged to form a "global sport monoculture."

As a consequence of the processes noted above, international (and many national) sports organizations found themselves with far more money than had been available previously. Many professional sports organizations managed to professionalize their governance, or at least their financial governance, often taking advantage of the autonomy of sport to avoid the type of laws that regulated non-sport corporations. Non-professional sports organizations used the same autonomy of sport exemptions to avoid regulation of their governance practices and new-found wealth and, following the bidding process for the Sydney 2000 Olympics, Sunder Katwala (2000, 90) felt empowered to state that, "it is difficult to find anything else in the world quite so badly governed as international sport."

Katwala (2000, 13) argued that[4]

> There are two crucial issues in sporting governance – those of legitimacy and of efficiency. Sport is a public good and so the goal of sporting governance is to ensure that sport is run effectively and in accordance with its values, while taking advantage of the ability to bring in additional private resources and spread participation of markets.

Debates about sport governance tend to present *legitimacy* and *efficiency* as alternatives where "sport must choose between its values and traditions or its commercial viability" (Katwala, 2000, 15); whereas legitimacy and efficiency are in fact overlapping and necessary characteristics of good governance. Many sport organizations appear to find it difficult to deliver both efficiency and legitimacy. They seem to focus on efficiency at the cost of legitimacy; but that focus can occur in a self-serving manner among unaccountable executive boards where efficiency can provide increasing opportunity for personal gain (e.g. Geeraert, Alm, & Groll, 2014). Sport as a public good (legitimacy) may be sacrificed when a sport organization focuses on efficiency as a commercial enterprise.

Sources ranging from Geeraert *et al.* (2014) to Play the Game (2011) have outlined the key organizational problems of the monopolistic and monopsonistic IFs: first, a lack of equitable representation and democratized governance; and second, corruption and problems with financial transparency and accountability. The consequences of these inadequacies of governance include the following widely publicized problems (in addition to the corruption noted above):

- problems with the integrity of sport (doping, gambling, and match fixing);
- problems with athlete health, safety, and violence control;

- problems with labor relations, team selection, and other aspects of due process for athletes;
- problems of athlete maltreatment and child protection in sport; and
- the general problems of the human rights of athletes and the overall lack of democratization of sports organizations.

The human and labor rights of athletes

The human rights, including the labor rights, of athletes have routinely been violated by those who stand to "profit" from athletes – gamblers, team "owners," and investors expecting increased revenue, and all those whose status, prestige, or pride is contingent, at least in part, on the success of athletes. It should be noted that athletes have sometimes been complicit in this. They have often conspired in their own subordination (in terms of their failure to assert their rights) because they have also often acknowledged that there was potential "profit" to be derived from accepting, without question, treatment from those in positions of authority that would not be acceptable in, for example, the classrooms, clinics, and legal workplaces in civilized society. Such acknowledgment has become so routine in many sectors of sport that it may be naturalized as *the culture of sport*.[5]

Hunt (2007, 208) reminds us that, "human rights are still easier to endorse than to enforce." However, she goes on to point out the essential paradox of human rights: the success of human rights lies in the fact that it is no longer possible to ignore them; it is no longer possible to pretend that some humans are less human than others: "you know the meaning of human rights because you feel distressed when they are violated" (Hunt, 2007, 214). In the era of human right – that is, since the 1948 Universal Declaration on Human Rights – there are numerous cases of athletes and others recognizing that the human rights of athletes are being violated, and challenging sport and political authorities to recognize their rights. These challenges may be divided into two general types: first, challenges by various classes of persons to assert their right to participate in sport; and second, challenges concerning rights associated with the circumstances of participation.

The first and perhaps the most prominent example of a challenge over the right to participate was part of a much larger protest over apartheid South Africa. Since South Africa only included minority White participants on its representative teams, a sport boycott became part of the wider campaign against apartheid. Many sport organizations were initially reluctant to participate, citing the spurious claim that sport and politics should not mix, but they eventually joined the boycott as a result of political and public pressure. "In locker rooms too, where athletes and coaches initially drew back from the campaign – the sportsperson's first instinct being to play – most came to understand when the case was explained in terms of human rights" (Kidd & Donnelly, 2000, 138). Having secured, in principle, ethno-racial inclusion in sport, campaigns turned to the rights of girls and women to participate in more equitable ways (in competition and in leadership positions), followed by children, persons with a disability, and most recently the rights of homosexual athletes.[6] A current campaign concerns the rights of transgendered individuals to participate.

Challenges to assure the rights of athletes appear to be everywhere now. For example, women athletes are actively challenging the return of gender testing in international sport; there are potential challenges to WADA's violation of athletes' rights in terms of privacy through its *whereabouts* and *biological passport* regulations; former speed skater Claudia Pechstein has successfully challenged the independence of the Court of Arbitration for Sport (CAS) by arguing that its members are appointed by the IOC and the IFs; and, in the recent O'Bannon case, the courts have recognized the right of ("amateur") university athletes to be paid for the commercial use of their images in the highly professionalized world of US university sports.

Athletes are recognized in the International Standard Classification of Occupations as Unit Group 3421, which gives examples of the tasks performed by *Athletes and Sports Players* (ILO, 2008, 210), and the International Labor Organization asserts that its international conventions apply to the sports sector. Some professional and Olympic athletes are represented by Players' Associations or unions, but their rights as workers are routinely violated. For example, professional athletes are often exempt from the rights that protect employees in other settings (e.g. the right to choose where you work, and workplace health and safety regulations). Recent examples of challenges include national team footballers' successful attempt to include breaks for water during games where the temperature was above 31 °C during the Brazil 2014 World Cup, despite FIFA's attempts to prevent this; and FIFPro's recent success in asserting the right of professional footballers to break their contract (and seek employment with a new team) if their own team has failed to pay them on time.[7]

National team athletes may have contracts, but often have even fewer rights than professional athletes. In Canada, national team athletes have contracts with Sport Canada, the Canadian Olympic Committee (COC), and sometimes with sponsors. But the government of Canada denies them status as employees, and thus employee rights. Here are a few of the rights identified and *not* enjoyed by one of Canada's top athletes – the right to: free speech and expression; privacy and health privacy; dignity and ownership of representation (images); make a living; having clarity of contractual obligations; and receiving due process when penalized for social media *faux pas*. In terms of the right of free speech, the IOC (and the COC) *encourages* accredited athletes to post social media in "first person, diary-style format." Athletes should not take on the role of journalist; are not permitted to report on competition; are not permitted to disclose information about people and organizations; and must use no vulgar words or obscene words/images.

Conclusion: the future of sport imagined

This chapter started with an example from the NFLPA. Player salaries have increased significantly, the health and safety of NFL players is now a matter of concern, and retired players have recently won a major lawsuit against the owners over health and safety issues. And yet, in 2013, one player (Troy Polamalu) was cited as follows: "There are rule changes every year. I do wish, however, that the NFL did have a voice from the players' side, whether it's our players' union president, or team captains, or our executive committee on the players' side. Because we're the guys that realize the risk, we're the guys on the field." This is a long way from "We are the game"; players are not even represented when rule changes are discussed and implemented.

However, I believe that there is reason for optimism. There is so much recognition of players' rights, and so much diverse action in an attempt to achieve them, that we may have reached a tipping point. Concern about good governance in sports goes hand-in-hand with players' rights, and includes concerns about democratic representation, and about the inclusion of athletes in discussions about decisions that affect them, and in approving decisions that affect them. I imagine a future of sport where democratized athletes are key figures in negotiating the form, the circumstances, and the meaning(s) of their participation.

Notes

1 This phrase is taken from the title of a booklet published by the National Football League Players' Association (in the United States) before the 1982 strike: "Q. Why 55% of the gross; A. Because *We are the Game*" (NFLPA, 1981; emphasis added).
2 Ted Turner, whose Turner Broadcasting network was independent of the major television networks in the United States, purchased the rights to broadcast the games, and guaranteed players $2,500 per game.
3 For example, Rick Gruneau interviewed Canadian Gus Marker, a journeyman professional ice hockey player who traveled between teams in the 1920s (Hockey, 1990); and Jan Eisenhardt from Denmark, who later became well known in Canada as a leader of the fitness movement, played professional football for Olympique Marseilles, and for the Stuttgarter Kickers during the 1920s.
4 Parts of the following are adapted from Donnelly (2015).
5 Parts of the following were adapted from Donnelly (2008).
6 These campaigns were backed up by the moral and legal authority of United Nations conventions that helped to give force to the Universal Declaration on Human Rights: the 1965 Convention on the Elimination of All Forms of Racial Discrimination; the 1979 Convention on the Elimination of All Forms of Discrimination Against Women; the 1989 Convention on the Rights of the Child; and the 2008 Convention on the Rights of Persons with Disabilities. Sexuality rights in sport were affirmed by the IOC in the lead up to the 2014 Sochi Olympics, but the *Fundamental Principles of Olympism* are both more inclusive and more limited in scope: Article 4 states: "The practice of sport is a human right. Every individual must have the possibility of practicing sport, without discrimination of any kind..."; and Article 6 states: "Any form of discrimination with regard to a country or a person on grounds of race, religion, politics, gender or otherwise is incompatible with belonging to the Olympic Movement" (IOC, 2013, 11–12).
7 Parts of the following were presented at the Play the Game conference (Donnelly, 2013)

References

Donnelly, P. (1996). "Prolympism": Sport monoculture as crisis and opportunity. *Quest*, *48* (1), 25–42.

Donnelly, P. (2008). Sport and human rights. *Sport in Society*, 11 (4), 381–394.

Donnelly, P. (2013). The democratization of athletes: What if athletes determined who governed their sports? *Play the Game Biennial Conference*, Aarhus (Denmark), October 28–31.

Donnelly, P. (2014). Buen vivir [Sumak Kawsay]: Notes on the consideration of sport as a cultural commons. *Movimento*, *20*, 211–226.

Donnelly, P. (2015). What if the players controlled the game: Dealing with the consequences of the crisis of governance in sports. *European Journal of Sport and Society*, *12* (1), 11–31.

Donnelly, P., & Kidd, B. (in press). In: M. Talbot & R. Bailey (Eds.), *The two cultures: Bridging the gap between sport for all and elite sport*. Abingdon: Taylor & Francis.

Ford, M. (2001). The two-day P.A.S.S. *The Coffin Corner*, *23* (6), 3–7. Retrieved December 10, 2014 from http://profootballresearchers.com/archives/Website_Files/Coffin_Corner/23-06-912.pdf

Geeraert, A., Alm, J., & Groll, M. (2014). Good governance in international sport organizations: An analysis of the 35 Olympic sport governing bodies. *International Journal of Sport Policy and Politics*, *6* (3), 281–306.

Gruneau, R. (1984) Commercialism and the modern Olympics. In A. Tomlinson and G. Whannel (Eds.), *Five ring circus: Money, power and politics at the Olympic Games* (pp. 1–15). London: Pluto Press.

Gruneau, R., & Neubauer, R. (2012). A gold medal for the market: The 1984 Los Angeles Olympics, the Reagan era and the politics of neoliberalism. In H.J. Lenskyj & S. Wagg (Eds.), *The Palgrave handbook of Olympic studies* (pp. 134–162). Houndmills: Palgrave Macmillan.

Hockey (1990). *Hockey: The Canadian game*: Episode 2, "The only game in town." Vancouver, BC: T.H.A. Media Distributors.

Hunt, L. (2007). *Inventing human rights: A history*. New York: W.W. Norton.

ILO (2008). *International standard classification of occupations*. Geneva: International Labor Organization.

IOC (2013). *Olympic Charter*. Lausanne: IOC.

Katwala, S. (2000). *Democratising global sport*. London: The Foreign Policy Centre.

Kidd, B., & Donnelly, P. (2000). Human rights in sport. *International Review for the Sociology of Sport*, *35* (2), 131–148.

NFLPA (1981). *Q. Why a percentage of the gross? A. Because we are the game*. September.

Play the Game (2011). *Cologne consensus: Towards a global code for governance in sport*. Retrieved December 10, 2014 from http://playthegame.org/theme-pages/the-sports-governance-observer/cologne-consensus/

Polamalu, Troy (NFL: Pittsburgh): ESPN (2013). Troy Polamalu talks rule changes. March 29. Retrieved December 10, 2014 from http://espn.go.com/nfl/story/_/id/9111820/troy-polamalu-pittsburgh-steelers-says-players-say-rule-changes

Wilson, J. (1994). *Playing by the rules: Sport, society, and the state*. Detroit, MI: Wayne State University Press

PART III

Fair (financial) management in a globalized sports world

Introduction

Stefan Kesenne and Bart Vanreusel

This part of the book addresses management deficits in global sport and develops proposals for a renewed future management of sport. Organizing models and principles, the quest for fair finance, policy choices and changes, and legal issues are discussed. Three chapters present different and contrasting cases: the private management of professional soccer, the paradoxes in professional road cycling, and the public management of sport for all. A concluding chapter outlines growing interconnections between international sport and legal issues.

Stefan Kesenne deals with the growing gap between professional soccer teams from large and small countries in European soccer. He studies the consequences of disproportionate budgets and performances. A European competition model such as the UEFA Champions League has almost turned into a closed league, limited to a small number of teams with top-level budgets from England, Germany, Italy, and Spain. Teams with lower budgets cannot make it to the quarter finals of the UCL. The author discusses future perspectives for soccer teams from small countries. Can they survive this financial gap? What can and should be managed to correct the unbalanced and unfair competition model of European soccer?

The plea by **Wim Lagae** and **Daam Van Reeth** for a renewed management in professional road cycling starts with the observation of paradoxes between a highly popular but poorly managed race cycling industry. The high turnover of sponsors, the failing redistribution of revenues and the over-exposure of a doping image create an unstable management model for this professional sport. The authors present a five-step management plan for a fair and stable race cycling industry in the future.

Bart Vanreusel explores how sport for all can remain a guiding principle for a future sport culture. He argues that recent sport for all developments tend to overlook the original human rights perspective, often resulting in sport for all who can afford it, who have an education, who are healthy enough, who fit into the dominant sport system, and who are targeted as potential consumers. The author advocates a renewed management of sport for all as a human right.

Taking a legal perspective, **Frank Hendrickx** complements the issues raised by the three cases above. Given the management complexity and the growing economic, social, and cultural significance of sport, he studies the increasing reliance of sport on the legal rules of public authorities. To what extent can sport bodies remain immune from public regulation and from legal rights and obligations as they apply to many other aspects of public and private life? The author argues that legal discourses will only intensify in the future management of sports.

Together, the chapters clearly point to a need for new, multifaceted management models in sport. Old intersections, such as the contrast between private and public enterprise, will eventually become obsolete and will be replaced by a demand for new management approaches, such as public and private cooperation. New interdependencies between diverse issues for fair management will feature in the future of sport.

12 The growing gap between small- and large-country football teams in Europe

Stefan Kesenne

Introduction

It is a well-known fact that professional football clubs of small European countries can no longer compete with top clubs in large countries. The gap, both in budget and in international performance, has grown dramatically over the last decennia. Many clubs in small countries run into financial problems by hiring players in order to compete with the top clubs in the European championships, and by paying high salaries to prevent the loss of their best players. However, even with the help of open and hidden subsidies from regional or local governments, the exodus can't be stopped. The international player migration from small to large countries has created a very unbalanced competition in European football. Even UEFA's Financial Fair Play – if it is ever implemented, given its legal problems – will not be able to restore the competitive balance.

Other constraints in some small countries are the lack of quality youth training in clubs, and the high number of teams migrating between the first and second national divisions. Between 1995, the year of the *Bosman* verdict, and 2010, no fewer than 34 teams have played in the Belgian top division of 18 teams, and only four teams have managed to stay permanently in the top division. This permanent migration causes a huge loss of football money invested in talent. In many cases, relegation to the second division means near bankruptcy.

In this chapter we will consider and discuss the most important causes of these problems, and suggest possible solutions that are based on published economic research.

The *Bosman* verdict

Many insiders have asserted for too long that the *Bosman* verdict of the European Court of Justice (CJEU) in 1995, which abolished the transfer system for end-of-contract players, is responsible for most problems. However, if the *Bosman* verdict has had any impact on professional football in Europe, it was not on the abolition of the transfer market, but rather on the opening of the European player market by ending the limitation of the number of foreign players that a team can field. The migration of players from small to large countries has increased dramatically since 1995 (Berlinschi, Schokkaert, & Swinnen, 2013). Even a large country like France has not been able to stop the exodus of its top players to the Big Four (England, Spain, Italy, and Germany) after the *Bosman* verdict, as can be seen in Figure 12.1.

All the players except one on the Belgian National team, the Red Devils, are playing in foreign clubs. This exodus is the economic consequence of freeing or deregulating the European labor market of football players, while keeping the European football product market closed or nationally protected (Kesenne, 2007a). An interesting side-effect of this international player migration is that it has had a positive effect on the international performances of the small countries' national teams (Berlinschi *et al.*, 2013). There can hardly be a better example of this side-effect than the recent World Cup performance of the Belgian national team.

The abolition of the transfer system for end-of-contract players has only resulted in the lengthening of player contracts (restricted by FIFA in 2001 to a maximum of five years), and in forcing players to sign a new contract before the existing contract expired. This way, talented players never reach the end of their contract, and can be transferred to other teams for ever higher transfer fees – nearly €100 million for the transfers of Ronaldo and Bale. Since the *Bosman* ruling of 1995, the football clubs' annual spending on transfers has increased from €400 million in 1996 to €3 billion during the 2010–2011 season. Over the same period, the number of deals has more than tripled, from 5,735 to 18,037.

If the *Bosman* verdict liberalized the labor market of football players in Europe, but kept the product market of football games and championships closed or

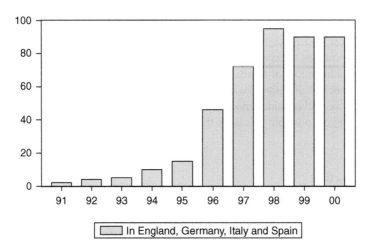

Figure 12.1 Number of French players in the Big Four (Primault, 2004)

nationally protected, the only sensible solution can be the liberalization of the football product market in Europe. The attempts of some football federations to close the player market again, by introducing the so-called home-grown rule, would be a big mistake, turning the clock backwards in a unifying European Union. There are no reasonable arguments to exempt the professional football industry from the rules that apply to all other industries. It follows that, given the pyramid-shaped structure of provincial and national divisions, pan-European divisions should be at the top of the pyramid in a unified Europe. The winners of a national championship should be promoted to the lowest European division, thus leaving their national championships. This would enable top teams in small countries to be competitive again by getting their share of the huge broadcast rights, sponsorship, and other commercial revenue of the European championships.

A first step in the direction of an open European product market for small countries such as Belgium and Holland would be a BeNe league, where both countries together create a supra-national top division and a championship with the best Dutch and Belgian teams. Together, Belgium and Holland have a population of 28 million, which would narrow the gap with the larger European countries. Media tycoon Rupert Murdoch, who bought the broadcast rights of the Dutch competition in 2013 for €1 billion over the next 12 years, has declared that he is willing to spend more money on the BeNe league's broadcast rights. In the European market, with free trade of goods and services, a team that is willing to play in a foreign league cannot legally be prevented from doing so.

Some people consider the UEFA Champions League (UCL) as an opening of the European product market of football. However, the opposite is true; the UCL has closed the European football market for all teams that are not at the top in the Big Four football countries. After December 1995, the year of the *Bosman* verdict, only one non-Big-Four team (Porto in 2004) has played in the final of the UEFA Champions League.

The UCL has even accelerated and consolidated the closing of the European football championship by its perverse prize system, which rewards winning rich teams more than winning poor teams. In this way, the European football league resembles more and more the closed major leagues in North America.

The lack of professional club management

It seems that in sport in general, and in football club management in particular, passion and emotion rather than sober reasoning prevail. Sloane (1971) has argued that the common profit-maximization objective in economic theory does not apply to European football teams, which are rather utility- or win-maximizers (Kesenne, 1996, 2007b). It follows that, in the race to build the best team and to win, managers tend to overspend on player salaries. Not only are too many players hired, but these players are overpaid in an effort to keep them from running off to a richer and better-paying foreign club (Kesenne, 2010).

If football clubs in Europe act as win-maximizers, even staying within their budgets, a simple figure can show that win-maximizing teams spend more money

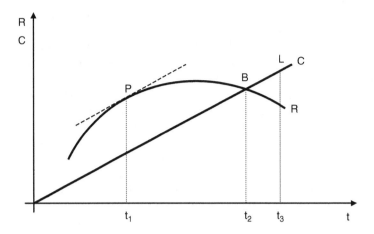

Figure 12.2 Win maximization versus profit maximization (Sloane, 1985)

on talent than profit-maximizing teams. In Figure 12.2, the number of playing talents, or the money spent on talent, is set on the horizontal axis. On the vertical axis, the total season revenue and cost of the team are measured. The cost curve (C) is assumed to be a simple linear increasing function of talent. The revenue curve (R) is an increasing function of talent, but the slope (that is, the marginal revenue of talent, which is the extra revenue of one more talent) falls with the number of talents in the team. If a team already has 20 talented players, one more talent will not add much to the team's playing strength and revenue.

A profit-maximizing team will hire talents until the marginal cost of talent (the slope of the linear cost curve) equals the marginal revenue of talent (the slope of the revenue curve) at point P. At that point, one can see that profit, or the difference between total revenue and total cost, is maximized. A win-maximizing club will hire as many playing talents as possible within the limits of its budget, which is at point B. A win-maximizing club clearly hires more playing talents than a profit-maximizing club, with a risk to overspend on talent such as at point L.

Many clubs ran into financial problems shortly after the *Bosman* verdict; the reason was that team managers had the short-sighted and one-sided idea that they could now spend more money on player salaries because it was no longer necessary to reserve money for paying transfer fees, while neglecting the fact that there was also no money from transfer fees. Many professional clubs in several European countries faced (near) bankruptcy because they raised player salaries when there was no money to do so. In the North American major leagues, player salaries increased dramatically after the abolition of the Reserve Clause in the mid-1970s, because the monopsonistic exploitation of players by team owners was stopped and players managed to get their legitimate share of the revenues and profits of the team owners (Quirk and Fort, 1992; Scully, 1974, 1999). A monopsonistic player market is created when there is only one demander for playing talent, which is the league in a highly regulated player market. A monopsonist, without a competitor in the market, has the power to underpay and exploit its players.

Furthermore, after *Bosman*, many clubs reduced their youth training programs, based on the false idea that, if players can leave at the end of their contract without any compensation, investment in training young talent would no longer pay off. In an attempt to stimulate youth training, FIFA introduced a new and hopelessly complex arrangement in 2002 to compensate all teams that have contributed to the training of a young player when transferred at the end of his contract. Unsurprisingly, this FIFA regulation came into conflict with the free movement of end-of-contract players in the so-called *Bernard* case of the European Court of Justice in 2010 (Kesenne, 2011). The CJEU found itself caught between two objectives: on the one hand, the European competition laws, including the free movement of players and, on the other hand, the stimulation and compensation of youth training.

Nevertheless, the way out of this dilemma is fairly simple if one separates youth training compensation from the transfer of a player. The league could simply create a youth training fund, to which all teams contribute, on a yearly basis, an amount of money as a percentage of their budgets. The league redistributes the money based on the quantity and quality of the teams' youth training programs. This way, the training of a player is compensated even if the player is not transferred, players are free to move, and transfer payments can be abolished altogether, even for players who are still under contract. Nevertheless, contracts should still be honored; the player, or the team, that unilaterally breaks a contract should be punished by suspension for a number of games, or a loss of points in the ranking, respectively. Furthermore, player transfers during the season should be forbidden because it falsifies the championship as much as a player changing teams during the half-time break of a match. Each team should finish the championship with the same players as it started the championship.

In order to prevent emotional and unprofessional club management, good governance suggests that the separation of the financial and sportive management of a club would better serve the model. The financial manager sets the financial limits and draws the lines, wherein sportive management can give rein to its passions and emotions.

The league size

It has been argued that small European countries are also too small for the current number of professional teams in their first divisions. Given the limited supply of talent in a small country, divided over too many teams, the average quality of the participating teams is reduced. As a consequence, so the argument goes, the number of teams in the national top division should be reduced. The more talented teams would then be able to compete with the European top clubs. When Belgium reduced the number of teams in the first division in 2010 from 18 to 16 teams, together with the introduction of a complex play-off system, quite the opposite happened. The general observation is that, over the last three years, the quality of the national championship has diminished. Economic research has also shown that the optimal number of teams in the top division is larger than the number of teams decided by the league authorities, if not only the interests of the large teams, that don't like to share money with the small teams, are taken into account (Kahn, 2007; Szymanski, 2003; Kesenne, 2009b).

So, in the spectators' interest, which is vital for the financial health of a sports league, Belgium should have more than 20 professional teams in the first division. In a rich country of 11 million people, more than 20 professional teams can survive. The yearly player cost of a team with 22 professional players, and a wage cost of €100,000 per player, amounts to €2.2 million. With a healthy wage-turnover ratio of 65 percent, the clubs' budget is only €3.5 million. There are also enough young, unschooled football players who are willing to play professionally for the salary of a university professor with 40 years of seniority.

In order to avoid bankruptcy of relegated teams in the cemetery of the second division, all clubs that can survive professionally, and perform accordingly, should play in the professional division of, say, 22 teams in Belgium. This top league should be semi-closed, or semi-open, in order to capture the advantages of both systems. Every year, one team is promoted and relegated, but a team promoted to the top division should be guaranteed a stay in the top division for at least three seasons. Only the team with the poorest performance over each overlapping three-year period is to be relegated to the second division. This way, the investment in playing talent, needed to compete in the top division, will have more time to adjust to the top competition and to yield a return.

The monopolization of broadcast rights

Football and other sports leagues in Europe and North America all tend to centralize the selling of broadcast rights to the highest bidding broadcaster or television channel. In most cases, this monopolization of the market of broadcast rights creates another monopoly on the downstream market of televised sports, if the rights are sold to just one broadcaster who can (mis)use its monopoly power to limit the number of televised games and to charge a high viewing price to television spectators. This practice is clearly causing a welfare loss.

The argument for the centralization of the selling of broadcast rights is that it allows the league to collect more TV-money than all teams together can collect individually and, moreover, to redistribute the money among all clubs to guarantee a more balanced competition. While the first argument is probably true, the distribution argument is certainly false. It is not necessary to monopolize broadcast rights if the league wants to distribute TV-money. The selling of broadcast rights can be left to the individual teams, as they are also the legal owners of the broadcast rights of their home games, according to several court verdicts in Europe. After the teams have sold their broadcast rights individually, the league should force the teams to contribute a percentage of their broadcast revenue to a fund that can be equally redistributed among all teams. Even if the total amount of broadcast rights is lower, this scenario avoids the welfare loss caused by monopolization (Kesenne, 2009a; 2015).

Empirical research has also shown that there is no connection between the monopolization of broadcast rights and competitive balance in the European national championships (Peeters, 2011).

Conclusion

If the objective is to restore the competitive balance in European football and to narrow the financial and sporting gap between the top clubs in the Big Four and all other European countries, UEFA should act, not with its Financial Fair Play (FFP) regulation, but by opening the European football market after *Bosman* has opened the European player market.

In 2010 UEFA announced its FFP plan, a set of financial restraints which clubs must respect when seeking to enter the UEFA Champions League (UCL). The most important restraint is probably the break-even constraint based on a team's structural football revenues only – that is, without the money of the so-called "sugar daddies." Even if the FFP regulations are implemented and enforced successfully, substantially reducing clubs' average payrolls and wage-to-turnover ratios, the financial and sporting gap between the top teams in large and small countries will hardly be narrowed. The revenues from broadcast rights, sponsorship, and merchandizing in the large countries are so far above those revenues in small countries (Peeters & Szymanski, 2014) that the sporting impact in European football will only be that the existing dynasties will stay in place. For example, Manchester City would never have been able to compete with Manchester United without the financial input of its personal sponsor. So, in a way, FFP could worsen the competitive balance in European football.

So, part of the solution is to be found in revenue-sharing among large- and small-budget teams. It has been shown that revenue-sharing improves the competitive balance in a league with win-maximizing teams, as opposed to profit-maximization. Furthermore, leagues should also stop monopolizing the market of broadcast rights, but tax the clubs' individual broadcast rights and distribute the collected money equally among all teams in one expanded half-open professional league.

Moreover, the famous *Bosman* lawyer, Jean-Louis Dupont (2013), has already called the FFP regulation illegal, which forewarns of future change.

References

Berlinschi, R., Schokkaert, J., & Swinnen, J. (2013). When drains and gains coincide: Migration and international football performance. *Labour Economics, 21*, 1–14.

Dupont, J-L. (2013, May 6). Press Release. Retrieved from www.FourFourTwo.com/features/bosman-lawyer-battling-ffp

Kahn, L.M. (2007). Sports league expansion and consumer welfare. *Journal of Sports Economics, 8* (2), 115–138.

Kesenne, S. (1996). League management in professional team sports with win maximizing clubs. *European Journal for Sports Management, 2* (2), 14–22.

Kesenne, S. (2007a). The peculiar international economics of professional football in Europe. *Scottish Journal of Political Economy, 54* (3), 388–400.

Kesenne, S. (2007b). *The economic theory of professional team sports: An analytical treatment.* Northampton, MA: Edward Elgar.

Kesenne S. (2009a). The impact of pooling and sharing broadcast rights in professional team sports. *International Journal of Sport Finance, 4* (3), 211–218.

Kesenne, S. (2009b). The optimal size of a sports league. *International Journal of Sport Finance, 4* (4), 264–270.

Kesenne, S. (2010). The financial situation of football clubs in the Belgian Jupiler league: Are players overpaid in a win-maximization league? *International Journal of Sport Finance, 5* (1), 67–71.

Kesenne, S. (2011). Youth development and training after the Bosman verdict (1995) and the Bernard case (2010) of the European Court of Justice. *European Sport Management Quarterly, 11* (5), 547–553.

Kesenne, S. (2015). The collection and distribution of media rights in a win-maximization league. In P. Sloane & J. Goddard (Eds.), *Handbook on the economics of professional football.* Northampton, MA: Edward Elgar.

Peeters, Th. (2011). Broadcast rights and competitive balance in European soccer. *International Journal of Sport Finance, 6* (1), 23–39.

Peeters, Th., & Szymanski, S. (2014). Financial Fair Play in European football. *Economic Policy, 29* (78), 343–390.

Primault, D. (2004). Les consequences de la dérégulation du marché du travail, données de cadrage [Consequences of the labor market deregulation, basic policy data]. In: J.J. Gouguet (Ed.), *Le Sport Professionel après l'Arrêt Bosman* (pp.87–94). Limoge: Pulim.

Quirk, J., & Fort, R. (1992). *Pay dirt: The business of professional team sports.* Princeton, NJ: Princeton University Press.

Scully, G. (1974). Pay and performance in Major League baseball. *American Economic Review, 64* (6), 915–930.

Scully, G. (1999). Free agency and the rate of monopsonistic exploitation in baseball. In C. Jeanrenaud & S. Kesenne (Eds.), *Competition policy in professional sports* (pp. 59–70). Antwerp: Standaard Editions.

Sloane, P. (1971). The economics of professional football: The football club as a utility maximiser. *Scottish Journal of Political Economy, 17* (2), 121–146.

Sloane, P. (1985). Informal seminar at the Economics Department, University of Antwerp.

Szymanski, S. (2003). The economic design of sporting contests. *Journal of Economic Literature, 41* (4), 1137–1187.

13 Paradoxes in professional road cycling

A plea for a new cycling industry

Wim Lagae and Daam Van Reeth

Introduction

Professional cycling is one of the oldest professional sports. It is hugely popular in some core European countries and gaining momentum in various countries all over the world. Yet, the sport is understudied in comparison to other sports like soccer or basketball. Road cycling, an outdoor sport that takes place on public ground, is an individual sport practiced in teams. This implies that while cycling races serve as team events, it is the individual performances and titles that are most important in the end. Contrary to other sports, the world calendar of races consists of a non-homogeneous set of one-day events and stage cycling events (Rebeggiani & Tondani, 2008). Even within both categories of events, some races are considered to be more important than others in terms of historical significance, number of spectators, and media exposure (Lagae, 2005). The Tour de France is more important than its Italian and Spanish counterparts, namely the Giro d'Italia and the Vuelta a España. Also, within one-day races a similar heterogeneity is detected between "historic classics" such as the Tour of Flanders and smaller regional races.

Until the 1970s, road cycling was characterized by limited team budgets and the sport was geographically concentrated in Belgium, France, Italy, the Netherlands, and Spain. The entrance of multinational corporations in the 1980s resulted in an increased demand for top riders, which in turn led to higher team budgets (Lagae, 2005). At the end of the 1980s, the Union Cyclist International (UCI), under the presidency of Hein Verbruggen, aimed to speed up the internationalization of road cycling and implemented various reforms, inspired by tennis and Formula 1, from which the current structure of road cycling developed (Brewer, 2002). Besides the introduction of a UCI ranking to determine the (market) value of riders and teams, the UCI aimed at maintaining the cycling fan's attention all year long, and at increasing cycling sponsorship (Brewer, 2002). The UCI ProTour competition, re-labeled as the World Tour from 2011 onwards, was seen as a way to promote cycling throughout the world and to attract more international teams and raise television revenues.

Professional sport is by its nature a representation of conflict in which multiple stakeholders are involved. Professional road cycling, in particular, is character-ized by a large and heterogeneous set of stakeholders with various interest inten-sities and resource relationships (Brewer, 2002; Morrow & Idle, 2008; Benijts & Lagae, 2012). As such, cycling provides an interesting microcosm that allows researching stakeholder strategies in detail. In the following section we analyze four paradoxes of professional road cycling. The final section concludes with a plea for more financial fair play and more professional organization through a structural strengthening of the cycling sector.

Paradoxes in professional road cycling

While cycling has coped with several doping crises during the last two decades, team budgets continued to increase

Brewer (2002) argues that the introduction of a UCI ranking and a year-long calendar did not only facilitate the commercial development of cycling, but also resulted in extra pressure on team managers and riders to resort to doping prac-tices. The Festina affair (1998), Operación Puerto (2006), and the Armstrong case (2012) are three notorious examples of how, during the last couple of decades, doping was present at the highest level of professional road cycling. From 2008 onwards cycling also had to deal with the consequences of the banking and economic crisis and with a decreasing spectator interest in the Tour de France. In fact, overall Tour de France TV audiences in Belgium, the Netherlands, the UK, the USA, and Australia fell by 22 percent between 2011 and 2014 (Van Reeth, 2014). It is a paradox that despite all these high-profile doping crises and other trouble-some evolutions, team budgets continued to increase. In nominal terms, the aver-age budgets of the best ten cycling teams grew slowly from about €4 million in the early 1990s to €7 million in the early 2000s. A more significant increase occurred with the introduction of the ProTour and the World Tour. Between 2005 and 2010 average budgets for the best ten teams increased to €10 million (Benijts, Lagae, & Vanclooster, 2011) and have since soared to over €14 million in 2014.

While some sponsors have left the sport, benefactors came into road cycling

Disgusted by recurrent doping crises, major commercial team sponsors like Deutsche Telekom or Rabobank left professional cycling in, respectively, 2007 and 2012. Other title sponsors abandoned cycling because of a change in market-ing strategy (Vacansoleil in 2013, Belkin and Belisol in 2014) or because of the economic crisis (Euskaltel-Euskadi in 2013). Although a few new sponsors entered cycling (like Soudal and Etixx from 2015 onwards), on balance the cycling sector lost commercial sponsors in recent years. It is a paradox that benefactors entered professional cycling instead. For benefactor-financed cycling teams, sponsorship is the toy of the CEO or the politician. Their personal (dis) likes shape the course of corporate finance and sponsorship activities in professional road cycling. Currently, almost one-third of the 18 World Tour teams (accounting for approximately half of all team budgets) are supported by wealthy individuals or oligarch business owners. The benefactors in today's professional road cycling are Zdenek Bakala (Omega Pharma – Quick-Step), Andy Rihs (BMC Racing Team), Gerry Ryan (Orica-Green EDGE), Igor Makarov (Katusha), and Oleg Tinkov (Tinkoff-Saxo). In 2014, the 18 World Tour teams can be subdivided into purely commercial sponsored teams (e.g. Lotto-Belisol), oligarch- and Maecenas-financed teams (e.g. Astana), and hybrid-financed teams (e.g. Omega Pharma – Quick-Step). As a result, we now witness a race between the deep-pocket sponsors promising ever-increasing wages to a selected group of top cyclists, as illustrated by the transfer of Tour de France green jersey winner Peter Sagan from Cannondale to Tinkoff-Saxo in 2015. This transfer will earn him an estimated yearly salary of €4.2 million.

While the UCI is mandated to have the political power in cycling, the organization of cycling is monopolized by a private media group

In theory, the UCI should be responsible for managing world cycling, similar to other international sport federations. However, in practice Tour de France organizer Amaury Sports Organization (ASO) seems to influence in a decisive way the democratic process within the UCI, sometimes even exercising a veto. The organization is considered to be the most powerful actor in professional cycling. ASO is often accused of being an arrogant monopolist that vigorously protects its superior position in the distribution of the marketing and television incomes from organizers. Neither the participating teams, nor anyone else in cycling, are currently aware of the amount of television revenue the Tour generates. In fact, the ASO successfully blocked discussion on the distribution of revenues toward teams and riders for years.

ASO is a for-profit organization that specializes in the organization and promotion of, among others, motor sports, athletics, equestrian sports, golf events, and cycling. With regard to cycling, the ASO organizes the Tour de France as well as five other prestigious cycling races in France and Belgium: Paris–Nice, Paris–Roubaix, Paris–Tours, la Flèche Wallonne and Liège–Bastogne–Liège. It also holds a majority stake in the Vuelta a España and is involved in the organization of many smaller cycling races. But it is the Tour de France that is the cash cow in professional cycling, with a rumored market share of two-thirds of all television revenue and sponsorship income generated by other World Tour organizers. Since the Tour de France has substantial freedom in deciding whether or not to invite a team to participate, the sponsors of cycling teams not invited suffer greatly. Due to this uncertainty about participating, sponsors became reluctant to invest, thereby creating an unstable financial context for the non-World Tour teams. This was especially problematic as professional cycling teams relied upon (one might even say were addicted to) sponsorship money as the main source of income. It is a paradox that neither the teams nor the riders, obviously essential ingredients of a cycling race, nor the national and international cycling federations, as regulatory bodies, have been able to challenge this dominant position of ASO.

While doping (perception) problems in cycling are overexposed, scandals in other spectator sports remain underexposed

Professional road cycling has had a long-lasting association with doping and, as already explained above, has witnessed some major doping crises in the past couple of decades. There is little research evidence on public reaction to doping, but a recent study in Flanders did show that most spectators prefer a "clean" performance in the Tour over exceptional results, such as those of Lance Armstrong, achieved by doping (Van Reeth & Lagae, 2014). Thus, although the public is aware of doping in cycling, they believe it is here to stay. Yet, this belief does not really affect whether they watch it on TV, as a further study (Van Reeth, 2013) has shown. Newly revealed doping cases during the Tour de France appear to have practically no impact on its average TV audiences, but are correlated with a 7 percent decrease in peak audiences.

Although it has not strongly affected Flemish audiences for cycling so far, doping is seriously threatening cycling in the long run. This is even more the case at the international level since it is very likely that public interest in cycling-crazy Flanders does not properly reflect the situation in other parts of the world, where professional cyclists are often considered to be doping-addicted junkies. It is worrying that, although a lot has changed in the past ten years, such as the introduction of a whereabouts system, the biological passport and the no-needle policy, professional road cycling does not seem to be able to free itself from this doping image with the general public. Other sports are facing similar problems too. In recent years, multiple medal-winning track and field athletes at the Olympics or the World Championships have been suspended for doping use, and match fixing is the biggest problem soccer is facing at this moment. However, both sports do not seem to have an image problem nor suffer from a decline in public interest, probably because these issues are hardly picked up by the media. It is a paradox that cycling's image remains tainted so strongly by its dark doping past, while other sports escape so easily from similar problems (Lagae, 2013).

A plea for a new cycling industry

More sports marketing efforts and an intense cooperation is needed between the different stakeholders in professional cycling in order to cope with its structural problems and develop a better future for cycling. We suggest an action plan for a new cycling industry that comprises five elements.

A better representation of teams and riders

One of the peculiarities of professional cycling in comparison with other spectator sports is its hybrid character as an individual sport practiced in a team context. However, neither the riders nor the teams are organized in a professional way. The riders are represented by the CPA (*Cyclistes Professionnels Associés* or *Association of Professional Cyclists*), an international association created during the Giro d'Italia of 1999. The CPA, led by two-time world champion Gianni Bugno, aims to defend and improve the riders' status and the riders' relationships with the employers. However, the CPA lacks any real power, as do the many interest groups of cycling teams, such as the AIGCP (*Association Internationale des Groupes Cyclistes Professionnels*), the IPCT (*International Professional Cycling Teams*), the MPCC (*Mouvement Pour un Cyclisme Crédible*) or Velon (a newly formed interest group of top cycling teams).

The cornerstone of a new cycling industry needs to be a new institution to guide the future of cycling from the perspective of top teams and riders, in addition to the regulating UCI and race organizers. Since cycling teams currently lack that sector perspective (contrary to, e.g. soccer leagues representing the clubs), a pro rata percentage of sponsorship and benefactor money should be invested in a fund in order to build and operate this new institution.

A better financing of cycling teams

Cycling teams warmly welcome the investments of wealthy benefactors and powerful oligarchs. Paradoxically, on a sector level, deep-pocket investors in cycling teams generate a crowding-out effect, pushing out sponsors seeking exposure/visibility for their brand through professional cycling, such as Vacansoleil-DCM or Belisol. Moreover, the current system in which cycling teams are almost exclusively financed by sponsors also creates a highly unstable sector model. For instance, in June 2014 Belkin decided to end sponsorship of the Rabobank cycling team, which it had taken over for a bargain only a year before.

Accompanied by professional negotiators and change managers, a new cycling institution representing all World Tour teams and riders should therefore look for new ways to get some additional external financing for cycling teams. The new institution needs, for instance, to exert pressure on race organizers and the UCI to make a fair deal on sharing media rights. It is astonishing that ASO, the main actor doing business with the organization of professional cycling, lacks transparency. Apart from its shareholders, nobody seems to know what television rights the Tour de France derives. However, it would be a mistake to focus all attention on the major stakeholder in cycling. The importance of the race makes a boycott of the Tour de France by teams or cyclists, similar to the NBA lockouts witnessed in the past, an ineffective threat. It would, in contrast, be much easier to negotiate such deals on media rights with (relatively) new races that want to be part of a new World Tour calendar of races. A key asset for cycling teams in these negotiations could be the content they can deliver themselves, such as the streaming of in-race (live) images, radio communication, and pre- and post-race interviews.

A better cycling product

At this moment, many stakeholders in cycling have an unrealistic view of the popularity of cycling, misled by the inflated TV audiences that the UCI and race organizers claim. In fact, only about a dozen cycling races have worldwide TV audiences of over one million viewers, almost entirely concentrated in Europe. It is symptomatic of cycling in general, but not surprising, that although the World Tour has existed since 2005, a sponsor for the event has never been found. Therefore, instead of fighting for little bits of the current (small) cake, we think the focus should be on increasing the size of the cake for all.

Media rights and sponsor money can only increase if professional road cycling becomes a product media really want to pay for. Although tradition has to be respected, enough newly created races outside of Europe need to be part of a new worldwide calendar to free cycling from its European cocoon. This top league of cycling races can then be sold to broadcasters as a product bundle, as a year-long take-it-or-leave-it package, to get professional road cycling away from the current situation of cherry-picking by the media. Moreover, much more than other sports, professional road cycling is a sport that can only be appreciated through the media. So both cycling races (the core product) and TV broadcasts of cycling races (the derivative product) have to change. More interesting coverage of a race is possible through the use of social media and new technologies, such as in-race cameras. New and shorter race formats are necessary to attract new and young audiences. If media and race organizers are ready for such a change, teams should commit themselves to line up their best riders as much as possible. While in tennis, skiing, or Formula One the same players take part in all events, even the ones in which they are less likely to be successful, the superstars of cycling often focus on a limited number of important races only. Why not make the sharing of TV-money contingent upon the participation of a team's top riders? This calls for a combined commitment by all stakeholders. In 2013, team Sky took the initiative to increase the size of the cake with the so-called "Avignon project." It succeeded in getting most of the cycling teams on the same page, but unfortunately did not get the support of ASO or the UCI.

A safer and healthier cycling

There are many dangers in the sport of road cycling, like bunch sprints, dangerous descents, road furniture, spectator control, or the organization of feed zones. Although not all health and safety matters in road races can be pre-determined, we are convinced that a series of new safety measures and communication controls need to be developed. Hiring experienced safety managers, who should try to diminish or control unfavorable racing conditions, is a necessary element of a new cycling sector. Comparable to the organization of Formula One races, there should be a clear ruling on (the communication of) safety problems and solutions in professional cycling, such as safety cars or motorbikes, more visual safety signals and the introduction of neutralization scenarios. After Milano–San

Remo 2013 and the debacle of the Stage 16 descent of the snowy Stelvio mountain-pass in the Giro d'Italia 2014, many called for new rules to regulate road cycling in icy weather. During the Tour of California 2013 and 2014 there was intense discussion on the issue of racing in too hot weather. It is clear that team managers and team doctors have to take sector responsibility and share their thoughts and experience with the new health and safety specialists. The cycling sector also has to measure, explain, and reduce the number of crashes during professional road cycling races.

Coping better with the doping past

One of the toughest problems cycling faces is how to come to terms with its long doping past and how to free itself from this doping image with the general public. Although a lot has changed for the better in the fight against doping, the way professional road cycling deals with riders caught, or sanctions riders who confess to having taken forbidden substances in the past, is a real PR disaster. It was unfortunate that, after the Court of Arbitration for Sport (CAS) suspended Alberto Contador in 2012, UCI president McQuaid publicly announced that, in his opinion, Contador was innocent and was a victim of contaminated meat. And it was wrong to take away the seven Tour de France victories of Lance Armstrong while at the same time allowing Richard Virenque to keep his seven king-of-the-mountain jerseys.

We do, of course, not want to minimize the doping problem, but the seemingly arbitrary way in which doping use has been sanctioned makes the rolls of honor of cycling races a joke. What's the use of removing Lance Armstrong from the list of Tour de France winners if we know by now that, of all the cyclists who had a podium finish between 1996 and 2005 (30 spots in total), only the Spanish Kelme cyclist Escartin in 1999 has never been accused of or confessed to doping? We therefore call for an independent truth and reconciliation commission of sports historians, sports ethicists, sports economists and marketers, former cyclists, and policy-makers. This commission should produce a report that once and for all draws a line under the past and clearly communicates what really happened without turning it into a manhunt. The UCI should also develop a clear policy on the communication of future doping issues to re-establish the reputation of not only the federation, but also of professional road cycling in general. Setting up such a commission was, in fact, one of the first decisions made by Brian Cookson, the newly elected president of the UCI in 2013. Unfortunately, the report by the Cycling Independent Reform Commission, published in March 2015, presents mainly well-known facts and primarily focuses on the historical role of the UCI and its presidents in the fight against doping. The report is not substantial enough to draw a line under the dark doping past of cycling, nor does it bring forward any elements to solve cycling's doping perception problem. Finally, the report did not succeed in proposing fundamental reforms of professional cycling either.

References

Benijts, T., & Lagae, W. (2012). Using program theory to evaluate league reforms: The case of professional road cycling. *European Sport Management Quarterly, 12* (1), 83–109.

Benijts, T., Lagae, W., & Vanclooster, B. (2011). The influence of sport leagues on the business-to-business marketing of teams: The case of professional road cycling. *The Journal of Business & Industrial Marketing, 26* (8), 608.

Brewer, B.D. (2002). Commercialization in professional cycling 1950–2001: Institutional transformations and the rationalization of "doping." *Sociology of Sport Journal, 19* (3), 276–301.

Lagae, W. (2005). *Sports sponsorship and marketing communications: A European perspective.* Harlow: Pearson Education.

Lagae, W. (2013). Actieplan voor een nieuwe wielersector. In: H. Vandeweghe (Ed.), *Wie gelooft die coureurs nog? Doping!? [Who still believes those racing cyclists? Doping!?]* (pp. 270–281). Gent: Borgerhoff & Lamberigts.

Morrow, S., & Idle, C. (2008). Understanding change in professional road cycling. *European Sport Management Quarterly, 8* (4), 315–335.

Rebeggiani, L., & Tondani, D. (2008). Organizational forms in professional cycling: An examination of the efficiency of the UCI ProTour. *International Journal of Sport Finance, 3* (1), 19–41.

Van Reeth, D. (2013), TV demand for the Tour de France: The importance of stage characteristics versus outcome uncertainty, patriotism, and doping. *International Journal of Sport Finance, 8* (1), 39–60.

Van Reeth, D. (2014). *Evaluation of TV viewing for the 2014 Tour de France: An international perspective.* Brussels: KU Leuven Campus Brussel.

Van Reeth, D., & Lagae, W. (2014). Public opinion on doping in cycling: Differences among population groups. In: Budzinski, O. & Feddersen, A. (Eds.), *Contemporary research in sports economics (Proceedings of the 5th ESEA conference)* (pp. 247–268). Frankfurt am Main: Peter Lang.

14 Sport is not for all

Toward a renewed future of "Sport for All" as a right

Bart Vanreusel

Introduction

This chapter explores whether or how Sport for All can be a leading principle for the development of a renewed sport culture in the twenty-first century. It traces back the original ideas of Sport for All and confronts these ideas with actual observations. Suggestions for a renewed vision of Sport for All are formulated.

The global expansion of Sport for All as an ideology, a social movement, and a common practice can be considered as one of the most remarkable cultural innovations in modern sporting culture. The traditional sporting culture for a long time was monopolized by "prolympism" (Donnelly, 1996), a mixture of professionalism and Olympism as the standard, with an outspoken emphasis on elite sport, obsessed with high performance and records. Prolympism is the subject of ongoing and intense commodification and globalization, resulting in today's global arena of sport events as commoditized spectacles, run by transnational corporations (Borgers, Vanreusel, & Scheerder, 2013).

In contrast to this, the Sport for All movement originally emerged as a reaction to the dominant culture of prolympic sport. In the slipstream of pop art, pop music, and other expressions of popular culture, in the 1960s and 1970s, Sport for All represented the rise of popular culture in physical activity and sport (remarkably, the concept of pop sport was never used). Since sport in its original and traditional meaning was not invented nor intended to be for all, a whole new social configuration of a sporting culture was introduced by the Sport for All movement. Traditional sport concepts such as athletes, competition, winning, and records were complemented by new sport concepts such as participation, recreation, physical activity, and health. The dominant meritocratic ideology of sport culture was based on exclusion, governed by the power elite of sport organizations and corporations. Gradually, a new sport ideology was created, founded on inclusion, equal opportunities and open participation in sport, play, and physical activity for all. Grass roots initiatives by civil society groups such as recreational sport organizations were the most important support for the early adoption of the

Sport for All movement. But a subsidizing policy by local and national governments, messages from the public health sector, and the growth of a consumer market for active sport participants gave wings to the expansion of Sport for All.

Sport for All as a right

However, the crucial and consolidating moment for Sport for All was the declaration of the European Sport for All Charter, first presented by the Council of Europe in 1975 with slightly adapted versions in later years. The first two articles of this eight-article charter declare that every individual has the fundamental right to participate in sport and that participation in sport must be encouraged as an important factor of human development and should be supported with public funding. This charter created a momentum that launched Sport for All as a new but durable sport concept for the future of sport, attractive enough to be embraced and flexible enough to be adopted. The Sport for All Charter was put into practice in Europe and gradually translated into policy and practice all over the world.

Perhaps the most striking feature of the Sport for All Charter is that it was inspired by human rights. The Human Rights Charter indeed was the source of inspiration for the Sport for All Charter. It was the first time that the sporting culture presented itself as a rights-based culture. This fundamental approach of sport as a right was a clear contrast with the traditional features of sport as a prerogative of "the young and the strong happy few." By referring to human rights, it was accepted that Sport for All should not exclude or discriminate against people, and that the right to participate should be safeguarded as a primary objective (*European Sport for All Charter*, 1975; Oja & Telama, 1991)

More than 20 years later, in a worldwide study of Sport for All trends and experiences, Da Costa and Miragaya (2002) showed how Sport for All, over the years, had turned into a well-established mainstream sporting culture. The new rights-based approach clearly had a significant and globalized impact on Sport for All developments in a variety of ways and was often put into practice with local color and flavor. Although programs and practices of Sport for All were different, similar basic social patterns could be recognized worldwide.

Sport for All was initially adopted and realized at the grass roots level by civil society groups, often outside of the traditional sport organizations. New social groups organized and experienced sport. This resulted in new participants that would not have been recruited by the traditional sporting culture.

State interventions at national and local levels provided support such as financial subsidies, facilities, staff training, and communication. In many countries, sport policy was changed fundamentally toward a Sport for All approach. This resulted in new perspectives on facility planning and a shift from the stadium to the neighborhood, a major benefit for Sport for All.

Creative and inviting promotion campaigns raised awareness of the need to be physically active and to participate in sport. Such promotion campaigns, often professionally targeted at specific groups, were sustained over many years and contributed to the positive vibe around Sport for All. Sport for All services, delivered by governments and markets, reached out with targeted Sport for All programs for groups with limited or no access to sport.

Warnings from the public health sector on the detrimental impact of the lack of physical activity and advice on the benefits of physical activity for everyone contributed to the impact of Sport for All. The conceptual differences and similarities between sport and physical activity were debated and the need for a healthy and physically active lifestyle took over the social scene as the new version of a Sport for All idea.

In addition to such observations, national and international large-scale sport participation surveys revealed increasing participation figures in sport over time and new modes of sport involvement, more in tune with a Sport for All idea. Furthermore, underrepresented groups in sport participation, such as women, senior citizens, and people with a disadvantaged socio-economic background, were slowly reducing the gap (Scheerder, Vandermeerschen, Van Tuyckom, Hoekman, Breedveld, & Vos, 2011). Longitudinal lifespan surveys have started to discover whether and how physically (in)active lifestyles are continued or discontinued over the lifespan (Vanreusel & Scheerder, 2015).

In sum, the fundamental idea that active involvement in sport is a right for every person has changed sport culture in all its aspects. Sport for All as a right was accepted, promoted, and implemented in many countries and cultures worldwide. It created access to sport and physical activity by groups in society that were not reached before by traditional sport culture. It contributed to the development of active lifestyles and it changed minds and policies in a durable way. Sport for All appeared to be an overall success.

Sport: not for all

The observations above might suggest that Sport for All had reached its objectives. The impression that the social transformation of sport culture toward a more democratic, inclusive, and open culture was a complete success has dominated discourses in popular and academic work on Sport for All. However, in contrast to the euphoric discourses on the spirit and the realizations of Sport for All, other sources have expressed their doubts. In 1999 Houlihan pointed out six reasons why the Sport for All movement lost momentum: (1) long-term objectives were not followed by short-term observable effects; (2) overambitious expectations resulted in a loss of interest and efforts; (3) a declining interest by governments because of a lack of clear progress; (4) a sneaking privatization of access to sport resulting in a less dynamic attitude by civil society; (5) a fragmenting and blurred vision on Sport for All; and (6) doubts about the measurable and significant positive public health effects of Sport for All policies.

Our reflection on 25 years of Sport for All policy in 2002 (De Knop, Renson, Taks, & Vanreusel, 2002) came to similar conclusions. The four basic objectives of Sport for All were only partially realized: (1) increasing sport participation levels were inconsistent, only observed in specific countries or regions, and might not necessarily be caused by Sport for All; (2) opportunities to participate for many groups in society were still remarkably unequal – age, gender, ability, culture, religion, and socio-economic difference still caused unequal opportunities; (3) exclusion and discrimination were still present in sport culture; and (4) civil society initiatives were countered and discouraged by consumer culture. In sum, the Sport for All ideology was only to a small extent matched by observable social realities.

To these early critical comments on Sport for All, I want to add my personal observations as an academic in the sociology of sport and as a field observer for over 30 years, with a specific interest in Sport for All. Over these years I observed Sport for All initiatives in various countries and settings, from industrial democracies to developing countries and conflict-ridden regions, from government interventions to non-governmental organizations, from educational to public health settings, from established transnational sport organizations to local neighborhood sport. My conclusion from these observations is simple and straightforward: sport is not for all. Or even stronger: sport is not for all at all. A brief overview of a failing Sport for All concept follows.

Blatant social exclusion still prevails in many areas of sport and in many regions in the world. Organized sport settings such as clubs and federations often are preoccupied with efforts to acquire the best athletes and to win, leaving no opportunities for the majority of others to participate and enjoy. Not only organized sport, but simple physical play is denied to millions of children and youth who grow up with unfavorable life conditions, caused by natural disasters, conflict, harsh socio-economic situations. or simply a lack of education.

Discrimination resulting in unequal opportunities to participate in sport has far from disappeared. Sometimes explicit, but more often implicit, socially hidden forms of discrimination based on skill, age, gender, ability, culture, religion, national or local identity continue to be part of the discriminating realities of sport. The equal-opportunity objective of Sport for All is not realized.

Socio-economic inequalities diminish opportunities to participate in sport as they cut through many issues of life and society. Those in poverty or with limited socio-economic means participate less or not at all in any kind of sport or physical activity. Social inequality of access to sport, play, and physical activity is everywhere. Differences in opportunities to participate in sport and physical activity between socio-economic groups in one particular city, for example, are as big as differences between rich and poor countries. Those with higher needs for a physically active and healthy lifestyle often experience inequality more intensely.

Mega sport events worldwide use enormous resources to run their facilities and spectacles with little or no return or impact on Sport for All. Often, these events use public finances that are no longer available to support Sport for All. Such events take place at the expense of Sport for All. Research on the potential social benefit of sport events, in favor of Sport for All, is just emerging (Taks, 2013).

Organizations and initiatives with a clear emphasis on Sport for All often suffer from a lack of support and resources, limited public attention and media, and little or no support from the traditional sport system. Special reference is made here to NGOs as new and creative providers of grass roots Sport for All initiatives.

School-based physical education programs do not sufficiently succeed in creating a lasting Sport for All lifestyle. The drop-out rate from sport and physical activity after school age remains dramatically high. Basic physical education as a ground for Sport for All is missing for a large number of schoolchildren worldwide.

This overview is in sharp contrast with the widespread claims for Sport for All by institutions inside and outside the world of sport. The claims for Sport for All are now echoed by cultural practices such as the health and fitness industry, world mega sport events and their organizers, the sport tourism economy, and the sporting goods industry. In many cases these claims of Sport for All are little more than a marketing tool, not matched by a serious engagement to take Sport for All as a right for every individual to participate in sport. The abuse of Sport for All as a window dressing marketing slogan has an extra negative effect on those initiatives that take the idea seriously.

In sum, in contrast to its original objectives, Sport for All today appears to be understood as Sport for All who can afford, who have an education, who are healthy enough, who fit into the dominant sport system, and who are targeted as potential consumers. Such new cultural interpretations have abused and degraded the Sport for All idea and they deny the original and fundamental ground of Sport for All as a right for all.

Toward a renewed future for Sport for All

If we want Sport for All to be a guiding principle of a future sport culture based on universal values, then it becomes clear that the Sport for All movement needs to be revitalized and renewed. Such a renewed approach needs to take the rights-based origin of Sport for All into consideration again. If sport really wants to be for all, the original Sport for All Charter must be a sharpened guiding tool, defending and realizing the right to participate, particularly for those who experience difficulty getting involved, fighting all kinds of social exclusion and discrimination. Some indicative measures to reinstall a true Sport for All spirit and to put it into practice are listed here. We invite scholars, policy-makers, and practitioners to complement this list.

The original Sport for All charter needs an updated version, clearly based on universal rights such as the right to play, the right to participate in sport, and the right to develop a healthy lifestyle. That charter needs to be published and endorsed worldwide and by the major players in the field. The declaration by Panathlon International on ethics in youth sport may serve as a guiding example (Panathlon International, 2004).

A renewed focus is needed on basic issues in order to realize rights-based Sport for All in the future. The glamour of the sports entertainment industry and the profit of the professional sport industry, no matter how attractive they are, do not qualify to be the guiding principles for the sporting culture of the future. Sport for All is a needed, valuable, universal, and viable alternative.

Public and private resources for sport should be redirected and redistributed to Sport for All. Such a reorientation of resources, away from elite sport events which can be carried out by the market, contributes to a sport policy based on good governance, social justice, and durability principles.

All sport organizations, from local sport clubs to transnational sport corporations, should develop a corporate social responsibility (CSR) program with a focus on Sport for All issues. Sport for All must be a common and permanent future agenda and responsibility for all sport organizations. In 2014, only 30 percent of international sport organizations were running a CSR program. Since sport organizations receive valuable support from society, a social return on investment can be expected from them, and Sport for All should be the focus of this social return (Gofry, 2009; Levermore, 2011; Taks, 2013).

New players and future actors in the field of Sport for All should be welcomed and supported. In particular, civil society is invited to come up with local actions that need global support. The emergence and growth of sport-related NGOs worldwide, who carry out Sport for All programs within a wider scope of development, peace, health and community-building goals, is a clear example of such new players on the Sport for All scene (Kidd, 2008; Sanders, 2012).

A renewed culture of Sport for All can learn from other fields in society in order to cope with exclusion, unequal opportunity, and discrimination. The underlying social processes are pretty similar across different cultural fields.

Conclusion

To conclude, in order to build a future of Sport for All, we call for a global coalition for Sport for All as a right for every person, without exclusion or discrimination. This coalition must include the commitment of local and transnational sport organizations, of national and international public authorities, of cultural organizations, and of private and commercial corporations. The commitment for Sport for All should at least be equal to commitments for mega sport events. This coalition must subscribe to four guiding principles: (1) create opportunities to participate for everyone; (2) take away unequal opportunities and discrimination; (3) promote and organize an inclusive sport system; and (4) root the Sport for All idea in civil society at the grass roots level. If it is the ambition of sport to play a significant role in twenty-first-century society, in accordance with human needs and values, a renewed and vital future for Sport for All will be the appropriate response to this call.

References

Borgers, J., Vanreusel, B., & Scheerder, J. (2013). The diffusion of world sport events between 1891 and 2010: A study on globalization. *European Journal for Sport and Society, 10* (2), 101–120.

Da Costa, L.P., & Miragaya, A. (Eds.) (2002). *Worldwide experiences and trends in Sport for All*. Aachen: Meyer & Meyer Sport.

De Knop, P., Renson, R., Taks, M., & Vanreusel, B. (2002). Sport voor Allen (Sport for All). In P. De Knop, B. Vanreusel, & J. Scheerder (Eds.), *Sportsociologie, het Spel en de Spelers (Sociology of Sport, the Play and the Players)* (pp. 204–220). Maarssen: Elsevier.

Donnelly, P. (1996). Prolympism, sport monoculture as crisis and opportunity. *Quest, 48* (1), 25–42.

European Sport for All Charter (1975). Brussels: Council of Europe.

Gofrey, P.C. (2009). Corporate social responsibility: An overview and key issues. *Journal of Sport Management, 23*, 698–716.

Houlihan, B. (1999). Sport for All in the United Kingdom. Paper presented at the *Symposium Sport for All, Exchanging Canadian and European Experiences*, University of Toronto.

Kidd, B. (2008). A new social movement: Sport for development and peace. *Sport in Society: Cultures, Commerce, Media, Politics (Special issue: sport and foreign policy in a global world)*, 370–380.

Levermore, R. (2011). The paucity of, and dilemma in, evaluating corporate social responsibility for development through sport. *Third World Quarterly, 32* (3), 551–569.

Oja, P., & Telama, R. (Eds.) (1991). *Sport for All. Proceedings of the World Congress on Sport for All*. Amsterdam: Elsevier.

Panathlon International (2004). *Panathlon declaration on ethics in youth sport*. www.panathlon.be.

Sanders, B., Philips, J., & Vanreusel, B. (2012). Opportunities and challenges facing NGOs using sport as a vehicle for development in post-apartheid South Africa. *Sport Education and Society, 19* (6), 789–805.

Scheerder, J., Vandermeerschen, H., Van Tuyckom, C., Hoekman, R., Breedveld, K., Vos, S. (2011). *Understanding the game, sport participation in Europe: Facts, reflections and recommendations*. KU Leuven: SPM sport policy and management editions.

Taks, M. (2013). Social sustainability of non-mega sport events in a global world. *European Journal for Sport and Society, 10* (2), 121–142.

Vanreusel, B., & Scheerder, J. (2015). Tracking and youth sport: The quest for lifelong adherence to sport and physical activity. In K. Green & A. Smith (Eds.), *Youth sport*. London: Routledge.

15 What if sport and the law have become interlocked?

The case of the EU

Frank Hendrickx

Introduction

The relationship between sport and the law has received growing attention over the years. Against this background, a discipline is emerging, called sports law. This field of study is concerned with the relationship between law and sport, and more precisely with the role of law in the field of sport. This is still an area under construction, but plays an important role in sports governance issues. The growing societal relevance and (public) policy concerns in the area of sport has not only led to an increasing role of the law in the sports arena, it has also made claims for autonomy in sport more prominent. In this debate the notion of "sports specificity" arises.

This chapter focuses on European Union law, as in this field the tension between sporting autonomy and (public) regulatory intervention is quite prominent. In the EU, this has been given shape by a legal debate on the specificity of sport, which has served the desire of sports bodies to be shielded from public regulatory intervention. It has been triggered by emerging case law of the Court of Justice of the EU (CJEU), which has played an important role in applying European law in the area of sport. Building further on earlier work (Hendrickx, 2009; 2012), this chapter will reflect on the dominant trend in sports law and how the future of sports law in the EU should be imagined. The main normative framework is derived from EU law and use is made from existing sources in the EU legal order, such as policy texts, legislation (such as the "sport article" in the Treaty on the Functioning of the European Union (TFEU)), case law, and legal doctrine related to sports law from the last ten years.

Sports law as a hybrid system

The sports and law debate is highly influenced by the hybrid character of sports law. Sports law deals with both autonomous as well as state-created rules regarding the variety of economic, social, commercial, cultural, and political aspects of sports activities. It thus concerns both private (relations between private actors) and public law (relations with or rules from governmental actors). However, in essence, sport originates from private initiative. Sports law, therefore, emanates primarily from the sports movement. This sports movement has established, sometimes powerful, organizations which have powers to determine and regulate the activity of sport and its stakeholders. One can think about the International Olympic Committee (IOC), the World Anti-Doping Agency (WADA), or the International Football Association (FIFA).

The private regulations of sports bodies, including organizational and disciplinary rules as well as rules of play, are sometimes labeled as "lex sportiva" (Nafziger, 2006; Foster, 2005) and one may argue that they constitute themselves a kind of legal order. Nevertheless, the trend toward more professionalism in sport and the growing economic, social, and cultural relevance of sport, have prompted an increasing reliance on legal rules adopted by governments. Not only the lex sportiva, but also the specific interplay between private and public rule-making, thus characterizes sports law as a subject.

It is assumed that there is a strong reciprocal relationship between sport and societal values (Mitten, 1997). This marks a special feature of sports law. Sport is a human activity resting on a wide variety of social, educational and cultural values. It contributes to integration, involvement in social life, tolerance, the acceptance of differences and playing by the rules. It can also be seen as a vehicle for personal fulfillment, physical and social wellbeing and cultural identity. The interdependence between sport and societal values and norms has triggered the question of to what extent sports bodies may remain immune from public regulation and the rule of law which follows from the application of certain a government-based set of rights and obligations.

Public policy and sporting autonomy in early EU case law

The Court of Justice of the European Union (CJEU) has played a major role in the development of sports law in Europe and in the discovery of the boundaries between public policy interventions in sport versus autonomy of sports organizations. The Court had to define to what extent EU legal rules and principles, or more generally the rule of law governing our societies, would be applicable to the sports world. The professionalization and commercialization of sport and related public policy concerns have activated case law of the European Court.

The first European Court case, *Walrave and Koch* (C-36/74), started an interesting debate about the relationship between EU law and sport. The case is known for the European Court's (early) position that, with regard to the objectives of the Union, sport is subject to EU law only insofar as it constitutes an economic activity within the meaning of the treaties. This approach in *Walrave and Koch*, confirmed in later case law, allowed the European Court to exclude certain matters from the scope or operation of the European Treaty and thus to create exceptions for sport.

In this early case law sporting exceptions seemed to be based on a rather pragmatic approach in which common sense would be the rough guideline.

In *Walrave and Koch*, the Advocate-General (Opinion of October 24, 1974) asked himself whether the signatories of the founding European Treaty intended to preclude a requirement that, in a particular sport, a national team should consist only of nationals of the country it represented. His response was that "common sense dictates that the signatories, with their pens poised, would all have answered impatiently 'Of course not' – and perhaps have added that, in their view, the point was so obvious that it did not need to be stated." In the view of the Advocate-General, the inapplicability of non-discrimination provisions thus seemed to be self-evident.

The lack of real conceptual guidance on defining the relationship between sports and law also appeared in *Dona v. Mantero* (C-13/76). The Advocate-General stated, rather rhetorically:

> I confess my inability to see what justification there would be, in a private sector where Community law directly applies, for action by State authorities other than judicial bodies. It would be difficult to imagine administrative authorities intervening in the affairs of private parties which were being conducted wholly within the field of private law.
>
> (Opinion of July 6, 1976)

Nevertheless, both in *Walrave and Koch* as well as in *Dona v. Mantero*, the Court applied the provisions of European free movement law, though with exceptions.

The specificity of sport

The issue regarding the relationship between law and sport in the context of EU law has led to a debate about what has been called the "sporting exception" (Parrish & Miettinen, 2008). This presumed exceptional status of sport under EU law is also discussed under the so-called "specificity of sport" concept (Siekmann, 2008; 2011). This concept implies the view that sport has specific characteristics that make deviations or exceptions from normal legal principles justified or necessary. It has been defined as "the sum of the unique and inherent aspects of sport which distinguish it fundamentally from all other areas of activity and service" (Zylberstein, 2008, 95, 96).

The specificity of sport was recognized in a declaration at the occasion of the European Council meeting in Nice (December 7–9, 2000). It was stated that

> even though not having any direct powers in this area, the Community must, in its action under the various Treaty provisions, take account of the social, educational and cultural functions inherent in sport and making it special, in order that the code of ethics and the solidarity essential to the preservation of its social role may be respected and nurtured.

The fact that the concept of "specificity" is strongly related with the relationship between the law and sport becomes clear in the Commission Staff Working

Document accompanying the 2007 White Paper on Sport: "The Community Courts and the Commission have consistently taken into consideration the particular characteristics of sport setting it apart from other economic activities that are frequently referred to as the 'specificity of sport'. Although no such legal concept has been developed or formally recognized by the Community Courts" (SEC, 2007, 935).

The specificity of sport is a dynamic concept and it has been under development since the sports case law of the European Court emerged. Its emergence can be explained by the European Union's limited competences or because of the specific regulatory interaction between EU law and the member states (internal market law is often driven by techniques of deregulation). As European integration models influence the integration of social, cultural, and economic values through EU law (Hepple, 1995) sport specificity can also be connected with substantial models of regulation, such as a market model, a welfare model, a socio-cultural model, or a political model (Parrish, 2003b). But a conceptual approach behind the European case law is not easy to point out, as the Court does not make theoretical assumptions, if any, explicit and also because the Court uses different wording or phrasing throughout its case law.

In the early cases, the "market model" was probably dominant, although subject to corrections. In *Walrave and Koch*, the Court's position was that sport does not, in principle, fall under EU law unless it concerns an economic activity. Sport was seen as a phenomenon that obeys the legal principles of the (EU) market order, but not if the non-economic dimension is at stake. The *Walrave* case also implied that, even within the economic dimension of sport, matters pertaining purely to sport could not be regulated under the provisions of EU (market-modeled) law. The Court established the *purely sporting interest* concept to preserve the tradition of national teams in sport. It decided that, "the Treaty does not affect the composition of sport teams, in particular national teams, the formation of which is a question of purely sporting interest and as such has nothing to do with economic activity." The concept of *purely sporting interest* suggests that there is no public policy interest. The approach was confirmed in *Dona v. Mantero*, where it was accepted that there are "reasons which are not of an economic nature, which relate to the particular nature and context of such matches and are thus of sporting interest only."

In the *Bosman* case (C-415/93), the Court threw more light on the subject. Advocate-General Lenz stated that

> it is certainly undeniable that the sports associations have the right and the duty to draw up rules for the practice and organization of the sport, and that that activity falls within the association's autonomy which is protected as a fundamental right.

> (Opinion of September 20, 1995, §216)

But he argued that "only an interest of the association which is of paramount importance" could justify a restriction on freedom of movement (§216).

The Court limited itself to stating that the debated EU "provisions … do not preclude rules or practices justified on non-economic grounds which relate to the particular nature and context of certain matches." It stressed, however, that such a restriction on the scope of the provisions in question must remain limited to its proper objective (§76).

The Court's concept of what constitutes an economic activity has been quite broad, as can be seen in the *Meca-Medina* case (C-519/04) concerning the International Olympic Committee's rules on doping control. The Court held that

> it is apparent that the mere fact that a rule is purely sporting in nature does not have the effect of removing from the scope of the Treaty the person engaging in the activity governed by that rule or the body which has laid it down.

This leaves a lot of room for interpretation, but the Court seemed to allow European legal intervention in areas of a purely sporting nature (Siekmann, 2008).

The EU sport article and the *Bernard* case

With regard to the politics of sports regulation in the EU, Parrish argued that the body of sports aspires, either implicitly or explicitly, to integrate social, cultural, and economic policies (Parrish, 2003a). In light of this, the "sport article" (article 165 TFEU), adopted in the Lisbon Treaty, may be seen as a shift. The EU took a step away from the spillovers of internal market law toward a more socio-cultural approach of sport (García, 2007).

The sports article (article 165, TFEU) provides that

> The Union shall contribute to the promotion of European sporting issues, while taking account of the specific nature of sport, its structures based on voluntary activity and its social and educational function.

It is further provided that

> Union action shall be aimed at developing the European dimension in sport, by promoting fairness and openness in sporting competitions and coopera-tion between bodies responsible for sports, and by protecting the physical and moral integrity of sportsmen and sportswomen, especially the youngest sportsmen and sportswomen.

There is a double aspect in this sport article, relevant for the development of sports law and governance. The European Treaty explicitly not only recognizes "the specific nature of sport" and refers to its "social and educational function"; it also provides a basis for positive policy intervention from the EU institutions, although this cannot lead to legislation (but only to incentive measures and recommendations) and harmonization. A positive (even soft) regulatory approach can give more legal certainty compared to a case-by-case approach by the Court (Cuendet, 2008). The European Commission's 2007 White Paper, however, takes a rather modest European governmental role, referring to the autonomy of sporting organizations and their responsibility (Wheatherill, 2008). The exclusion of harmonization is also a sign that EU action may remain limited (Vermeersch, 2009).

In light of this, it is relevant to look at the potential impact of article 165 TFEU on the case law of the Court of Justice and the acceptance of sports specificity. The *Bernard* case (C-325/08) shows that the Court was more willing to accept training compensation in professional football, compared to *Bosman* (Hendrickx, 2010). The impression that the issue of specificity of sport played a role is strengthened by the Court's reference to article 165 TFEU. In her opinion before the Court, the Advocate-General tempered the notion of specificity of sport, indicating that they must be considered carefully "just as the specific characteristics of any other sector would need to be borne in mind when examining the justification of restrictions applicable in that sector" (Opinion of July 16, 2009, §30). She nevertheless stated that "professional football is not merely an economic activity but also a matter of considerable social importance in Europe" (§47).

Specificity of sport will, therefore, not be a magic concept to exclude sport from EU law, but it is a reality that is codified in the EU's sport article.

Future prospects

The case of the EU shows that the dominant trend in sports law is a growing infiltration of law in sport. It is inevitable for sports governing bodies to take legal rules from the public legal system into account. Sports and the law have become interlocked, and this often means that sport bodies have to adapt policies and practices. As this has not historically gone smoothly, governance in sport will deal with a growing tension between private sports regulation and public regulation. An increasing reliance or attempt to rely on specificity of sport arguments in order to recognize the specific characteristics of sports will be a likely consequence.

Sports bodies have a right to autonomy and the right to establish their own sporting rules. This follows from the freedom of association and the freedom of enterprise. But with freedom comes responsibility. If the CJEU intervenes in sport, it is to secure the rule of law and to avoid abuse (Kehrli, 2014). It is evident that the sports world cannot be immune from fundamental legal provisions and principles. The many challenges and problems in sport will quite likely lead to new Court cases. Notwithstanding the criticism about legal uncertainty, the "case method" will (and should) thus not be ignored.

The EU Treaty has recognized specific characteristics of sport, and the sports movement may see this as recognition that special treatment under the law is required. This is a justified expectation. However, the sport article also means that the sports world may face more governmental intervention. Although the EU approach is still cautious, a bigger role for the (EU) government in sport could be defended. This should be dependent on whether the sport governing bodies themselves have their house in order. Subsidiarity may be a core principle in the desired governance model: As long as sport governing bodies guarantee good governance and respect for the rule of law, government can be distant. Self-regulation, but with control by the EU institutions, is a defendable way forward. The sports world still has a long way to go to integrate fundamental legal principles in its governance framework. The EU itself can facilitate and guide this by using its current soft competences. The EU can even borrow its structures, such as social dialogue. However, the EU should not hesitate in using its hard legal competences in various economic and (labor) market-oriented fields. Sport has become a global phenomenon and transnational legal responses are necessary. EU law has proven to be legitimate and effective in addressing legal problems within the frameworks of sport bodies, even outside the EU, such as the IOC, FIFA or UEFA have experienced. Some (international) sports bodies have such a societal impact that legal control should be similar as for any other (big) business.

References

Cuendet, S. (2008). The EU Commission's White Paper on sport: An official coherent, yet debated entrance of the commission in the sports arena. *International Sports Law Journal, 1–2*, 9–13.

Foster, K. (2005). Lex sportiva and lex ludica, the Court of Arbitration for Sport's jurisprudence. *Entertainment and Sports Law Journal, 3* (2), 1–14.

García, B. (2007). From regulation to governance and representation: Agenda-setting and the EU's involvement in sport. *Entertainment and Sports Law Journal, 5* (1), 1–12.

Hendrickx, F. (2009). Future directions of EU sports law. In R. Blanpain, M. Colucci, & F. Hendrickx (Eds.), *The future of sports law in the EU: Beyond the EU Reform Treaty and the White Paper* (pp. 9–20). The Hague: Kluwer Law International.

Hendrickx, F. (2010). The Bernard case and training compensation in professional football. *European Labour Law Journal, 1* (3), 380–397.

Hendrickx, F. (2012). Rules of law in the business of sport. In B. Segaert, M. Theeboom, C. Timmerman, & B. Vanreusel (Eds.), *Sports governance, development and corporate responsibility* (pp. 177–195). London: Routledge.

Hepple, B. (1995). The development of fundamental social rights in European labour law. In A.C. Neal & S. Foyn, *Developing the Social Dimension in an Enlarged European Union* (pp. 23–34). Oslo: Universitetsforlaget.

Kehrli, K. (2014). The unspecified specificity of sport: A proposed solution to the European Court of Justice's treatment of the specificity of sport. *Brooklyn Journal of International Law, 39*, 403–441.

Mitten, M.J. (1997). Sports law as a reflexion of society's laws and values. *South Texas Law Review, 38*, 999–1006.

Nafziger, J. (2006). Lex sportiva and CAS. In: I. Blackshaw, R. Siekmann, & J.W. Soek (Eds.), *The Court of Arbitration for Sport* (pp.409–419). The Hague: Asser Press.

Parrish, R. (2003a). The politics of sports regulation in the European Union. *Journal of European Public Policy, 10* (2), 246–262.

Parrish, R. (2003b). *Sports law and policy in the European Union*. Manchester: Manchester University Press.

Parrish, R., & Miettinen, S (2008). *The sporting exception in European Union Law*. The Hague: Asser Press.

Siekmann, R. (2008). Is sport special in EU law and policy? In R. Blanpain, M. Colucci, & F. Hendrickx (Eds.), *The future of sports law in the European Union: Beyond the EU reform treaty and the white paper* (pp. 37–49). The Hague: Kluwer Law International.

Siekmann, R. (2011). The specificity of sport: Sporting exceptions in EU Law. *International Sports Law Journal, 3–4*, 75–85.

SEC (2007). Commission Staff Working Document: The EU and Sport: Background and Context – Accompanying Document to the White Paper on Sport. COM(2007) 391 final, SEC/2007/935final.

Vermeersch, A. (2009). The future EU sports policy: Hollow words on hallowed ground? *International Sports Law Journal, 9* (3–4), 3–7.

Weatherill, S. (2008). The white paper on sport as an exercise in better regulation. *International Sports Law Journal, 1–2*, 3–8.

Zylberstein, J. (2008). The specificity of sport: A concept under threat. In R. Blanpain, M. Colucci, & F. Hendrickx (Eds.), *The future of sports law in the European Union: Beyond the EU reform treaty and the white paper* (pp. 95–106). The Hague: Kluwer Law International.

PART IV

Sport and body enhancement

Ethics and possibilities

Introduction

Jan Tolleneer and Bengt Kayser

Fostered by the International Olympic Committee (IOC), the worldwide efforts to combat doping in sport have led to a tightening of the application of the anti-doping rules. This is now overseen by the World Anti-Doping Association (WADA) and legitimized by UNESCO's International Convention Against Doping in Sport, ratified by no fewer than 177 countries. By adopting regulation and legislation measures these countries are expected to contribute to the "prevention of and the fight against doping in sport, with a view to its elimination."

Despite persistent doping use on a wide scale, belief in the necessity and feasibility of the zero-tolerance principle still seems deeply rooted in public opinion and elaborately underpinned by certain philosophers. In his chapter, **Jan Vorstenbosch** (the Netherlands) adds an inspiring point to the long list of anti-doping arguments. He analyzes the sport phenomenon from the perspective of Oakeshott's philosophy of practice and concludes that lifting the doping ban would damage the very heart of sport as being a "language of self-disclosure." Permitting performance-enhancing technology goes against "nature" and leaves athletes, both as a group and as individuals, alienated from the very meaning of the game and their own contribution to the outcomes of this particular practice. Vorstenbosch's article opens interesting perspectives for future explorations in this direction.

When it comes to performance-enhancing drugs and their future in sports, **Bengt Kayser** (Switzerland) gives an almost diametrically different point of view. Without being enticed into the trenches of bio-liberal philosophers, he provides arguments in favor of a "pragmatic approach" based on human rights and public health principles. The war on doping, he argues, should learn from the harms and benefits the war on drugs generated for individuals and for society. The author pleads for a reform of anti-doping policy and for experiments with alternative regulations and harm-reduction measures, as have been successfully applied in the sphere of psychoactive drugs. In the latter, according to the Global Commission on Drugs Policy, repression and criminalization have brought significantly more harm to society than prevented. Worldwide tendencies for relaxation here are now perhaps contained by the mounting war on doping. Kayser also expresses concern about how anti-doping may have possible negative side-effects outside the sports realm and questions whether the peculiar societal status of sport is worth such a hefty price tag.

Rather than discussing the broader role of sport, **William J. Morgan** (USA) focuses on the game itself and illustrates how enhancement practices and the efforts to restrain them can pervert the game and the relations between players. He uses the iconic case of Lance Armstrong to examine the moral aspects of doping use. Morgan's penetrating analysis concludes that Armstrong is a bully, but not necessarily a cheater. Yes, he violated the official rules but, given the plausible hypothesis that his opponents did the same, he acted not in an offensive but in a defensive way, making his use of illicit means what Morgan calls morally appropriate: Armstrong just played the game of the peloton. The author, interestingly, further opens a "moral book on anti-doping regulators." Instead of the regular analytical methods, doping authorities have started to use other techniques like applying heavy pressure on athletes to testify against fellow sportsmen. Herewith they pit the athletes against each other and make an already highly toxic competitive athletic environment even more toxic, which is morally objectionable, and even treacherous according to the author. By carefully balancing the moral books between dopers and anti-dopers he discloses the complexity of the moral problem and takes away the hope for simplistic solutions in the future.

Given the decisiveness of the current anti-doping authorities and the recent transnational political consensus they successfully wrested, one can hardly expect a relaxation of regulations in the near future. To the contrary, the systems and institutions centered on the zero-tolerance principle will probably gain further momentum in the coming years. Even if public opinion changed and researchers reported more convincing evidence against the zero-tolerance approach, the law of inertia will not easily allow drastic changes in the next decades.

However, arguments can be found for a projection of a certain turning point further in time. This can be related to changes outside sports, such as the influence of technological innovations and the zeal with which they have been embraced in medicine and in daily life. It can especially be connected to changes within the realm of sport. Sports historical examples show that principles and norms gradually change and give cause to an adaptation of written and unwritten rules. In the beginning of the twentieth century, athletes rejected intensive training and the calling in of professional trainers, but this specific fair-play norm gradually dissolved when they "started to take sport seriously." This is discussed by Morgan as an example of the process of normative delegitimization. Kayser mentions that in the second half of the twentieth century a similar development took place. The amateur rule was gradually undermined by state-sponsored amateurs, which led to the acceptance of professional athletes by the Olympic Movement. Sports are getting more serious. One could extrapolate these developments and predict that the current anti-doping policy might disappear in the course of the century.

Anyhow, today's continuation of widespread doping use undermines the anti-doping ideals and indicates the weakening normative force of the current rule. Will this lead to a relaxation of those rules? Sports are getting even more serious.

16 The practical self-understanding of athletes and the future of sport

Jan Vorstenbosch

> Life can only be understood backwards; but it must be lived forwards.
>
> (Søren Kierkegaard, *Journalen* JJ, 167, 1843)

Introduction

This chapter deals with the future of elite sport. The time horizon for the prospective view presented here is the next 25–30 years and its theme is the influence of the increasing technological, and in particular the pharmacological possibilities of enhancing athlete performance by the use of drugs, on the future of sport proposed.[1] For several decades performance-enhancing drugs (PEDs) have been widely discussed. There is considerable support in the academic literature, on principled or pragmatic grounds, for lifting the current ban on PEDs.[2] However, developing a system in which PEDs are allowed and combined with health control of athletes is a dubious alternative, for reasons of implementation and effects on non-elite sport that are fairly put forward by the advocates.[3] This chapter is best viewed as based on three counter-arguments against this pragmatic position.

First, the proposal runs the risk of moral hazard, that is: it might lead to ignoring the possibilities of more morally defensible strategies, aimed at aligning the athletes and other stakeholders by collective and democratic action to overcome the conflict of interests regarding the use of PEDs.

Second, the pragmatic-liberal approach pays insufficient attention to the inner logic of competitive sports practices, which will probably encourage a competition in PEDs, this time within the new conditions.

And third, the approach is not based on a positive and explicit normative view of sport as a social practice. It is premised on the negative effects of current zero-tolerance anti-doping policy and on the conflict of this policy with human rights such as privacy and freedom of movement. My own perspective on the matter focuses on an elaboration of the second and third argument.

There is also a systematic and more radical position, that of *trans-humanism*, which holds that PEDs are not a threat to the fairness and spirit of sport and its future. Rather, PEDs are conceived by these authors as a preferable way of developing sports because they contribute to realizing the value of human excellence which supposedly founds the practice of sports (Savulescu, Foddy, & Clayton, 2004).

Contrary to these positions, I propose some arguments for a future in which PEDs are not accepted. This view is based on the idea that conceptions of excellent performance in sport are always relative to sport as a social practice, as a particular rule-governed historical and cooperative human activity. As such, sport is an original and autonomous social practice, and it is worthwhile to protect this practice from the overriding influence of considerations from other practices such as science, law, and economy. The full richness of human abilities, differences, talents, and qualities that sports disclose is worthy of being salvaged. A sport contest is a social, public, and rule-governed practice in which agents are challenged to prove the superiority of their athletic and strategic abilities in overcoming obstacles in an encounter with other agents.

But excellence in sport is realized not in an absolute way, a view suggested by an emphasis on world records, but always in the historically and socially relative context of concrete matches, games, and races. As to the future, the system of rules for sports is inevitably subject to change and these changes should be argued for on the basis of adaptation, continuity, and a coherent view of what the sport is about and what gives it meaning, or so I will defend. Sports are only intelligible and meaningful against the background of an understanding, both by the participants and by the public, of what the performance involves. An agreement on the internal coherence and the particular attractions that makes it meaningful, engaging, exciting, and varied is a necessary condition for this meaning. I will defend the position that the free use of PEDs in the long run is in conflict with the conditions of sport as a practice, using the conception of practice developed by the English philosopher Oakeshott (1975).

Sport as an essentially contested concept

Sport is an example of an essentially contested concept, a notion introduced by Gallie (1955/1956) with respect to concepts such as democracy and justice. These notions are used for social or political arrangements that historically and conceptually contain a diversity of dimensions or elements. Because of this complexity the concepts are inevitably in need of interpretation, often on the basis of an "exemplar," such as the democracy in Ancient Greek city-states. Interestingly, Gallie (1955/1956) himself uses football as an example of an essentially contested concept because it contains various dimensions (technique, strategy, willpower, style, beauty) which may be defended as more or less important by different adherents of the sport. Conceptions of sport emphasize different dimensions of a sport (or of sport in general), and propose a certain (re-)configuration of the importance and role of the different dimensions. By a change of rules some challenges and capabilities will be foregrounded and others become less pertinent to the sport. All this goes to show that we should be careful with the interpretation of "excellence" as a single and uniform standard in sports.

As historically constructed, rule-governed practices, sports mirror the general ideas in society about what human beings essentially are, or are up to. The conceptions reflect the self-realization and self-understanding of human beings. Explicitly defended conceptions will propose changes in, or conservations of, the rules on the basis of the normative sources of this conception. But often changes of rules are supported and discussed without referring at all to a systematic conception of the sports practice as an interesting practice of its own. Often economic reasons, general moral grounds of justice, legal grounds of rights, or some empty reference to innovation and "the spirit of the time" are given instead of developing arguments on the basis of a coherent, holistic, and reflective view on the connections between the rules and the meaning of the sport as such. One of the ideas that stimulate my own view on the future of sport is that there is a need to sustain and not reduce the plurality and multidimensionality of sports. We need to pursue the quest for balance of these dimensions. Lifting the ban will lead to a less interesting, less unique and ultimately meaningless sport, or so I will argue.

The human body and the argument from naturalness

Sports are in a special sense related to the body, or rather to the embodiedness of human beings and their actions. They motivate agents to develop their bodies in a very particular way: they discipline it by intensive training and preparation to develop superior abilities for meeting the challenges of a particular sport. Because the human body is generally seen as more based on a given, genetically or biologically determined, structure of the species than the human mind, talk of *naturalness* is often prominent in debates on doping and enhancement. The positions of conservative opponents of PEDs and trans-humanist proponents seem premised on this scheme of nature versus culture, respectively arguing for respecting the naturalness and genetic integrity of the body, and overcoming it. There are scientific as well as philosophical reasons to doubt this static conception of the workings of the body that is uncritically presupposed by both camps, although with a different evaluation.

An important source for an alternative idea of the role of the body is the phenomenological view of the French philosopher Merleau-Ponty. For Merleau-Ponty the way of being-in-the-world in general, perceiving and acting, is very much based on the body, not as a thing-like given reality, but as a dynamic field of interacting structures, orientations and capabilities. The impact of such a view on the evaluation of PEDs is often ignored in the debate on the effects of doping on the way the sport will develop itself in the future. A phenomenological view of the body that is less keen on changing the body but respecting its possibilities and the subtleties of style and diversity in bodily performance and achievement of athletes, encourages a different way of conceiving the future of sports.

While human embodiedness is certainly a common element in sports, it is important to take into account the diversity of ways in which the body is challenged and how the future of sports is differentially influenced by technological developments.[4] The future of sports is most at issue in those sports that are premised on, or conditioned by, strongly physical parameters of the human body, such as endurance and muscle strength, without negatively influencing other important capabilities such as coordination, communication, and fine motor skills. Examples are cycling and weight lifting. Because many sports require a subtle interplay between a diversity of physical, mental, and emotional capacities, it is likely that it is more difficult in those sports to control the positive effects of a PED and not affect other capacities negatively. The side-effects of most substances on the performance will then prevail. For many other sports, especially team sports that presuppose a broader array of competences, mentally, physically, and socially, in terms of coordination, in terms of strategic plans, in terms of communication, the future with respect to the influence of PEDs will thus look very different.

This said, the kind of general story that I want to tell about the future of sport is neither a prediction of the most likely future, nor a visionary sketch of an imaginary, possible future.[5] It is a normative view of what sports are about and what the limits are of what it can become without losing its plausibility and attraction as a meaningful human activity. This approach is best contrasted with the prospect of a visionary story of a possible future. My objection to such a future would be that it can be doubted whether it can count as a future of *this* sport as we know it from history and from the current way it is played. We touch here on deep philosophical questions about identity and sameness – is the game "Quidditch" in *Harry Potter* a kind of handball, or is it a completely different sport, or a sport at all?[6] Fortunately, my approach to the philosophy of sport makes it possible to avoid these questions by regarding sport as a particular genus of social practices, social practices being human activities that can only be identified and understood against a historical and cultural background or tradition. So a social practice necessarily and unavoidably is bound to historical conditions and rules, and changes by way of (re-)consideration of its traditional rules on the basis of reasoned decisions in response to influences from within or from without. These reasonable responses, in my view, should be based on the idea of sport as an original, unique, and autonomous practice. The responses must be based on some kind of interpretation of the game as we know it, an interpretation that has to be convincingly defended as guaranteeing its continuity and connectedness with the meaning of the game. Holism and balance, and sensitivity to the coherence and inter-connectedness of the rules, are the key to these responses. In the following, however, I will focus on some more basic arguments why PEDs, besides risking making a sport more one-dimensional, are in conflict with the conditions of sport. These arguments turn on the notion of a social practice.

Oakeshott on practice and the self-understanding of agents

In the social-philosophical literature on practices, different accounts of practices can be found. Nicolini (2012) summarizes the features that these accounts have in common, of which two are especially relevant here. Practices are "meaning-making, identity-forming and order-producing activities." This implies that practice-accounts block ontologically the idea that there is a straightforward observational access to reality or action *as it is*. Furthermore, practices are necessarily social. They cannot be understood and explained by derivation from what goes on in the mind or brain of individuals, they presuppose a joint and reciprocal acknowledgment of a set of rules by which the actions of practitioners are guided, or even by which the actions are only made possible, or make sense in the first place.

These generic features of practices as such are not sufficient to claim that transhumanists are on the wrong track by the lights of a practice-oriented approach. It has to be shown that the proposals of trans-humanism regarding sport, or of a liberal position on PEDs, are somehow in conflict with these premises. I will use a particular account of social practices, that of the British philosopher Oakeshott, to develop some arguments against PEDs.

To expose in a few sentences Oakeshott's complex philosophical view (1975), perhaps it is best to refer to the controversy between essentialist and trans-humanist conceptions of *nature* and naturalness. Against these conceptions, Oakeshott starts with the idea that all knowledge of human nature is mediated and grounded in the experience of agents, which in itself cannot refer to any "outside" objectively given reality of nature. Experience is only possible within the frame of historical understandings and traditions which are transferred and socially acquired by learning. This dimension of learning is associated with the practice-conception, in a literal sense, in that agents become acquainted with and get well-versed in practices by practicing, by shaping and developing themselves on the basis of an authoritative already existing framework, and with the help of experienced authorities. *Natural*, as it figures in our experience, is always a matter of "second nature," an internally organized, "logical" way of understanding practical things.

Actions within practices are purposive and have a substantive objective – they aim at realizing a telos, a wished-for satisfaction, such as knowledge in science and proving superior athletic abilities in sport. But they also, and this is essential, have a formal dimension which relates to their being enacted by humans, who are associated on the basis of a commitment to certain rules and procedures. Oakeshott uses *procedure* in a wide sense, as a reference to all "prescribed conditions for the substantive choices and performances." Procedural conditions do not determine in a strict sense the performances, which are always purposive. Performances can also be enacted outside the practice, in which case they may have a different meaning taken from another context.[7] These conditions are *formal* qualifications for the performance being part of a practice. The achievements within practices therefore may be better expressed in adverbial terms: knowledge may be had in different ways, but scientific knowledge is knowledge that is had *scientifically*, and so superior athletic ability may be acquired and possessed but not proven within the practice *fairly*.[8] Oakeshott gives the example of the most well-known practice that we participate in, that of speaking a vernacular language. The formal conditions of speaking a language, the vocabulary, the syntax, do not in themselves determine what is said and with what purpose.

They determine what is said *correctly*. As such, speakers of a language are party to a common practice, shared by the members of a linguistic community, and their linguistic performances can also adverbially be qualified from different procedural viewpoints as *considerately*, *poetically*, or *judicially*.

Although among the many examples that Oakeshott gives of practices, sport is not mentioned, I think that sport is an excellent example of a practice in this sense. When Oakeshott calls a practice a "language of self-disclosure," I think that this applies in a special sense to sport as a practice, and the idea of self-disclosure throws a different light on the meaning of practices such as elite sport than that of self-creation.

The very meaning of a practice, then, may be held to be conditional on the understanding of practical agents, in our case sporting athletes, of what they are doing together and what makes these doings meaningful. Not in the sense that they know every detail of what determines their performance, and certainly not in the sense that they are individually *in control* of everything that happens in the performance, least of all the actions of their adversaries. But understanding is meant minimally in the sense that they know from each other that as participants in the practice of sport (1) they are party to a formal association in which they can trust to engage on fair and equal terms, and (2) they know for themselves what their performance is about, and they can understand their own practical conduct and relate their efforts and abilities in an intelligible way to their performances and achievements – to the "point" of the game.

While the meaning of the practice is mediated by this historical understanding and the knowledge of what one is doing, the ongoing historical conditions always challenge the way this meaning can or ought to be sustained in a coherent and meaningful way. A constant worry of Oakeshott, especially concerning the practice of politics, the analysis of which he is most well-known for, is that it will go out of bounds with tradition by intruding upon the practice with abstract, rationalist conceptions. To draw a parallel between the fate of politics and that of sport will help us to clarify the two conditions above. Rationalism in politics is associated by Oakeshott with theory and the availability of a "technique" that makes understanding of the practice on the basis of a connection with a tradition superfluous. For Oakeshott, the concept of familiarity, acquired by understanding and practicing in relation to activities that presuppose the use of "tools" in a wide sense, is central to the meaning of the practice. In the context of sport we can regard the material tools and equipment as tools but also, with reservations, one's body can be seen as a tool with which one becomes familiar under the conditions of particular challenges. Familiarity with tools does not require unquestioning acceptance of existing tools and rejection of new insights. The very point of sports is to find out the possibilities, conditions, and limits of one's abilities and to improve one's achievements. But, Oakeshott submits, in all tool-using activities, there is no *immediate* application of one's craft – it is always mediated by the skill and practical understanding of the agent.

The application of this, admittedly complex, philosophical position to the role of PEDs in sport practices can only be sketched here in a few sentences. But the

main ideas follow. By lifting the ban on PEDs, the mutual understanding postu-
lated above, and needed to sustain an association and the self-understanding
needed for meaningful enactment of the practice, the meaning of the game gets
lost in the following way. As to the first condition, it is, on logical grounds,
unlikely that information about the substances used will be shared, because it is
exactly the point of lifting the ban to enable professional athletes to prepare
themselves more successfully by gaining a physical or physiological edge over
their rivals.[9] Moreover, installing the right to use PEDs will lead to imbalance
as well as lack of transparency concerning the different factors that contribute
to the chances of athletes to win and the results of the game. This will erode
the trust of the athletes themselves in what they are collectively doing and
achieving. But also, as the right for everyone to use PEDs will force the athletes
to compete on these new terms and use them to be successful, they will no
longer know what they are individually doing. The performance of the agent
will start to be the result of a mix of the *preparation* with PEDs, and his or her
own contribution and effort, which is difficult to unravel and understand.
In time, a future of sports with PEDs will more and more be the result of
processes whose workings within the body are not known to the agent, and will
less and less be mediated by the athletes' own understandings.[10] In time, and
almost by definition, for PED-sensitive sports the focus on successful *preparation*, by means of increasing scientific knowledge and technological abilities,
will crowd out the meaning and import of other aspects of interest of a particular
sport, and what's more it will replace the autonomy and multidimensionality of
sport by the growing influence of the practices of science and technology. The
association of sporting athletes will no longer be based on a higher-order interest of pride and honor to which they are collectively committed on the basis of
their formal relations, but on the individual fear of falling behind and of not
keeping up with the technological development.

The message argued for here, on the basis of Oakeshott's account of practices,
is this: Sport is a practice of its own, separate from other practices, and it should
be wary of technological developments which stand in the way of the understanding of the agents themselves, or that put into question the inner meaning of the
practice as a challenge, not only to show superior ability but also to show what
human beings on terms of self-enactment and self-disclosure can achieve with
understanding, individually and collectively. A future with PEDs, by which
athletes are prepared by experts in a way that they don't understand themselves
and that destroys the multidimensional, vulnerable, but unique balance of challenges that traditional sports should cherish, will unleash a race on a quite different base.

Conclusion: the message for the future of sport

In this chapter I have argued for what I have called a practice-oriented view on
the future of sport, more particularly a view inspired by some notions of
Oakeshott's philosophy of practices. I have developed some arguments turning

on the kind of meaning and intelligibility that underpins the meaning of sport and that point in the direction of a specific, viable future of sports, one in which the tendency to pursue the *telos* of sport in a technology-based, more specifically *PED-driven* way is countered, and the changes in rules are invented and evaluated on the basis of a practice-account – that is, on the basis of (1) historical continuity with the interpretation of the meaning of the game; (2) rivalry and excellence as basically time- and place-relative, not absolute notions; and (3) meaning and interest as dependent on certain aspects of sport as a special and autonomous practice and manner of self-disclosure such as fairness and the intelligibility of the practical action by the agents themselves.

Notes

1 In the remainder I will use PEDs, short for *performance-enhancing drugs*. I will not go into the issue of germ-line genetic modification, which as yet is only an option for a future much further away, but the main argument applies a fortiori to this development.
2 More pragmatic are Kayser and Broers (2013). A more principled view is that of Brownsword (2013).
3 See Kayser in this volume.
4 A good example is chess, which after the defeat of Kasparov against the computer Deep Blue in the 1990s suffered from a fall in public interest.
5 Frankly, I believe that with the increasing scientific knowledge and technological possibilities to measure and change the human body, "parametric" sports will inevitably lose much of their interest, to the advantage of more complex and multidimensional and esthetic sports.
6 This is a weak spot in the vision of the future of sports in the sign of enhancement that Pieter Bonte defends in his contribution (2013).
7 One may think of performing gymnastics in a circus or of "wrestling" in a show.
8 "A practice is a prudential or a moral adverbial qualification of choices and performances, in which conduct is understood in terms of a procedure" (Oakeshott, 1975, 55).
9 Of course, the authorities can try to enforce a new balance of relative equality to prevent an "arms race" by trying to control the use of PEDs, enforce transparency of substances, and keep the use within certain bounds, but (1) this situation would re-install the situation as we know it and all the problems that come with it of "cheating," costs of control, etc.; and (2) nothing is won by that detour with regard to the meaning of the sport. The only thing that is won would be that a higher level of *absolute* excellence of performance could be reached (mirrored, for instance, in records) but this only goes to show that the absolute conception of excellence is limitless; it does not contain any limit in itself. In theory, if not in practice, the PEDs to be developed for the sake of excellence and legitimately used by *all* elite athletes would only lead to the same result as the free and liberal use of PEDs: a one-sided and pointless concentration on a particular dimension of the sport, that can be influenced by these means, to the exclusion of other dimensions of meaning and beauty in sport such as style of running or cycling, of mental and cognitive abilities. In Oakeshott's terms, it would lead to an all-the-way-down purposive enterprise association at the cost of the formal association that is essential to a practice and its meaning.
10 The workings will not be "unintelligible" from the point of view of theoretical understanding of scientists, but they will be unintelligible and therefore meaningless from the point of view of the practical understandings of the agents (and, for that matter, the public).

References

Bonte, P. (2013). Dignified doping: Truly unthinkable. In: J. Tolleneer, S. Sterckx, & P. Bonte (Eds.), *Athletic enhancement, human nature and ethics* (pp. 59–88). Dordrecht: Springer.

Brownsword, R. (2013). A simple regulatory principle for performance-enhancing technologies: Too good to be true. In: J. Tolleneer, S. Sterckx, & P. Bonte (Eds.), *Athletic enhancement, human nature and ethics* (pp. 291–310). Dordrecht: Springer.

Gallie, W.B (1955/1956). Essentially contested concepts. *Proceedings of the Aristotelian Society*, 167–198

Kayser, B., & Broers, B. (2013). Anti-doping policies: Choosing between imperfections. In: J. Tolleneer, S. Sterckx, & P. Bonte (Eds.), *Athletic enhancement, human nature and ethics* (pp. 271–290). Dordrecht: Springer.

Nicolini, D. (2012). *Practice theory, work and organization: An introduction.* Oxford: Oxford University Press.

Oakeshott, M. (1975). *On human conduct.* Oxford: Clarendon Press.

Savulescu, J., Foddy, B., & Clayton, M. (2004). Why we should allow performance enhancing drugs in sport. *British Journal of Sports Magazine, 38*, 666–670.

17 A glimpse into the morally ambiguous future of elite sport

The Lance Armstrong story

William J. Morgan

Introduction

The official start of the struggle to staunch the use of performance enhancing drugs (PEDs) in elite sport dates back to the 1960s. Today, that struggle, which set in motion a hunted–hunter relation between dopers and regulators, has only intensified as each side seems undeterred in their effort to outwit the other. And as it has intensified it has taken on an unmistakable one-sided moral edge that favors the regulators, who have managed successfully to brand their campaign against dopers as a moral one upon which the very integrity of sport depends. The public and most of the media have largely bought into this view, which is why athletes caught using PEDs are routinely and summarily condemned without a second thought as cheaters.

I want to claim, however, that this picture is misleading to say the least, and, therefore, needs to be corrected. For on closer inspection, I argue, dopers are not the moral villains, nor are their testers the moral saviors, they have been frequently made out to be. That neither of these parties warrants moral sainthood goes without saying. Nevertheless, a balancing of the moral books is necessary if we are going to find some way out of the impasse created by the current struggle between regulators and dopers.

The recent Lance Armstrong case is, I think, instructive in this regard as to how to rethink the received view of both of these warring sides, notwithstanding its sordid details and controversial nature. For while there is no doubt that Armstrong is indeed the ruthless bully and consummate liar he has been depicted to be – the most egregious of his lies, that after chemo the idea of putting anything foreign in his body was especially repulsive (Runciman, 2012), was also, alas, his most effective lie – there is or should be real doubt that he is a cheater. That's because Armstrong doped for the same reason his peers most certainly did: It was the only way he could ensure he had a competitive chance to win prestigious cycling events like the Tour de France. That is, he doped not to gain an unfair advantage but rather to make the competition fairer than it otherwise would have been – to, as it were, level the playing field. And in doing so he remained faithful to the conception of sport that dominates not just cycling but all elite sports nowadays, a conception that in the oft-quoted words of the fabled Green Bay coach Vince Lombardi says "winning isn't everything, it is the only thing." There are good reasons to take issue with what I regard to be a morally impoverished conception of sport, but it's the view that currently governs high-performance sports like cycling, and one that Armstrong and his counterparts ignore only at their own competitive peril. And, perhaps more importantly, it's a moral conception of sport that isn't likely to go away any time soon. Indeed, I argue that if one wants a glimpse of what the likely morally fraught future of elite sports will look like, the Lance Armstrong debacle might well be our best clue.

The Armstrong case is further instructive in the light it shone on the regulators of doping; on the tactics they used to catch high-valued targets like Armstrong. For while understandably frustrated by their inability to catch Armstrong and other elite athletes suspected of doping by the standard analytic method – drug tests – despite the considerable amount of money they poured into devising ever more sophisticated tests and testing regimens, their turn to non-analytic methods such as criminal investigations and getting athletes to rat on one another, while often more successful, violated the rights of these athletes in ways we wouldn't tolerate with regard to their fellow citizens. That it further poisoned the already toxic social relations between athletes and their competitors, and between athletes and regulators, in which no one, and I mean no one, trusts anyone else, only made their troubling legal tactics that much more troubling. This anti-doping side of the current struggle to reshape elite sport also gives us a window into the tenuous moral future of elite sports, which is again why the Lance Armstrong saga warrants our close critical scrutiny.

The moral book on dopers

My argument that Armstrong was no doubt a scoundrel but not a cheater has to do, as I have already suggested, with the competitive conditions and environment that he and his compatriots faced on the racing circuit. Those conditions and the competitive environment they created were made up of the following key elements, each of which I want to argue is crucial to evaluating whether or not Armstrong and his athletic peers resort to doping qualifies as cheating.

The first of such features may be the most obvious if not the most significant one, which is that a very good living indeed could be had by winning major cycling events like the Tour de France. Armstrong, for example, has supposedly accumulated a fortune of around $125 million in prize money and endorsements in his cycling career. But the promise of a lucrative standard of living also extended to his teammates and those of other star riders. That's because cycling is a team sport in which the main task of a star rider's team is to put that rider in the best position to win, to give him the best chance to dominate his main competition. And if they do their job well, as, for example, Armstrong's teammate Tyler Hamilton did, they go from living on the edge as a cyclist to a six-figure salary. In Hamilton's specific case, when he did successfully become a member of

Armstrong's US Postal team he was rewarded with a $150,000 salary, and when Armstrong won the Tour de France his already respectable salary shot up to a hefty $450,000 (Runciman, 2012). So the incentive to dope in cycling is very much an economic one.

That explains a second feature of the elite cycling circuit, which is that PEDs were a regular part of each team's so-called medical program. The job of dispensing PEDs and monitoring was usually shared between team doctors and the team masseur. And as Voet (2002), the Festina masseur, makes plain in his book, his duties included routinely giving intramuscular injections of corticoids, providing riders saline bags the night before a competition to dilute the PEDs in their system in the event testers show up at their hotel the next morning, and administering and monitoring the various drug cocktails prescribed by the doctors for the riders to take before and during the actual competition.

A third aspect of the elite riding scene is that there is a constant and fierce competition among the members of a racing team to maintain their coveted spots on the team. This means that the incentive to dope is even greater for team members on the bubble, namely those who are likely to be cut if their performances don't improve dramatically in short order, than it is for the star riders they serve.

The fourth constant of elite cycling is the prevalence of doping not just among the top riders and teams, but those riders and teams vying for the spotlight, for their day in the sun. That doping is pervasive in elite cycling is not sheer conjecture, since one can reasonably tell who is doping by comparing their present performance and split times to their past ones. The fact that such telltale signs are not, however, conclusive enough for testers to charge them with doping offenses is one reason most of them are reasonably sure they won't be caught so long as they are careful and vigilant about how they dope. In fact, dopers who do fail drug tests can mostly blame themselves or their handlers for being either careless or unlucky. For example, one of Tyler Hamilton's failed doping tests was due to the fact that the bag of blood he was given before the race to boost his performance, which he thought was his own stored blood drawn earlier in his training when he was in peak condition, was in fact a bag of his teammate's blood that a handler had mistakenly given him (Runciman, 2012). So he was caught red handed with someone else's blood in his system, which is why he was suspended for blood-doping.

The final thing to note about the cycling world in which Armstrong and his competitors did their bidding was that because PEDs were illegal a strict code of silence among riders was maintained at all times. That meant that communication about who was doping and what sort of drugs they were using was *verboten*. There was no opportunity, then, for cyclists to communicate with one another regarding their doping decisions and regimens. Riders who did get caught doping thus had to fend for themselves, since getting caught meant they were effectively excommunicated from the cycling world.

What we are to glean from these features of the contemporary cycling scene, then, is how the riders' incentives to dope line up perfectly with the competitive conditions in which they found themselves. In other words, doping was a perfectly rational way to cope with these current competitive conditions, and, more importantly, a fair way to do so since no one would be disadvantaged by doing so. For if everyone knows that doping is a part of the competitive situation, part of the shared expectation of what is required of an elite rider to be competitive, no one can legitimately claim after the fact that they were treated unfairly.

A critic might immediately object, however, that all I have shown is that cyclists have strong incentives to dope as things presently stand, but not that they have moral license to do so. That is, my would-be critic might plausibly complain that while I might have made a case for why no one should be surprised under the present circumstances that riders like Armstrong end up doping, what I have not made a case for is why Armstrong and his peers should not be regarded as cheaters. After all, such a critic might point out further, doping is against the rules, and the fact that just about everyone in elite cycling is breaking the rule is no justification for violating it. Indeed, the claim that since everyone is doing it, therefore, we're justified in doing it as well has a distinctive adolescent ring to it, and is, in any event, hardly a persuasive reason to condone doping.

This retort has some force. For there is, of course, a rule against doping, which means that some will obey it, perhaps out of naiveté or as a matter of principle, and will be thus unfairly disadvantaged by those who break it. But this begs the important question presently at issue, which is whether there should be such a rule in the first place.

What, though, about the critic's other point, that widespread defection from a rule doesn't justify breaking it, nor, therefore, does it tell against labeling those defectors cheaters? Again, this looks like a trenchant rejoinder. But the confounding factor is that defection from a norm or rule on such a large scale as we see with respect to doping might well be a sign that the rule or norm itself has lost its normative grip on us. The defection from the doping norm significantly weakens if not nullifies our obligation to adhere to it, since such adherence is in part conditional on others doing the same. Further, since the riders' non-compliance is keyed in this case to this one particular prohibition against doping, and not to other rules or norms that govern sport presently, it cannot be rejected as morally reckless. This suggests something like Kavka's distinction between morally inappropriate offensive rule violations and morally appropriate defensive ones (Holley, 1997). Offensive rule violations are morally suspect because they give the offender an unfair advantage over others who are mostly complying with the relevant rule, whereas defensive rule violations are morally on the up and up because those who break them do so in order not to be disadvantaged because there is good evidence to suggest practically everyone else is breaking them as well. Since Armstrong's and his peers' violation of the doping rule falls, or so I argue, in the defensive category, their actions meet this moral test, which means, therefore, that calling them cheaters is unjustified.

But there is an even stronger argument to be made regarding Armstrong's and his fellow elite cyclists' moral standing in not abiding the prohibition against doping, one that suggests not only that it is morally permissible but perhaps morally obligatory to disregard this prohibition, given the reigning conception of elite sport. This has to do with two points relevant to our discussion – one about cycling itself and the other about the effect taking PEDs like EPO have on a rider's body.

With regard to the first point about cycling itself, an important ingredient in determining a rider's success in long-distance endurance events of this kind, and especially of the herculean demands placed on riders in premier events like the Tour de France, is the capacity of riders to endure the tremendous suffering such contests call for.

With regard to the second point, while doping does nothing to mitigate this suffering, it does give those riders who were not endowed by nature, who, in other words, did not win the genetic lottery at least in this one respect, a greater capacity to push their bodies further before their body shuts down despite their will to keep going. In the lexicon of cycling this is called "bonking," in which the rider's metabolic system essentially stops working before their will to go on does (Runciman, 2012). That means that doping essentially neutralizes the genetic component of athletic success that favors certain athletes and riders over their less fortunate counterparts, and puts the entire onus on effort as the determining factor of who wins or loses.

The lesson to be drawn from conjoining these two points is ably made by the aforementioned Tyler Hamilton, who in an especially acute passage insisted EPO made cycling fairer since it "granted the ability to suffer more; to push yourself farther and harder.... Races [as a consequence] weren't [anymore] rolls of the genetic dice, or who happened to be on form that day. They didn't depend on who you were. They depended on what you did – how hard you worked, how attentive and professional you were in your preparation" (Runciman, 2012, 5). If Hamilton is to be believed, then it seems that PEDs like EPO allow elite riders like Armstrong and Hamilton to make the race less about one's genetic stock and more about who has the stronger will to push beyond the pain and agony that are a characteristic feature of long-distance cycling races and come out on top.[1]

If my account to this point is on the mark, then Armstrong's and his peers' embrace of doping in their cycling pursuits is both morally permissible and perhaps even morally virtuous. That means, therefore, that those of us who, none-theless, insist on calling them cheaters are wrong to do so, and are further guilty of calumny, that is, of issuing not only a groundless accusation but a scurrilous one. I realize this last bit might especially be hard for the sporting public to swal-low, since it not only exculpates Armstrong and company from the charge of cheating, but comes awfully close to singing their praises. I think such a moral qualm is justified, because while I don't think Armstrong is a cheater, I also don't think he is by any stretch of the imagination a moral exemplar of the sporting world. But I want to suggest that our moral misgivings in this regard should not be directed at the elite athletes themselves but at the dominant conception of sport they labor under. For it is that conception, which puts such a premium on winning, that explains why most elite athletes dope. Those moral misgivings should also be aimed at ourselves, those of us who make up the sporting public and never tire of putting winners like Armstrong on a pedestal and, just as tire-lessly, mixed with more than a little *schadenfreude*, knocking them off of that pedestal when caught doping, all the while conveniently ignoring our own complicity in furthering "the win at all costs athletic mentality" that incentivizes elite athletes to dope in the first place. This, I suppose, is just another way of saying that when it comes to elite sports at least we want to have it both ways, which is why, I conjecture, we get the athletic heroes we deserve.

The first moral to be drawn from Armstrong's doping case, then, is that accusing dopers like him of cheating is off the mark because the use of PEDs is fully in step with the development of the Lombardian win at all costs ethos that presently dominates elite sport. For if winning is as important as this conception claims, then the resort to doping is both a perfectly rational move and a perfectly fair one. But if there is any doubt that Armstrong's do-whatever-it-takes-to-win approach to sport furthers rather than departs from that dominant ethos, compare Armstrong's own rendering of that ethos – losing and dying, it's the same thing – with that of one of his predecessors, former coach of the University of Minnesota's basketball team Bill Musselman – losing is worse than dying, you have to live with it – and finally with one of his former and biggest corporate sponsors, Phil Knight, head of Nike, who commissioned the following advertising slogan for the Olympics: "You don't win silver, you lose gold."

The moral book on anti-doping regulators

Let journalists Longman and Fressenden (2004) explain, for they anticipate the critical point I want to make here when they note how the USADA's strategy to get the goods on suspected dopers in this manner sets in motion a morally unseemly chain of events that closely approximates what happens when legal authorities try to get the goods on street drug users. More specifically, what they noticed is that the way PED cases play themselves out when athletic authorities adopt this non-analytic strategy starts to look more and more like the way street drug cases play themselves out with one important twist: "whereas street drugs rivals kill off one another, steroid drug rivals rat off one another" (Longman & Fressenden, 2004, 4). For in the cut-throat, do-whatever-it-takes-to-win world of elite sports, the chance to smear one's opponents, to destroy their athletic reputations and fortunes by carefully crafted allegations of drug use, is, and no doubt will continue to be in the foreseeable future if the status quo prevails, too tempting for today's jaded elite athletes to pass up. That is why we should be especially chary of appeals to fairness in this context, since in this Hobbesian-like setting such appeals are just as, or perhaps even more, likely to be used as rationalizations to justify exacting revenge on one's rivals rather than ridding sport of the scourge of doping. And that is why we should be similarly chary about the Armstrong case.

If there is any doubt that the USADA's effort to goad athletes to betray one another locks them into a morally fraught and unwinnable game of tit-for-tat, one in which the self-serving interests of each party trumps the interest in the moral welfare of sport, then consider the fact that Armstrong himself, long before USADA instituted this new policy, used it to good effect to advance his own cycling career. For when Armstrong grew suspicious that his competitors and even his teammates might be using new PEDs that he did not have access to, he would swiftly inform the authorities and request that they be checked out (Runciman, 2012). He did this very thing to his teammate Tyler Hamilton after the latter's winning performance in 2004, in which Hamilton was summoned to the Cycling Federation headquarters in Switzerland and read the riot act for his dalliance with PEDs. It was only later that Hamilton found out that it was Armstrong who had turned him in. This only goes to show, or so I argue, that anti-doping initiatives of this kind, which pit the win-at-all-costs will of dopers against the win-at-all-costs will of anti-dopers, are unworkable, since neither side in this soul-destroying contest of wills has any reason to play a very different kind of game, one in which the aim is to ensure the moral flourishing of sport.

A critic might complain, however, that I have overlooked at least one important difference between these two cases that tells against my criticism of USADA non-analytic effort to stem the tide of doping. For it seems clear that Graham's secretive effort to put the testing authorities on the trail of dopers he was not coaching was explicitly intended to give the doped athletes he was coaching a decidedly unfair competitive advantage, whereas Armstrong's teammates' testimony against him was not, and could not have been similarly motivated, given that most of them were already in the twilight, if not the end, of their own athletic careers. That is, they had nothing to gain competitively by revealing the details of their own or of Armstrong's doping. So my charge that this is just another way in which the futile and ill-conceived game of dopers trying to evade detection and anti-dopers trying to catch them is played, my would-be critic would likely conclude, must be mistaken.

This retort has some force if only because it is true that Armstrong's teammates, unlike Graham's runners, were indeed no longer at the top of their game, and, therefore, were in no position to take competitive advantage of their testimony against Armstrong. But it would be a non-sequiter at best to jump to the conclusion that in fingering Armstrong in this bordering-on-forced confessional manner they were acting in the best interests of sport rather than feathering their own nests. Indeed, there are several good reasons to think they were doing the latter rather than the former.

To begin with, if their aim was to clean up elite cycling they could have voluntarily offered up what they knew to the authorities rather than having to be pressured to do so, and without, it should be said, having to betray anyone else in the process; after all, the entire lot of them doped, and so had plenty to tell the authorities without having to implicate anyone else. And at this late stage in their careers they had much less to lose by doing so, which is why it is no coincidence that most of what we know about the doping predilections of elite athletes comes from the lips of retired rather than active athletes.

Another reason we should be wary of their giving up Armstrong to the USADA is that by implicating Armstrong they deflected the attention away from their own doping transgressions, which might otherwise have garnered a sizable share of the mass media's coverage. Instead, Armstrong bore almost all of the media's fire and brimstone denunciations, and was made to appear, as previously noted, as the person virtually single-handedly responsible for tarnishing the reputation of elite cycling.

Yet a final reason, at least for my purposes, for being suspicious of Armstrong's teammates' intentions here is their prior silence regarding their own doping and that of Armstrong when they were arguably the foremost cycling team in the world. For when they were winning practically every elite cycling event they competed in, to include the biggest prize of all in the Tour de France, they were as tight lipped about their use of PEDs as Armstrong was of his. An important reason why, I think, has to do with how their own livelihood at that time very much depended on keeping their own doping under wraps, and especially Armstrong's, since the better he did the more they financially profited. Call me a cynic then, but their recent willingness to talk on the record mainly about Armstrong certainly appears at least to have a lot to do with the fact that their fortunes, economic and otherwise, were no longer tied to his.

Conclusion

I want to underscore that my effort here to balance the moral books between dopers and anti-dopers by featuring the recent Armstrong case was not intended to come down on one side or the other of this momentous struggle for the soul of elite sport, even though it does seek more modestly to turn down the voluble criticism of Armstrong's moral character a notch or two and to turn up the mostly muted criticism of the moral standing of the testers at least as much.

On the contrary, my ultimate aim was to show *why there is no winning this struggle as it is currently waged.* For both sides seem to think that this battle can be won by depending wholly on technical measures, that is, that dopers can keep the testers at bay by becoming ever more sophisticated in their evasive techniques to mask the drugs they are taking and to sabotage the testing policies foisted on them, and testers can defeat dopers by increasingly refining their tests and by employing quasi-criminal strategies to get athletes to police themselves, to do the tester's own dirty work.

But if my argument has any force at all, it should be all too apparent that the doping epidemic in elite sports today is mainly a moral problem. That means we need to rethink both the point and purpose of athletic enterprise and the values we wish it to express. And if taking this daunting moral step has any chance of succeeding at all, athletes and athletic authorities alike, as well as the greater sporting public, need to engage one another in a sustained moral conversation in which only the force of the better argument, rather than that of the yet more efficient strategy of evasion or detection, carries the day. That way those of us who claim we care – really care – about sport, will at least have a fighting chance of changing it into a social practice worthy of that care.

Note

1 I am not claiming here that Hamilton's argument for the fairness of using drugs like EPO is a knockdown argument that settles the matter once and for all, and for all at once. Rather, I'm only claiming that it is a forceful argument that warrants serious consideration. The main objection made against it is that it overplays the importance effort should be accorded in athletic contests and underplays, or denies altogether, the importance talent should play in these contests. This latter argument is forcefully made by Sandel (2007).

References

Holley, D. (1997). Breaking the rules when others do. *Journal of Applied Philosophy*, *14* (2), 159–168.

Longman, J., & Fressenden, F. (2004, April 11). Rivals turn to tattling in steroids cases involving top athletes. *New York Times*, 4.

Runciman, D. (2012). Everybody gets popped. *London Review of Books*, *34* (22), 5–10.

Sandel, M. (2007). *The case against perfection*. Cambridge, MA: Harvard University Press.

Voet, W. (2002). *Breaking the chain*. London: Yellow Jersey Press.

18 From zero-tolerance toward risk reduction of doping

Learning from the failure of the war on drugs?[1]

Bengt Kayser

Introduction

This chapter considers what the future of sport might be in 20–30 years time, with particular emphasis on technological advances for performance enhancement. "Citius, Altius, Fortius" or "Faster, Higher, Stronger" is the Olympic motto, chosen by Pierre de Coubertin at the time of the creation of the International Olympic Committee in 1894. This motto accurately describes the essence of elite sport. As a result, athletes engage in preparatory practices such as physical/ mental training, eating special diets, sleeping at (simulated) altitude, taking (licit) supplements, training in wind tunnels and exploiting other technological advances such as modern running shoes, low-friction garments or carbon fiber contraptions, all aimed at enhancing performance, to increase the chances to win. Even though sport claims a level playing field, athletes do not necessarily share or have equal access to such means. This is in keeping with the true nature of professional sport, which is the celebration of biological and artificial inequalities.

Choosing to dope

Since elite sport is essentially the celebration of differences between winners and losers, it is not surprising that what is known today as "doping," also aimed at performance enhancement, has been part of sport from its beginnings (Dimeo, 2007). Athletes may engage in doping if they consider that the potential effect outweighs the risk of discovery, and, importantly, if they are exposed and have access to the potential of doping (Hauw & Mohamed, 2015; Overbye, Knudsen, & Pfister, 2013; Mazanov & Huybers, 2010). Today's doping and anti-doping are consequences of Olympism and the general professionalization and commercialization of sport, which result in tremendous pressure on athletes to perform. They aim to be as fast, high, and strong as possible and will balance any decisions on what means to employ to attain those objectives on a cost–benefit analysis.

Certainly, human decision-making is not a pure rational process, but personal reasoning plays a part. Given the stakes at hand – gold medals, glory, and fortune – it is perfectly understandable that some athletes, who are just as human as any other member of society, will decide to take the risk. Doping is thus at least partly a rational choice, a logical consequence of the tenets of modern sport and, more generally, modernity. But apart from this *cognitive* model, which stipulates that athletes are accountable for their acts to attain their sporting and non-sporting goals, doping behavior is also explained by a *drive* model and a *situated dynamic* model. In the drive model, doping behavior is conceived as a solution to reduce unconscious psychological and somatic distress, while in the situated dynamic model the broader context of the athlete's life is taken into account, linking temporally critical life events with the athlete's actions (Hauw & McNamee, 2015).

Doping then, anti-doping now

Doping, in the sense of substance use with the aim of performance enhancement, was rather common last century (Dimeo, 2007). Even if more prevalent in some sports than others, it was generally more or less tacitly accepted, for example in professional cycling during most of the 100-year history of the Tour de France (de Mondenard, 2011). This is understandable, since for the first half of last century doping had not been clearly defined and there was no list of forbidden substances and methods, nor were there real anti-doping controls (Dimeo, 2007). The chances of discovery were low, and many athletes saw doping as being an integral part of their endeavor. Even though some early anti-doping voices were heard, only in the 1960s did a gradual development toward anti-doping start, which eventually led in 1999 to the inception of WADA and globalization of anti-doping efforts. A shift in official rhetoric: "doping is bad, period" (Pound 2006) echoed by the media, changed public perception about doping, which become more critical (Engelberg & Moston, 2012).

But today's official stance is that doping in elite sports is such a major threat to sports and to public health that it must be "fought" with a "war against doping." Important surveillance measures have been implemented, with collaborations between WADA, Interpol, and national intelligence and police services, and several countries have adopted specific criminal laws against doping (Alexander, 2014). The declared objective is eradication of doping and a future of drug-free sport. Based on a means-justify-the-end principle, anti-doping policies thus have become quite excessive (e.g. the obligation to inform about one's whereabouts 365 days a year and unannounced urine and blood sampling for testing purposes), and seem mostly driven by ideology and political convenience. But they are ethically problematic, insufficiently effective, costly, and possibly lead to more harm to society than they prevent (Kayser & Broers, 2015). Given the poor results from other attempts of prohibition, it is doubtful that a further increase of surveillance pressure and its extension to the general population would help.

Consequences of doping and anti-doping

Certainly, in elite sport the increased surveillance from anti-doping has led to changes in doping behavior, because certain practices can no longer go undetected. But it still remains possible to stay under the radar by using methods for which laboratory detection technology is currently insufficient (Berry, 2008). And even though the gap between dopers and anti-dopers is perhaps getting smaller, a perverse consequence of modern anti-doping cannot be prevented, which is the impossibility of excluding doping in a winner. This is because of the limits of surveillance and laboratory technology. A negative test does not exclude doping due to limited sensitivity and specificity of tests, and hence every winner is potentially a cheat. Thus anti-doping paradoxically directly undermines its ultimate goal, the celebration of clean champions.

Sure enough, it would all be simpler without doping, but as with other aspects of human behavior, doping exists, cannot be eradicated, and causes harm. There are several harms associated with doping (Kayser & Broers, 2015). Concerning the athlete, the substance may come with direct health risks. Harms can also occur from the way substances are used (e.g. injection of drugs with contaminated syringes) or from the use of impure or mislabeled uncontrolled substances. But harms can also be consequences of anti-doping regulation, with loss of autonomy and the practical consequences of the *whereabouts rule* for daily life (Valkenburg, de Hon, & van Hilvoorde, 2013). Harm can further result from positive tests and subsequent punishment, even when there was clearly no intent to dope (Pluim, 2008).

Another type of harm is that to other athletes. Doping may even force athletes to engage in doping, as coercion into risk is very common in sports endeavors in general (Kayser & Broers, 2015). There is also potential doping-induced bodily harm to one's opponent. For example, the use of anabolic steroids might induce increased aggressiveness, which could lead to harm to one's opponent. However, the distinction between other permitted techniques (such as physical and mental training or the use of permitted substances, aimed at enabling boxers to hit harder) and the prohibition of steroids would seem arbitrary, especially since the evidence for this alleged increased aggressiveness (so-called "roid rage") is so shallow (Tricker *et al.*, 1996).

There may also be harm to society outside sport. Fuelled by the media, there is a growing belief among amateur athletes and the public that "doping works," perhaps stimulating the use of performance-enhancing substances in wider society. Performance enhancement in the larger sense of the word is seen as an increasingly "normal" societal phenomenon (Greely *et al.*, 2008). Finally, anti-doping-related harm to society concerns international organized crime. There are important black and gray markets in different substances such as human growth hormone, EPO, anabolic steroids and insulin. Even if the doping market is less visible than the illicit drugs market, organized crime induces violence and feelings of insecurity, leads to corruption, adds to parallel money circuits, and finances mafia and wars (Paoli & Donati, 2013).

Overall it appears that much of the harm of doping for the individual athlete, other athletes, the image of sport or wider society, seems to be more related to anti-doping than to the use of the performance-enhancing methods or substances as such. This is also the case in the illicit drug field, even if the reasons for using the drugs are not similar. Whereas psychoactive substance users will use their chosen substance for the desired psychotropic effect or because they are dependent, athletes may turn to doping substances for the anticipated benefits of winning. The pressure on athletes to perform, the almost religious admiration for successful athletes, and the huge financial incentives for the winners can be considered indirect causes of harm (Kayser & Broers, 2015).

War against drugs, war against doping

There are therefore several areas where the global efforts against illicit drugs and those against doping in sports show similarities. In both cases the rhetoric used by those in favor of prohibition is rich in arguments attributing terrible consequences to the use of various substances, arguments frequently devoid of solid scientific evidence. Both tend toward an "ends justify the means" approach in an arms race between users and controllers, enforced by excessively strong repressive and surveillance measures. Both are unable to attain their declared objective, eradication of illicit psychotropic drug use and doping in elite sports, respectively. Both have unintended side-effects, with a high cost to society, certainly so for the war on drugs, likely so for the war on doping. Finally, they merge, as illustrated by the inclusion of non-performance-enhancing recreational psychotropic drugs like marijuana on WADA's list of prohibited substances and, in some countries like the USA, the classification of anabolic steroids as illicit drugs, on a par with psychotropic drugs such as cocaine.

There is thus considerable similarity and overlap between the war on drugs and the war on doping. Fundamental to the war on drugs is its discourse on the extraordinary danger of illicit drugs like cocaine, heroin, methamphetamine, or cannabis. But critical appraisal of the science for this position shows that there is a lack of evidence. Overall, the science on the effects of illicit psychotropic drug use suggests that controlled use is possible and is the rule for the vast majority of users. Most of the consequences of illicit drug use are not related to the substance itself but to the societal boundaries in which the substance is used. Three reports of the Global Commission on Drug Policy explain how most of the indirect harms of drugs (HIV,[2] HCV,[3] deaths from overdose and criminality, excessive incarceration rates, consequences in drug-producing countries) are fueled by the war on drugs (GCDP, 2011; 2012; 2013). This war on drugs has thus introduced more harm to society than it prevented.

Given these insights there are lessons to be learned from the way in which the use of psychotropic drugs has been dealt with and how modern policies are now moving away from a zero-tolerance war against drugs, toward more pragmatic policies. If the war on drugs has failed (Wood, Werb, Marshall, Montaner, & Kerr, 2009) and has caused important harm to society, the same may apply for the war on doping. The official anti-doping discourse also uses a scaremongering discourse of the danger of doping. Certainly, depending on substance, dose, and administration, significant health risk is possible, but that is also true for many licit substances. Also, most of the anecdotes of doping victims used in anti-doping discourse are modern myths (Kayser & Broers, 2015). The only documented evidence of significant doping-induced health harm in athletes beyond doubtful anecdotes is that of the East German state-run doping program. Such coercion of young athletes into doping is inexcusable, but it is important to understand that also the discovery of this state-supervised systematic doping led to its subsequent mythification and use for anti-doping rhetoric. The recent allegations that at that time similar doping practices were also prevalent on the western side of the Berlin Wall add to the complexity of the problem.

Relaxing rules and harm reduction

Given the impossibility of the eradication of doping and the negative side-effects of the zero-tolerance stance of anti-doping (Fincoeur, Frender, & Pitsch, 2013), there is a need for change. The discussions on doping and anti-doping should not ignore the imperfect practical outcomes of current anti-doping policies in elite and amateur sport, as well as outside sport. Today's anti-doping is not a solution, but an increasingly costly imperfection.

Of course, we all prefer a world without wars, drugs, or doping. But daily reality is quite different. Fifty years of war on drugs has had little effect on the prevalence of illicit substance use but has had many negative consequences. Consequently it makes sense to start exploring and evaluating alternative policies, like regulating drug use based on human rights and public health principles, with a combination of pragmatic policies including harm reduction, taking into account local socio-cultural and economic specificities, and continuously adapted to ongoing developments (e.g. in Portugal, Uruguay, and several states in the USA with the legalization of cannabis use). These principles apply possibly also to the field of performance enhancement.

So where might sport be in 20–30 years? WADA has been successful in giving universal value to its Code through the UNESCO International Convention Against Doping in Sport. The Convention's intention is the elimination of doping in sports and it refers to WADA's code, leaving it up to WADA to define doping and anti-doping. As for illicit drugs, this makes policy changes moving away from the hard line of zero-tolerance politically difficult. The inertia is such that in the next 10–20 years little change can be expected. But, given a future in which enhancement practices outside sport are likely to be increasingly viewed as normal (e.g. cognitive enhancement, anti-aging medicine (Greely 2010)), anti-doping ideology could well lose ground, since it is in such contradiction with developments outside sport. There is a precedent for such a shift. Just as in the early 1970s the sacred amateur status of Olympic sport was progressively dropped, zero-tolerance-based anti-doping might be abandoned one day (Tolleneer & Schotsmans, 2012).

How to go about such a paradigm shift? To begin with, the concept of performance enhancement by means of methods or substances should be seen as a logical consequence of elite sports endeavor and not be negated by a utopic ideological *spirit of sport* concept (Mauron, 2011). Second, the health of elite athletes should still be protected. This would imply some form of testing, but without going all the way as in today's testing. No-starting rules could be proposed to keep health risks below acceptable levels. Athletes will find ways to cheat a bit around such strategies, but that would be part of the play, as it is for many other rules in sport. The argument that it would change sports into an arena akin to Formula 1, where the best engineering team wins is only partly correct. It will still take talent, a lot of hard work and some luck to become a champion. And this happens anyway; today well-assisted athletes may engage in complex training regimes and strategic doping while remaining undetected. Third, the list of forbidden substances can be simplified, keeping only performance-enhancing substances with proven major health hazards. Recreational drugs can be taken off the list, allowing athletes to be dealt with in the same way as the general population. Instead of a crackdown on steroid use in gyms and fitness clubs, with compulsory testing as in Denmark, approaches such as in the UK where so-called steroid clinics offer mostly free and anonymous services, make it possible to provide harm-reduction measures with proven health benefits (Hope *et al.*, 2013).

There are obviously important questions to be asked. By how much would the prevalence and intensity of doping rise under a different regime? Would reduction in other costs outweigh the risks of increased doping? One would have to distinguish between elite athletes, amateur athletes, minors, gym users, and the public in general, since it can be expected that the answers to these questions will vary between groups. In elite athletes one might expect limited health problems since medical supervision and health-oriented testing would constrain use. In amateur athletes the possibility of refraining from sourcing substances from the black market and having access to general information and proper methods of use might have positive effects. It will be difficult to devise an optimal strategy to regulate for children specifically. Since athletic careers often start very early, the protection of young talents would be mandatory. Alternative policies should be continuously and extensively evaluated for desired outcomes and unintended negative consequences, carefully balancing the two.

Would such a shift change the nature of sport? It depends. If we take the Tour de France as an example, in which for most of its history doping was highly prevalent, it could be argued that relaxing the rules and introducing a health-centered and harm-reduction approach would allow the Tour to remain what it was for most of its history. Other sports might change. But sports are not fixed, they evolve. For sports measuring performance in grams and seconds this is surely the case. If today records can still be broken, this will end since there are biophysical limits to performance. The 100 m dash will never be run in zero seconds and hence records will cease to be broken at some point, depending on further selection of optimal genetic talent from a still growing recruitment base. It is impossible to predict if the 100 m dash will still enjoy the same popularity in the future when records will have ceased to be broken.

To summarize, even if sufficiently complete and accurate data on the negative aspects of anti-doping policy are still lacking, there is need for reform of anti-doping. We should start experimenting with an evaluation of alternative ways of dealing with doping in elite (and amateur) sports, inspired by the experience gained with alternative drug policies. These should be scientifically sound, respect human rights and public health principles, and treat athletes as ordinary humans and not as potential criminals. The modern globalized sport entertainment industry, with its almost unlimited financial means, should not be allowed to hijack worldwide legal frameworks and orient society toward a zero-tolerance approach to both psychotropic and performance-enhancing substances. Considering that a possible "de-sanctification" of elite sport will take time, that anti-doping will not be able to eradicate doping and the likelihood that doping will continue in amateur and elite sport, with the winners including some of the best dopers, more pragmatic approaches, as set out above, deserve serious consideration. Let's hope that in the meantime the side-effects of the war on doping will not worsen, and that the tendency for a fusion of the war on drugs with the war on doping, with excessive surveillance and harsh repression of a dystopian nature, will remain limited before achieving truly Orwellian dimensions.

Notes

1 This chapter is based on papers by the author published previously (Kayser & Broers, 2013; Kayser, Mauron, & Miah, 2007). The reader is referred to those papers for full lists of references.
2 Human immunodeficiency virus.
3 Hepatitis-C virus.

References

Alexander, B.R. (2014). War on drugs redux: Welcome to the war on doping in sports. *Substance Use & Misuse, 49* (9), 1190–1193.
Berry, D.A. (2008). The science of doping. *Nature, 454* (7205), 692–693.
de Mondenard, J.-P. (2011). *Tour de France, 33 vainqueurs face au dopage, entre 1947 et 2010 (Tour de France, 33 winners facing doping between 1947 and 2010)*, Paris: Hugo et Compagnie.
Dimeo, P.L. (2007). *A history of drug use in sport 1876–1976: Beyond good and evil.* London: Routledge.
Engelberg, T., & Moston, S. (2012). Public perception of sport anti-doping policy in Australia. *Drugs: Education, Prevention and Policy, 19*, 84–87.
Fincoeur, B., Frenger, M., & Pitsch, W. (2013). Does one play with the athletes' health in the name of ethics? *Performance Enhancement & Health, 2* (4), 182–193.
GCDP (2011). Report of the Global Commission on Drug Policy. Retrieved February 13, 2014, from www.globalcommissionondrugs.org/Report.
GCDP (2012). The war on drugs and HIV/AIDS. Retrieved February 13, 2014, from http://globalcommissionondrugs.org/wp-content/themes/gcdp_v1/pdf/GCDP_HIV-AIDS_2012_REFERENCE.pdf.
GCDP (2013). The negative impact of the war on drugs on public health: The hidden hepatitis C epidemic. Retrieved February 13, 2014, from www.globalcommissionondrugs.org/hepatitis/gcdp_hepatitis_english.pdf.

Greely, H.T. (2010). Enhancing brains: What are we afraid of? *Cerebrum: The Dana Forum on Brain Science, 14*, 1–10.

Greely, H., Sahakian, B., Harris, J., Kessler, R., Gazzaniga, M., Campbell, P., *et al.* (2008). Towards responsible use of cognitive-enhancing drugs by the healthy. *Nature, 456* (7223), 702–705.

Hauw, D., & McNamee, M. (2015). A critical analysis of three psychological research programs of doping behaviour. *Psychology of Sport and Exercise, 16*, 140–148.

Hauw, D., & Mohamed, S. (2015). Patterns in the situated activity of substance use in the careers of elite doping athletes. *Psychology of Sport and Exercise, 16*, 156–163.

Hope, V.D., McVeigh, J., Marongiu, A., Evans-Brown, M., Smith, J., Kimergård, A., *et al* (2013). Prevalence of, and risk factors for, HIV, hepatitis B and C infections among men who inject image and performance enhancing drugs: A cross-sectional study. *BMJ Open, 3* (9), e003207.

Kayser, B., & Broers, B. (2013). Anti-doping policies: Choosing between imperfections. In *Athletic enhancement, human nature and ethics: Threats and opportunities of doping technologies* (pp. 271–289). Dordrecht: Springer.

Kayser, B., & Broers, B. (2015). Doping and performance enhancement: Harms and harm reduction. In V. Moller, I. Waddington, & J. Hoberman (Eds.), *Routledge handbook of drugs and sport*. London: Routledge.

Kayser, B., Mauron, A., & Miah, A. (2007). Current anti-doping policy: A critical appraisal. *BMC Medical Ethics, 8*, 2.

Mauron, A. (2011). Le dopage et l'esprit du sport. *Les Cahiers du Centre Georges Canguilhem, 5* (1), 125–139.

Mazanov, J. & Huybers, T. (2010). An empirical model of athlete decisions to use performance-enhancing drugs: Qualitative evidence. *Qualitative Research in Sport and Exercise, 2* (3), 385–402.

Overbye, M., Knudsen, M.L., & Pfister, G. (2013). To dope or not to dope: Elite athletes' perceptions of doping deterrents and incentives. *Performance Enhancement & Health, 2*, 119–134.

Paoli, L., & Donati, A. (2013). *The sports doping market*. New York: Springer Science & Business Media.

Pluim, B. (2008). A doping sinner is not always a cheat. *British Journal of Sports Medicine, 42* (7), 549–550.

Pound, R.W. (2006). *Inside dope: How drugs are the biggest threat to sports, why you should care, and what can be done about them*. Mississauga: Wiley & Sons.

Tolleneer, J., & Schotsmans, P. (2012). Self, other, play, display and humanity: Development of a five-level model for the analysis of ethical arguments in the athletic enhancement debate. In *Athletic enhancement, human nature and ethics: Threats and opportunities of doping technologies* (pp. 21–43). Dordrecht: Springer.

Tricker, R., Casaburi, R., Storer, T.W., Clevenger, B., Berman, N., Shirazi, A., *et al.* (1996). The effects of supraphysiological doses of testosterone on angry behavior in healthy eugonadal men: A clinical research center study. *Journal of Clinical Endocrinology and Metabolism, 81* (10), 3754–3758.

Valkenburg, D., de Hon, O., & van Hilvoorde, I. (2013). Doping control, providing whereabouts and the importance of privacy for elite athletes. *The International Journal on Drug Policy, 25* (2), 212–218.

Wood, E., Werb, D., Marshall, B., Montaner, J., & Kerr, T. (2009). The war on drugs: a devastating public policy disaster. *Lancet, 373* (9668), 989–990.

PART V

Re-conceptualizing "sport for development"

Introduction

Karen Petry

The starting point of this part is the fact that sport has been linked by the United Nations to the realization of the Millennium Development Goals (MDGs), including the promotion of peace and human dignity. How do key sport scientists see the future of sport for development?

Despite the fact that development is not a unique term and has many definitional and semantic differences, the term as well as the concept of sport and development remains strongly debated and discussed. Whereas development as such is primarily understood in economic terms, the authors in this part advocate rather a comprehensive, theoretical as well as practical approach when it comes to the use of sport in the development context. As always, different authors provide contrasting views, such as a more skeptical and critical view about the overall theoretical as well as practical concept of sport for development (Fred Coalter), such as a critical view on the existing research paradigm and on the distinction between the Global North and the Global South (Oscar Mwaanga and Kola Adeosun) and a more practical (positive) view on the future role of research and the universities in the area of sport and development (Marion Keim and Christo de Coning).

Fred Coalter (UK) argues in his chapter that *outcome research* rather than an accumulation of descriptive studies of the impacts of sport-for-development projects is needed in order to enable the development of middle-range theories about the mechanisms of such programs. The need for greater specificity also relates to the urgent need to address the nature of relationships between "possible program impacts and broader individual and social outcomes" and their relationship to development. Coalter states that it is unrealistic to speak of a sport-for-development effect, despite its rhetorical appeal. Finally, he argues that even among those attracted by the potential of sport for development, there is a need to embrace the skepticism and discipline of sociology, if both theory and practice are to be improved.

The outlined skepticism from Coalter is further developed by **Oscar Mwaanga** (Zambia) **and Kola Adeosun** (UK) in their chapter. They argue that the inflated and growing popularity of this field in the last decade has led to a paucity of concepts as well as research activities. Both authors develop a critique of the hegemonic or dominant research paradigm(s) and introduce the Critical Participatory Paradigm (CPP) in order to progress the field. The main critique postulates that it is an undemocratic endeavor in which the Global North researches on and not with the Global South, and gathers knowledge which has limited application among the end users, especially in Global South communities. They argue for the future democratization of research through the CPP, which includes, *inter alia*, the complexity as well as the context of the developmental processes, mechanisms, and outcomes. They conclude the CPP by proposing a shift from the dominant research paradigm that privileges the Global North toward a more democratic paradigm that aims and works to engage all key stakeholders in partnership.

Marion Keim and Christo de Coining (South Africa) move more or less in the same direction. They represent again the Southern perspective and approach the sport and development debate using a research initiative initiated by UNESCO's Africa Office to establish a baseline for a global sport policy index with 11 African countries. This research can be regarded as a first step toward establishing a global index in the field. The authors argue that a "joint commitment" from the Global North and the Global South is required in order to learn from each other, and to share research as well as experiences from the field across continents.

The final contribution in this part, by **Karen Petry and Marius Runkel** (Germany), has been conceived as an attempt to draw an overall conclusion from the three former chapters. They discuss the concept of development and the sport-related (future) approach in a broader sense. In most definitions there is an assumption that development is characterized by positive change and progress and the concept of modernization can be seen as a form of development affecting individual and community improvement in terms of social and economic perspectives. However, the authors argue that the complex relationship between development and sport, as well as such positive claims, must be treated with some caution. Finally, a redefinition of development is proposed and a broader approach of global learning in all geographical directions around the world is introduced. They argue that, in future, the scientific community in the area of sport and development should avoid the term *development* and substitute a new one, such as *sport and global learning/cooperation* or to revitalize the sociological, philosophical as well as psychological debate about the role of sport participation in the respective area, such as *social development, community development, personal development, health-enhancing activities*, etc., which automatically brings a broader perspective and opens the field in a positive way.

To sum up: in future, the sport and development debate should stop complaining about ideological, geographical, and academic inequity, and begin a new phase of discussion about new terminology, and a future conceptualization of a scientific discipline, which for the next decades should lead the discussions about the area of sport and development.

19 The future of sport for development

From ideology to sociology

Fred Coalter[1]

How new is new?

Many, often self-interested, academics and consultants claim that sport-for-development is a "new field" in its "formative stage" (Kay, 2009, 1177; Woodcock, Cronin, & Forde, 2012). However, this seems an odd claim for several reasons. Further, it is a claim which stands in the way of the development of sport-for-development as an academic area of study and as an area of policy and practice.

First, the claims of the sports evangelists who promote a role for sport in "development" are based implicitly on long-standing assertions about the nature and contribution of sport; the legitimacy claimed by such conceptual entrepreneurs (Hewitt, 1998) surely rests on the fact that it is *not new*. The claims reflect popular beliefs about the supposedly *inherent* developmental potential of sport, which one presumes are based on assumptions of evidence.

Second, a striking aspect of this area is the widespread ignoring of a large body of research evidence about sport's rather limited contribution to personal and social development. Perhaps it is ignored because it raises difficult questions about many of the claims made by the conceptual entrepreneurs of sport-for-development (e.g. Coalter, 2007; Coakley, 2011; Hartmann & Kwauk, 2011). It might be argued that the widespread use of *sport plus* approaches (which have a variety of additional educational components) indicates recognition of the developmental limits of *sport*.

Consequently, the claim that sport-for-development is a new field serves to narrow the definition of "relevant" research. For example, Coakley (2011) highlights the need to look outside the limited field of sport-for-development; Tacon (2007) argues that many sport-for-change projects have much in common with social work practice. For example, although some place "peer leaders" at the symbolic heart of sport-for-development programs (e.g. Nicholls, Giles, & Sethna, 2011), there is little systematic evidence about their effectiveness (Kruse, 2006). Drawing on more robust theory and research in education and health education serves to de-mystify the role that they have been accorded, often on ideological grounds rather than educational effectiveness, and sets an agenda for research.

Cognitive, affective, and normative dimensions and ideological over-reach

Part of the reason for the relative isolation from mainstream social science is to be found in a form of *liberation methodology* among some sport-for-development academics, who argue that the attempt to define, measure, and quantify impacts and outcomes is illegitimate, even oppressive. Issues of ontology, epistemology, methodology, and methods are used in abstract ways and combined with diffuse notions of politics, power, and liberation. This results in the designation of quantitative research as being unavoidably part of "neo-colonialist hegemonic repression" and contributing to the reproduction of unequal power relations (Lindsey & Grattan, 2012; Darnell & Hayhurst, 2012; Nicholls *et al.*, 2011).

However, the symbolic weight attributed to sport-for-development and the viewing of certain approaches to evaluation as signifying neo-colonial oppression is a form of ideological over-reach. My response is that of Hammersley (1995, 19), who argues that "philosophy must be not be seen as superordinate to empirical research ... research is a practical activity and cannot be governed in any strict way by methodological theory." Allied to this is Sugden's (2010, 267) advocacy of a form of critical pragmatism which "places emphasis on theoretical development and refinement through critical, practical, empirical engagement, rather than fixating upon abstract debate and unmovable theoretical principles." It is worth noting that those promoting the supposedly liberatory "decolonizing, feminist-oriented, participatory action research" (Lindsey & Grattan, 2012) seem to have produced rather predictable data, which even some of these critics admit has rather limited analytical value (Kay, 2009).

Craib (1984) argues that social theory has three dimensions and that theorists do three different things simultaneously, with varying balances between them. The *cognitive dimension* seeks to establish objective knowledge about the social world. The *affective dimension* is one in which elements of the theories embody the experience and feeling of the theorist, which means that any debate involves more than rational argument. The third dimension is *normative* – any theory of the way that the world is, is also based on assumptions about the way that the world ought to be. Too often the affective and normative dimensions are predominant in sport-for-development writing, to the detriment of the cognitive. For example, even the critics of certain supposedly neo-colonialist policies and practices retain an affective and normative belief in the inherent developmental potential of sport. In this regard Hartmann and Kwauk (2011, 289) refer to the functionalist view of sport, which underpins much sport-for-development, as being based on "the normative vision of social life, social change, and the status quo embedded in this dominant vision." They also suggest that "given its history and ideology, sport is easily understood by the dominant class as a socially beneficial and culturally normative 'character builder'" (Hartmann & Kwauk, 2011, 292). Coakley (2011, 309) refers to the fact that commitment to neoliberal ideas "runs deep in ... the global social problems industry," reinforced by the cult of the individual used as a marketing tool by corporate sponsors. The importance of this is that:

> When organized into interpretive perspectives, these ideas constitute widely shared visions of how social worlds could and should be organized – much like other interpretive frameworks inspired by ideology more than research and theory. When combined with similarly shared emotions, identities, and dominant narratives, they tend to resist change, even when evidence contradicts them.
>
> (Coakley, 2011, 309)

Although the tensions between normative, affective, and cognitive perspectives are inevitable, within sport-for-development they are sub-optimally confused among those whose imperative is "to make a difference" (Black, 2010). The combination of neoliberal assumptions, the claim-making of conceptual entrepreneurs, the faith and beliefs of the sports evangelists, the cloistered self-referential environment of incestuous amplification (*Janes' Defense Weekly*, n.d.), organizational self-interest, liberation methodologists, and the notion that sport-for-development is *new* makes this a difficult research terrain. The truth of Pisani's (2008, 300) assertion that "doing honest analysis that would lead to program improvement is a glorious way to be hated by just about everyone" is obvious in sport-for-development.

Deficit models and environmental determinism

The dominance of normative and affective perspectives underpins what Black (2010) has referred to as the lack of clarity and precision relating to the definition of *development*. Nevertheless, it is clear that a core assumption of sport-for-development programs is that poor communities produce deficient people who can be *developed* through sport. However, there is a paradoxical danger of well-meaning projects being based on negative stereotypes of all young people from particular areas, with the attendant danger of misconceived provision, inappropriate performance indicators, and subtle forms of racism.

For example, in my survey data in three African countries and two cities in India (Coalter & Taylor, 2010; Coalter, 2013), the young people did not form homogeneous groups and had a range of positive self-evaluations. It is possible that some of these evaluations reflect a certain self-protective element, with a degree of denial and suppression (Hunter, 2001). However, at the very least, the data raise questions about the extent to which respondents are simply relatively normal young people living in often dreadful circumstances.

It is essential to avoid overly generalized deficit models which ignore the fact that the nature and extent of impacts on participants will depend not only on the nature of the experience, but also on the nature of the participants and their response to the various aspects of the programs, the key mechanism. To ignore this contains obvious ideological and pedagogic dangers. It raises important questions about how *need* and *development* are conceptualized and how desired impacts and behavioral outcomes are defined and measured. The need for greater clarity is also emphasized by the apparent diversity among the so-called Global South/Majority World/low-income participants, politically correct terms which lack the specificity required for empirical research. In such circumstances the universalizing anti-neo-colonialist analysis contains the danger inherent in "the know-it-all tendencies of normative theory" (Pawson, 2001, 11).

Program theory and necessary conditions

The implicit view seems to be that sport-for-development requires an accumulation of impact studies to address the supposed "evidence deficit" (Woodcock *et al.*, 2012) – whether this is via decolonizing, feminist-oriented, participatory action research (Lindsey & Grattan, 2012), the accumulation of well-selected "heartfelt narratives" (Hartmann & Kwauk, 2011, 286), or the simple accumulation of so-called *neo-colonialist* quantitative impact studies. However, the wide variety of sport-for-development programs – many of which are various forms of "sport-plus" (Coalter, 2007) – combined with a wide diversity of participants means that it is exceptionally difficult to make robust generalized statements about sport-for-development. The difficulties are emphasized by Coakley's (1998, 2) comment that we need to regard "sports as sites for socialization experiences, not causes of socialization outcomes" and Hartmann and Kwauk's (2011, 290) argument that "the educational experience within the sporting experience is the most critical space."

Therefore there is a need to consider the implications of Pawson's (2006) and Weiss' (1997) emphasis on middle-range mechanisms. Such perspectives shift our focus from *families of programs* (sport-for-development) to *families of mechanisms*, with apparently diverse interventions sharing common mechanisms and processes. Although Pawson *et al.* (2004, 7) argue that "rarely if ever is the 'same' program fully effective in all circumstances," Pawson also suggests that:

> There are probably some common processes (e.g. how people react to change) and thus generic theories (about human volition) that feed their way into all interventions. If synthesis were to concentrate on these middle-range mechanisms, then the opportunities for the utilization of reviews [of research] would be much expanded.
>
> (Pawson, 2006, 174)

A concern with mechanisms requires a shift from an emphasis on the dead end of politico-epistemological purity to a more pragmatic "logic of inquiry" (Pawson, 2006, 178). This would seek to understand the nature and theoretical robustness of the assumptions and practices underpinning interventions, the policy-makers' and practitioners' understanding of the presumed *mechanisms*, and consequently provide a framework for their evaluation (Coalter, 2006; 2007).

Weiss (1997, 520) argues that one of the clearest arguments for the development of program theories and theory-based evaluation is "when prior evaluations show inconsistent results" – clearly applicable to most sport-for-change programs (Coalter, 2007; 2013). The concentration on middle-range mechanisms would also enable a broader view of the world of evidence and encourage researchers and practitioners to draw on a wide range of generic research and practice. From this perspective, the supposed dearth of relevant research in sport-for-development is not a constraint. In fact, a broader knowledge of research and theory is necessary in order to evaluate critically the providers' program theories. This approach has significant advantages for both academic research and program effectiveness (Coalter, 2009):

- It emphasizes the critical distinction between necessary conditions and the *sufficient conditions* required to maximize the potential to achieve desired impacts.
- It requires a systematic re-consideration of the individual deficit model on which much sport-for-development is based.
- It identifies and seeks to resolve different theories of change held by program providers, policy-makers, and funders.
- It assists in the formulation of theoretically coherent and realistic impacts related to program processes.
- It helps evaluators to focus on key questions/mechanisms and it provides feedback about which chain of reasoning breaks down and where it breaks down.

Displacement of scope and going beyond the touchline

A theory of change approach would also assist in addressing issues implicit but largely ignored in sport-for-development rhetoric – displacement of scope (Wagner, 1964). This refers to wrongly generalizing micro-level (program) effects to the meso and macro levels. Wagner (1964, 582) argues that "the problem of differentiated scope is inherent in the tremendous range of sociological subject matter itself." This relates to long-standing debates within social science about the relationship between structure and action, between the individual and the social, or even between values, attitudes, intentions, and behavior. If I may extend Wagner's (1964) concept, the most basic questions related to sport-for-development programs seem to be:

- In what ways are which participants in need of *development*?
- Does participation positively affect the combination of values, attitudes, knowledge, and aptitudes contained in a notion of *development*, for all or some?
- How does the program achieve such impacts and for whom?
- Does this result in an intention to change specific behaviors, for all or some?
- Does this lead to an actual change in behavior, for all or some?

- Does the participants' environment enable desired changes in behavior (Mwaanga, 2003; Jeanes, 2011; Ungar, 2006)?
- If not, how does this contribute to broader processes of social and economic development?

Such questions clearly relate to an individualistic, blame-the-victim perspective of development which many argue is the dominant ideology of sport-for-development (Black, 2010; Kidd, 2008; Coakley, 2011; Darnell & Hayhurst, 2012; Jeanes, 2011). Here it is worth noting Ungar's (2006) comment that it might be better to "change the odds" rather than try to seek to enable individuals to "beat the odds" in environments which frequently do not support behavior change, or offer opportunities for *development*. Ungar's (2006) concern with the resilience of *environments* rather than individuals raises important questions about the manner and extent to which we can "go beyond the touchline."

This also reflects an attempt to address Black's clear and unambiguous warning that:

> DTS [development through sport] interventions will not be successful or sustainable for most participants in the absence of a much wider range of interventions, changes and improvements. DTS practitioners must themselves be persuaded to transcend the "myth of autonomy" to learn from, and collaborate much more systematically with, the diverse panoply of development agents.
>
> (Black 2010, 127)

The contingent nature of impacts

Much research has found no necessary connection between participation in sport and *personal development* (e.g. Fox, 2000; Bowker, Gadbois, & Cornock, 2003; Coalter, 2007; Coalter & Taylor, 2010). Simple assertions about sport and *development*, even at the level of the individual, over-simplify the differential impact of such programs and the strength and direction of the impacts on a variety of individuals. Coalter and Taylor's (2010) cross-national data illustrate a consistent mixture of increases, decreases, and no change in self-evaluations of perceived self-efficacy and self-esteem. Such data call into question the meaning and diagnostic value of the selective "heartfelt narratives" (Hartmann & Kwauk, 2001) often used as evidence of effectiveness by sport-for-development evangelists. As it is likely that *any* social interventions will produce individual successes, such *ad hominem* evidence tells us little about *how* various programs operate and for whom.

Further, the activity – sport – may be much less important than the *attractiveness factors* which encourage people to stay with such programs (Fox, 2000; Sandford, Armour, & Warmington, 2006). More fundamentally, Morris, Sallybanks, Willis, and Makkai (2003) suggest that *any* program where there had previously been none may be the most important factor. Further, research indicates that the nature of the social climate and the social and emotional relationships are as, if not more, important than the activity itself (Witt and Crompton, 1997; Pawson, 2006; Coalter, 2011; 2013). Once again we are drawn to a concern with middle-range mechanisms and Coakley's (1998) distinction between sports as *sites* for, but not necessarily causes of, socialization outcomes and Hartmann's (2003, 134) assertion that "the success of any sports-based social intervention program is largely determined by the strength of its non-sport components." Even the International Working Group on Sport for Development and Peace, unlikely critics, concluded that "the evident benefits appear to be an indirect outcome of the context and social interaction that is possible in sport, rather than a direct outcome of participating in sport" (SDPIWG, 2008, 4).

Consequently the search for a simple *sport-for-development effect* seems naïve. When we move beyond the universalizing rhetoric of the conceptual entrepreneurs, this is hardly a surprise – the presumption of such a general effect could only exist in the rhetoric of the evangelists. As in all forms of social intervention, the nature and extent of impacts will be contingent and vary between programs, a variety of participants, participants' experience, and cultural contexts. In addition, as few sport-for-development organizations seek to achieve their desired impacts and outcomes solely through *sport*, the nature and experience of such programs vary widely. As Pawson *et al.* contend:

> It is through the workings of entire systems of social relationships that any changes in behaviors, events and social conditions are effected.... Rarely if ever is the "same" program equally effective in all circumstances because of the influence of contextual factors.
>
> (Pawson, Greenhalgh, Harvey, & Walshe, 2004, 7)

Wider and more robust research in areas in which many in sport-for-development claim expertise raises significant issues about the universalizing rhetoric expressed by some in sport-for-development. For example, the almost absolutist conviction about the liberatory significance attributed to peer-leader approaches (Nicholls *et al.*, 2011) is in contrast to the more measured, nuanced, and skeptical analyses found in the much more robust health-related research (Wight, 2007). As with other areas of sport-for-development, the pedagogic effectiveness of such approaches is a matter for empirical investigation and cannot rest on affirmation rooted in normative and affective liberation theory.

Of course, even where programs lead to improved self-evaluations and increased knowledge or even intention to change behavior, we are still left with the question as to what this has to do with *development*.

Hope is not a plan: a defense of skepticism

Gramsci's advice to radicals was that they should combine pessimism of the intellect with an optimism of the will (Gramsci, 1994). This represents a succinct summary of the dilemmas which I have faced seeking to take an objective approach to the development of sport-for-development, while working with many innovative and optimist practitioners.

However, the source of my pessimism is not the many ever-optimistic, innovative, and generous practitioners. Rather, my pessimism relates to two issues: (1) the sheer scale of the issues left unexamined by the amorphous and ill-defined notion of *development* and the failure to address systematically issues of displacement of scope; (2) more significant are the evangelists, the self-interested conceptual entrepreneurs and the atmosphere of incestuous amplification in which research is reduced to the role of confirming what they already think they know (e.g. Koss in van Kampen, 2003) and where agnostics are banned from their narrow church.

I agree with Emler (2001, 3) that "we should be suspicious of any convenient convergence of self-serving interests with the greater good." I accept that evaluation is a rational exercise that takes place in a political context (Weiss, 1993). I also acknowledge that rhetoric partly reflects processes of lobbying, persuasion, negotiation and alliance-building. I understand that in a marginal policy (and academic) area such as sport-for-development such processes frequently produce inflated promises, unrealistic desired impacts and outcomes that lack the clarity and intellectual coherence that evaluation criteria should have.

However, the result of this has been that "in its contemporary manifestation, the SDP [sport-for-development-and-peace] emphasis on practice has come, for the most part, at the expense of critical and theoretically-informed reflection" (Black, 2010, 122). This does not imply that sport-for-development needs more cross-sectional descriptive studies of limited generalizability, more heartfelt narratives, or even de-colonizing, feminist-oriented, participatory action research – noble and caring as this might be. Rather, there is a need to step back and reflect critically on what we and, most especially, others might already know (Tacon, 2007; Crabbe, 2008; Coakley, 2011). There is a need to draw on more generic research and analyses on aspects of the processes, impacts, and outcomes often claimed by sport-for-development – to de-reify sport-for-development and raise important theoretical questions about its supposed *newness* and its effectiveness.

I strongly believe that this is a core requirement of academic practice and the pursuit of cognitive understanding – albeit struggling with the affective and normative components present in all social theorizing. It is the duty of an academic to apply informed skepticism to the claims of sport-for-development, and academics can contribute to this by working to privilege the cognitive. Such an approach can contribute to the intellectual and practical development of sport-for-development by placing it within a much wider world of knowledge and research and by theorizing its limitations, as well as outlining its *potential*. Perhaps also the critics of neo-colonialist funders and researchers need to be less imperialistic in their claims for this potential. In this regard I derive intellectual support for my position from one of the original practitioners of sport-for-development. Mwaanga argues that:

To claim that sport can combat HIV and AIDS is not only to overstate the limited capacity of sport but also to dangerously ignore the complexity of HIV and AIDS ... the fundamental question that confronts us ... [is] how can we better understand the interplay between sport, with its limited capacity on one hand, and HIV and AIDS, in its full complexity, on the other.

(Mwaanga, 2010, 66)

While this is related to HIV and AIDS, for me it serves as a general comment on sport-for-development. Further, it echoes Pawson's (2006, 35) more generic comment that "social interventions are always complex systems thrust amidst complex system" – a complexity not admitted by conceptual entrepreneurs, but an essential requirement for academics, researchers, and practitioners. One is reminded of Daniel Patrick Moynihan's comment and warning (http://jaypgreene. com/tag/national-review-online) to "beware of certainty where none exists. Ideological certainty easily degenerates into an insistence upon ignorance."

Leaving poorly defined *development* to hope and *sport* is a poor strategy.

Note

1 The arguments in this short piece are more fully developed in Coalter (2011), especially in the final chapter.

References

Black, D. (2010). The ambiguities of development: Implications for "development through sport". *Sport in Society*, *13*, (1), 121–129.

Bowker, A., Gadbois, S., & Cornock, B. (2003). Sport participation and self-esteem: Variations as a function of gender and role orientation. *Sex Roles*, *49* (1/2), 47–58.

Coakley, J. (1998) *Sport in society: Issues and controversies*. Boston, MA: McGraw Hill.

Coakley, J. (2011). Youth sports: What counts as "positive development?" *Journal of Sport and Social Issues*, *35* (3), 306–324.

Coalter, F. (2006). *Sport-in-development: A Monitoring and evaluation manual*. London: UK Sport.

Coalter, F. (2007). *Sport a wider social role: Who's keeping the score?* London: Routledge.

Coalter, F. (2009). Sport-in-development: Accountability or development? In: R. Levermore & A. Beacom (Eds.), *Sport and international development* (pp. 55–75), Basingstoke: Palgrave Macmillan.

Coalter, F. (2011). *Sport, conflict and youth development*. London: Comic Relief.

Coalter, F. (2013) *Sport for development: What game are we playing?*. Routledge, London.

Coalter, F. & Taylor, J. (2010). *Sport-for-development impact study*. London: Comic Relief, UK Sport and International Development through Sport. www.uksport.gov.uk/ docLib/MISC/FullReport.pdf

Crabbe, T. (2008). Avoiding the numbers game: Social theory, policy and sport's role in the art of relationship building. In: M. Nicholson & R. Hoye (Eds.), *Sport and social capital*. London: Elsevier.

Craib, I. (1984). *Modern social theory: From Parsons to Habermas*. Brighton: Wheatsheaf Books.

Darnell, S., & Hayhurst, L. (2012). Hegemony, postcolonialism and sport for-development: A response to Lindsey and Grattan. *International Journal of Sport Policy and Politics*, *4*, (1), 111–124

Emler, N. (2001). *Self-esteem: The costs and causes of low self-worth*. York: Joseph Rowntree Foundations

Fox, K.R. (2000). The effects of exercise on self-perceptions and self-esteem. In S.J.H. Biddle, K.K. Fox, & S.H. Boutcher (Eds.), *Physical activity and psychological well-being* (pp. 88–117). London: Routledge.

Gramsci, A. (1994). *Letters from prison*, Vols 1 and 2. New York: Columbia University Press.

Hammersley, M. (1995). *The politics of social research*. London: Sage.

Hartmann, D. (2003). Theorising sport as social intervention: A view from the grassroots. *Quest*, *55*, 118–140.

Hartmann, D., & Kwauk, C. (2011). Sport and development: An overview, critique and reconstruction *Journal of Sport and Social Issues*, *35* (3), 284–305.

Hewitt, J. (1998). *The myth of self-esteem: Finding happiness and solving problems in America*. New York: St Martin's Press

Hunter, J. (2001). A cross-cultural comparison of resilience in adolescents. *Journal of Pediatric Nursing*, *16* (3), 172–179.

Janes' Defence Weekly (n.d.) *Incestuous amplification*. Retrieved November 21, 2014, from www.cybercollege.com/ia.htm

Jeanes, R. (2011). Educating through sport? Examining HIV/AIDS education and sport-for-development through the perspectives of Zambian young people. *Sport, Education and Society*, June 13 (iFirst online), 1–19.

Kay, T. (2009). Developing through sport: Evidencing sport impacts on young people. *Sport in Society*, *12* (9), 1177–1191.

Kidd, B. (2008). A new social movement: Sport for development and peace. *Sport in Society*, *11* (4), 370–380.

Kruse, S.E. (2006). Review of Kicking AIDS Out: Is sport an effective tool in the fight against HIV/AIDS? Unpublished draft report to NORAD.

Lindsey, I., & Grattan, A. (2012). An "international movement"? Decentering sport for development within Zambian communities. *International Journal of Sport Policy and Politics*, *4*, (1), 91–110.

Moynihan, D. (n.d.) *The Moynihan Challenge: 5 Years Late*. Retrieved November 21, 2014, from http://jaypgreene.com/tag/national-review-online

Morris, L., Sallybanks, J., Willis, K., & Makkai, T. (2003). *Sport, physical activity and anti-social behavior*. Canberra: Australian Institute of Criminology.

Mwaanga, O. (2003). HIV/AIDS at-risk adolescent girls' empowerment through participation in top level football and edusport in Zambia. MSc thesis submitted to the Institute of Social Science at the Norwegian University of Sport and PE, Oslo.

Mwaanga, O. (2010). Sport for addressing HIV/AIDS: Explaining our convictions. *Leisure Studies Association Newsletter*, *85*, 61–67.

Nicholls, S., Giles, A.R., & Sethna, C. (2011). Perpetuating the "lack of evidence" discourse in sport for development: Privileged voices, unheard stories and subjugated knowledge. *International Review for the Sociology of Sport*, *46* (3), 249–264.

Pawson, R. (2001). *Evidence based policy: In search of a method*. London: Queen Mary, University of London.

Pawson, R. (2006). *Evidence-based policy: A realist perspective.* London: Sage.

Pawson, R., Greenhalgh, T., Harvey, G., & Walshe, K. (2004). Realist synthesis: An introduction. ESRC Research Methods Program University of Manchester.

Pisani, E. (2008). *The wisdom of whores: Bureaucrats, brothels and the business of AIDS.* London: Granta Books.

Sandford, R.A., Armour, K.M., & Warmington, P.C. (2006). Re-engaging disaffected youth through physical activity programs. *British Educational Research Journal, 32* (2), 251–271.

Sport for Development International Working Group (2008). *Harnessing the power of sport for development and peace.* Toronto: Right to Play.

Sugden, J. (2010). Critical left-realism and sport interventions in divided societies. *International Review for the Sociology of Sport, 45* (3), 258–272.

Tacon, R. (2007). Football and social inclusion: Evaluating social policy. *Managing Leisure: An International Journal, 12* (1), 1–23.

Ungar, M. (2006). Resilience across cultures. *British Journal of Social Work, 38* (2), 218–235.

van Kampen, H. (Ed.) (2003). *A report on the expert meeting "The Next Step" on sport and development.* Amsterdam: NCDO. Retrieved November 21, 2014, from www. toolkitsportdevelopment.org/html/resources/0E/0E00BE53-2C02-46EA-8AC5-A139AC4363DC/Report%20of%20Next%20Step%20Amsterdam.pdf

Wagner, H.L. (1964). Displacement of scope: A problem of the relationship between small-scale and large-scale sociological theories. *The American Journal of Sociology, 69,* (6), 571–584.

Weiss, C.H. (1993). Where politics and evaluation research meet. *Evaluation Practice, 14* (1), 93–106.

Weiss, C.H. (1997). How can theory-based evaluation make greater headway? *Evaluation Review, 21* (4), 501–524.

Wight, D. (2007). Theoretical bases for teacher- and peer-delivered sexual health promotion. *Health Education, 108* (1), 10–28.

Witt, P.A. and Crompton, J.L. (1997). The protective factors framework: A key to programming for benefits and evaluating results. *Journal of Parks and Recreation Administration, 15* (3), 1–18.

Woodcock, A., Cronin, O., & Forde, S. (2012). Quantitative evidence for the benefits of moving the goalposts: a sport for development project in rural Kenya. *Evaluation and Program Planning, 35,* 370–381.

20 The critical participatory paradigm and its implications

Oscar Mwaanga and Kola Adeosun

Introduction

The once high-flying Sport for Development and Peace (SDP) balloon may be deflating and hence descending due to several holes. In this analogy, the balloon represents the popularity of SDP in the last decade, while the holes represent flaws in the conceptualization and consequently the problematic practices and research of the SDP field.

One big hole that has been rupturing the field since its inception in the late 1990s is the failure to question the fundamental assumption of SDP relating to what knowledge is authentic, how this knowledge should be created, and who is researching and being researched. A case in point, the first author[1] has observed more than once SDP champions who pilot research endeavors, embrace the simple and rigid linearity of top-down research approaches, as opposed to negotiating balanced approaches, which is more in keeping with the rhetoric.

These top-down models tend to perpetuate the covert power relations that surround the Global North and Global South,[2] resulting in research that continues to flow one way, top-down, clearly exemplifying research done on, as opposed to done with, end-users (Mwaanga, 2012). Certainly Keim and de Coning (in this volume) emphasize this point, noting that in the SDP field, the majority of literature is published in the North, even though the majority of projects run in the South. Consequently, research endeavors reach their conclusions based on northern ideological standpoints, while viewing the Global South as stereotypically inferior or incapable, thereby reproducing the suppressive dispositions of neo-colonialism, the "cultural legacy of colonialism" (Mwaanga, 2012, 22). As a result, people subject to SDP, under this neo-colonial influence, are not the ones deciding the components of their progress (Mwaanga, 2012). Surely, an authentic SDP research will be one that emancipates all vested interests from the shackles of neo-colonialism.

This chapter presents three critiques of the dominant research paradigms that permeate SDP. These research paradigms draw canons from objectivist and positivist meta-theories, generally centering "on the idea of using scientific methods to gain knowledge" (Denscombe, 2010). Additionally, Kuhn (2003) argued that the dominant research paradigms are "predicated on the assumption that the scientific community knows what the world is like"; that its means to knowledge, for instance, are not socially constructed. This essentially situates them as undemocratic and devoid of political, cultural, and social location, which makes SDP researchers insensible to how such location affects research findings (Hunt, 2010). Consequently, we offer the critical participatory paradigm (CPP) as a tool and an alternative paradigm meant to democratize SDP research and knowledge development.

Indeed, *our first critique* stems from the neo-colonial blanket of SDP, replicated in current SDP research processes, which often silence indigenous voices, resembling the historical orthodoxy once associated with colonialist practices that place value on Northern approaches and view Global Southern ideas as inferior (Annett & Mayuni, 2013). Coalter (in this volume) further suggests that SDP research is subdued within neo-colonialist suppression, which acts as one of the causative factors of continual uneven power relations. Moreover, Darnell and Hayhurst (2012) recognize the neo-colonialist tendencies of SDP research and indeed submit that the time is ripe to pursue a decolonizing research process, one that displaces the antecedents of colonialism. This advocates a post-colonial approach to future SDP research processes, decolonizing the structures of hegemony that are in place.

Although we agree with these sentiments (and many more), enduring as a noble and justified cause, given the deep-rooted neo-colonial research of contemporary SDP, where the Global North dictates the development direction of the South (Mwaanga, 2012), we must outline that the current post-colonial critique offers little more than a series of ad hoc criticisms of the neo-colonial research process apparent in SDP. Indeed, McEwan (2008) suggests that the post-colonial critique has become institutionalized, representing the dominant Northern worldview, therefore making the current post-colonial critique of SDP research another barren academic endeavor firmly situated within hegemonic theorization. Consequently, we contend that to actually decolonize the research process there is a requirement for a philosophical and methodological framework to guide the critical engagement of end-users, whose transformed (or untransformed) lives are the paramount measure of authenticity in SDP interventions.

The second critique brings to the fore the undemocratic research propensity of SDP, where Northern perspectives are "privileged at the expense of other discourse" (Mwaanga & Banda, 2014, 175), especially within the knowledge-creation process. This is highlighted by Spaaij and Jeanes (2013), who point to the historical hierarchy of researchers as a limitation to authentic dialogue and genuine democratic action in SDP research, because those who consider themselves knowledgeable rarely consider the advice of those they consider to know nothing (Freire, 1970). Thus, this historical hierarchy further prevents the development of critical pedagogy in end-users (Spaaij & Jeans, 2013).

Nevertheless, the aim of this chapter is not simply to discredit current SDP research paradigms, but to draw attention to inadequacies in order to highlight effectively a framework for change. Indeed, it demonstrates ways in which the majority of SDP development scholars can begin to include their marginalized research subjects in the knowledge-creation process. The aim, of course, is to displace the long-standing undemocratic vertical relationship of SDP, where the SDP policy end-user knowledge is under-valued, replicating the arrogance that comes with many conventional Northern development programs (McGee, 2002).

The third critique recognizes the naivety of researchers and practitioners in SDP, where we (the Global North) neglect or refuse to subjectively critique our biographical background in the knowledge-creation process. Without doubt, this lack of encouragement to emancipate ourselves severely hinders the possibility of emancipating others through our research. In his research, Mwaanga has used participatory workshops as platforms where all vested interests in the research process present and discuss their biographical background. For that reason, Mwaanga (2012, 295) has called for scholars to step out of their "comfortable zones of privilege," a plea reflected in Freire's critique.

Freire (1970) suggested that all merchants of revolutionary change must first deconstruct themselves to attain the knowledge of reality before they can deconstruct the current practice at hand. Otherwise the cyclical process of SDP will continue with undemocratic research and faulty policies leading to ineffective outcomes. Easterly (2007) exemplifies this cyclical process in relation to *foreign aid*, where celebrities continually raise money in an attempt to abruptly end world poverty; but he details their misguided beliefs as ignorant to the knowledge of reality. Of course, if poverty and underdevelopment were that easy to solve it would have already been solved. Mwaanga's experience as a Global Southern practitioner has taught that cultural problems such as poverty, underdevelopment, or HIV/AIDS cannot be solved simply through funding, foreign aid, or intensified Global Northern campaigns. Those who still believe in these approaches need to emancipate themselves if we are to attain sustainable progress in international SDP (Mwaanga & Banda, 2014).

Easterly (2007) labels the unemancipated as "planners" who view the world homogeneously and believe they have in their research conclusions the answers to the Global South's problems. In contrast, the "searchers" are emancipated to recognize social reality, trusting their Global Southern opposites, asking questions as to how they can aid local communities and recognizing the need to include their Global Southern partners in the process of decision-making. Unquestionably, the dichotomy of the "planner" and the "searcher" is established out of the cultural divide between the outsider and the insider. Subsequently, outsiders tend to be planners while insiders tend to be searchers, and therefore the Global Northern outsider (the powerful) survey the world from the top and see almost nothing of the bottom (Easterly, 2007).

Mwaanga, an advocate of home-grown development, argues that is one reason why many Northern academics who have researched SDP in Zambia are not cognizant of Ubuntu, the organizational philosophy of the EduSport Foundation. Ubuntu's primary focus is the people; indeed EduSport programs are "centered on the interests and needs of the people we serve." Clearly this is crucial in understanding the developmental mechanisms within the EduSport Foundation, yet its presence has eluded many Northern academic research reports on the organization (www.edusport.org.zm).

Now we propose the critical participatory paradigm (CPP) both as a philosophical and pragmatic remedy for the critiques presented above. The CPP, through its set imperatives, encourages direct lines of communication and collaborative community-building (Mwaanga, 2012), and can be defined as *critical* because it does not pretend that history, culture, gender, race, geography, or power play no part in research, but rather looks to these important variables as launch-pads for a realistic option. Furthermore, the CPP is participatory because it aims to work in collaboration with indigenous people, allowing policy end-users to be placed alongside the researcher in the knowledge-creation process. In addition, the CPP is also *emancipatory* to the extent that it aims to awaken critical consciousness in indigenous people, so that they may adequately interact with others and change their social world. In this way the authenticity of research conclusions is validated because end-users have a sizeable input on such conclusions.

The critiques presented in this chapter are supported by two main sources of evidence. First, the chapter draws evidence from the empirical investigation of the first author's post-graduate research, which focused on empowering girls and people living with HIV/AIDS through SDP in Zambia. Second, the first author, as a colonized "other" and a leading sub-Saharan SDP activist of close to 20 years, has lived and struggled through the imperialistic notions which betray SDP, and thus provides critical insights from personal experiential knowledge. Indeed, the first author's development of several indigenous SDP initiatives, including Go Sisters, peer leadership, and Kicking AIDS Out, stand as testament to this struggle.

Critical participatory paradigm

This section will attempt to explain the CPP through its underlying philosophical principles, framed as ontological, epistemological, and political imperatives for research practice.

The CPP ontology, or simply the way we think or theories about what it means to exist in the social world, champions the idea of a subjective–objective ontology which submits that there is a deeply participatory feeling to all things, a felt "reciprocity" (Abram, 1996). In this subjective–objective ontology, Heron and Reason (1997) contend that to experience anything is to participate, and to participate is to mold, alter, and shape. Consequently the world is an interactive and participatory network that exists between the researcher and the indigenous people (Reason & Bradbury, 2008). This reciprocity is the connection *felt* between people and communities, it is a *fertile soil* through which to grow and maintain relationships that pave the way for positive mutual exchange with the potential to result in authentic collaboration in both development and knowledge creation. Hence the ontological imperative recognizes the importance of a positive connection with indigenous people leading to reciprocal partnerships, breaking what Freire (1970) called the "culture of silence." Besides, the indigenous understanding of their locality makes them invaluable for any potential social change. As Easterly (2007) demonstrates, reversing the effects of colonialism requires the indigenous people to participate in their own development, suggesting reforms influenced by home-grown knowledge and people, who recognize and respect local customs. It is partly this ontological belief that humbles "searchers" in their SDP engagement, and sets ontological cornerstones for the inclusion of research subjects in the research process, thus overthrowing the neo-colonial divide of SDP.

Indeed, Grix (2002) suggests that ontology forms the foundation of research endeavors, after which one's epistemological position must follow. Epistemology is what we think can be learned about the social world (Fleetwood, 2005). CPP epistemology, or what is called the "extended epistemology" extends beyond theory into experience and practice, obliging the researcher to engage in research *with* people as opposed to *on* or *about* them (Reason & Bradbury, 2008). This extended epistemology brings experiential knowledge to the center, and thus stands in opposition to common practices, which for example allows parachute academics to "float in and out" of local communities with preconceived and rigid notions of indigenous knowledge. This is a common practice opposed by Spaaij and Jeanes (2013), who have recommended that all so-called "researchers" should spend time in the community they are researching to gain knowledge and democratically engage with local groups. Therefore this imperative sees the production of knowledge as an interactive process, between the researcher and research subjects, in a collaborative exercise searching for truth (Mwaanga, 2012). All collaborators in this process must appreciate that the production of knowledge is a positive process of engagement, commitment, communication, action, and reflection (Finn, 1994), but also one that is underpinned by strong invincible current powers. In short, the extended epistemology forces us to see knowledge creation both as a relationship-building and emancipatory process.

Within the extended epistemology the "searchers" engage the world in four interrelated ways (experiential, presentational, practical, and propositional), allowing interaction with the social world – be it people, societies, or events – in a proximal manner (Reason & Bradbury, 2008). First, experiential knowledge is attained via direct contact with people and places, and is therefore subjective to the "searcher" and difficult to explain. Second, presentational knowledge develops through the filtering of experiential knowledge, represented as ideas, descriptions, and narratives told by the "searcher." Third, practical knowledge is developed through increased exposure to practical experiences and becomes the intricate knowledge of how things work and how to do certain things, embodied in the skills and practical capabilities (Breu & Peppard, 2001). Fourth, propositional knowledge is the "searchers'" theories regarding the social world that is expressed by the knowledge formulated in research conclusions. Therefore, this imperative challenges the positivist dichotomy that separates the researcher and the end-user, helping us to realize that knowledge is relative to surroundings and promoting this as "true knowledge" is power. Therefore, the epistemological imperative empowers policy end-users through the creation of a systematic framework that questions the dominant knowledge systems from the reference point of local knowledge.

Lastly, the political imperative represents the subjective consciousness of the CPP, underpinned by the philosophies of praxis and reflexivity. Praxis, according to Freire (1970), is the "reason for existence," a practice of freedom that advocates authentic liberation through awakening the critical consciousness of research participants, so that they might act and reflect upon their world, in order to transform it. It is this critical consciousness that begins the development of praxis, which is the organized struggle to regain power through the development of knowledge (Freire, 1970).

Giving the aforementioned neo-colonial origins of SDP research, which has allowed the *powerful* to interfere, decide, and state the development path of the *less powerful* (usually the Global South), it is essential that praxis is used to reclaim power, history, and knowledge (Mwaanga, 2012; Smith, 2012). Indeed, it is only when the *less powerful* discover their oppression by the *powerful* that there can be an illumination of intellectual understanding, beginning the struggle for freedom (Freire, 1970). Because praxis cannot be reduced to mere intellectual capabilities or the attainment of theoretical knowledge, the idea of true praxis is *action* committed through human activity, the meaning of praxis is the combination of theory and practice to develop critical awareness (Mwaanga, 2012; Freire, 1970). Together, praxis and reflexivity occur simultaneously, since the achievement of end-user praxis is reliant on the reflexivity of researchers to trust in their research participants' abilities to reason and contribute to their local community. As a result, end-user praxis will lead to the increased development and identification of local "searchers."

Reflexivity, on the other hand, urges the researcher to continually question their biographical make-up in relation to the construction of research policies, breaking down pillars of positivistic evidence and allowing the researcher to acknowledge their contribution as an outsider (Mwaanga, 2012). As indicated previously, there is a cyclical process to SDP research because the SDP movement does not offer clear guidelines for researcher reflexivity, which results in a positivistic research orientation, and that advocates the neutrality and objectivity of researchers (Mwaanga, 2012).

We acknowledge that any researcher who has recognized, researched, and written about the neo-colonial and hegemonic compression of SDP is truly committed to transforming the unjust order, but because of their background they believe that they must be in the vanguard of that transformation, as they do not trust the indigenous people to carry it out (Freire, 1970). This is a detrimental act, as Freire (1970) further explains that the necessary requirement of revolutionary change is *trust*. Therefore, reflexivity emancipates the researcher to attain the knowledge of reality, to trust in their research participants, and discover themselves simply as collaborators in the transformation; it is in this reflection that the dichotomy of the "planner" and "searcher" is bridged.

Ultimately, praxis and reflexivity function as instruments to view SDP from alternate paradigms, reminding the researcher to factor in their backgrounds, while awakening the critical awareness of end-users to the struggle for their liberation (Mwaanga, 2012).

Conclusion

This chapter has identified a number of flaws in current SDP research processes, bringing forth key issues that limit the development of effective and community-specific programs. As a springboard, this chapter has critiqued the neo-colonial compression of SDP research, which silences indigenous voices and gives precedence to "research experts" in deciding the development path of their research subjects. Further to this, the assumptions of knowledge made by the Global North corrupt social reality, circulating the myth that outsiders know best, and as a result there is an undemocratic research process that distances end-users in the knowledge-creation process. Unquestionably, unless SDP encourages its researchers to subjectively critique and deconstruct themselves, the uncontrollable descent of the SDP balloon will continue. In order to re-inflate the SDP balloon, this chapter has argued for the CPP, through its imperatives to decolonize, democratize, emancipate and subjectively critique in the research process, which draws us closer to authentic and legitimate development outcomes within SDP.

To sum up, the need to adopt a process which engages with end-users as the spearhead of policy development has been stated, and the CPP is a means to achieve this. First, the CPP presents a philosophical and pragmatic framework that permits end-users a sizeable input in documenting their existence and their future, deconstructing conventional power relations and ideologies, while conversely allowing researchers to humbly negotiate the complexities of the research phenomenon.

Second, its awakening of praxis and reflexivity aids the researcher in revising their conventional characteristics, which obstruct revolutionary change and maintain their position as "planner." However, as Mwaanga (2012) contends, the awakening of praxis and reflexivity must be followed with action. Certainly, to change social reality it requires a researcher who is willing to act and reconstruct themselves from their "traditional sovereign positions" (Mwaanga, 2012, 293) and equally join the struggle for liberation. It is in this show of solidarity that end-users will discover that they are themselves the praxis of their liberation, realizing human beings as the foundation of knowledge, information, enterprise, and labor (Freire, 1970).

At this juncture, though, it is important to state that SDP is still in its infancy (Kidd 2008), and the CPP is an early remedy to wrestle SDP from the shackles of neo-colonialism. Clearly, knowledge creation and research are a suitable starting point in the emancipation and empowerment of SDP end-users.

Notes

1 The first author, Dr. Oscar Mwaanga, is the founder of the EduSport Foundation, which is the first SDP organization in Zambia which he set up in 1997 and formally registered in 1999. Oscar is renowned as one of the leading activists of the sub-Saharan SDP movement of the last century.
2 The binary of Global North and Global South is "of course, geographically inaccurate and too generalised to encompass the complexities within and between nations, but it is perhaps the least problematic means of distinguishing between relatively wealthy countries and continents [Europe] and relatively poorer ones [Africa]" (McEwan, 2008, 13–14).

References

Abram, D. (1996). *The spell of the sensations*. New York: Pantheon.
Annett, E., & Mayuni, S. (2013). Sport, development and African culture. In A. Parker & D. Vinson (Eds.), *Youth sport, physical activity and play: Policy, intervention and participation* (pp. 96–110). London: Routledge.
Breu, B., & Peppard, J. (2001). The participatory paradigm for applied information systems research (pp. 243–252). *Paper at the 9th European Conference on Information Systems*, Bled, Slovenia, June 27–29.
Darnell, S., & Hayhurst, L. (2012). Hegemony, postcolonialism and sport-for-development: A response to Lindsey and Grattan. *International Journal of Sport Policy and Politics*, *4* (1), 111–124.
Denscombe, M. (2010). *Ground rules for social research: Guidelines for Good practice* (2nd edn.). Maidenhead: Open University Press.
Easterly, W. (2007). *The white man's burden*. Oxford: Oxford University Press.
Finn, J. (1994). The promise of participatory research. *Journal of Progressive Human Services*, *5* (2), 25–42.
Fleetwood, S. (2005). Ontology in organization and management studies: A critical realist perspective. *Organisation Articles*, *12* (2), 197–222.
Freire, P. (1970). *The pedagogy of the oppressed*. New York: Seabury Press.
Grix, J. (2002). Introducing students to the generic terminology of social research. *Politics*, *22* (3), 175–186.
Grix, J. (2010). Introducing "Hard Interpretivism" and "Q" Methodology. *Journal of Leisure Studies*, *29* (4), 457–467.
Heron, J., & Reason, P. (1997). A participatory inquiry paradigm. *Qualitative Inquiry*, *3* (3), 274–294.
Hunt, M.R. (2010). "Active waiting": Habits and the practice of conducting qualitative research. *International Journal of Qualitative Methods*, *9* (1), 69–76.
Kidd, B. (2008). A new social movement: Sport for development and peace. *Journal of Sport in Society*, *11* (4), 370–380.
Kuhn, T. (2003). A role for history, 1962. In: G. Delanty & P. Strydom (Eds.), *Philosophies of the social science: The classic and contemporary readings* (pp. 72–77). Maidenhead: Open University Press.
McEwan, C. (2008). Post-development. In V. Desai & R.B. Potter (Eds.), *Companion to development studies* (2nd edn.; pp. 124–128). London: Hodder.
McGee, R. (2002). Participating in Development. In U. Kothari & M. Minogue (Eds.), *Development theory and practice: Critical perspectives* (pp. 92–116). Basingstoke: Palgrave.

Mwaanga, O. (2012). Understanding and improving sport empowerment for people living with HIV/AIDS in Zambia. Unpublished PHD Thesis at Leeds Metropolitan University.

Mwaanga, O. & Banda, D. (2014). A postcolonial approach to understanding sport-based empowerment of people living with HIV/AIDS (PLWHA) in Zambia: The case of the cultural philosophy of Ubuntu. *Journal of Disability & Religion, 18* (2), 173–191.

Reason, P., & Bradbury, H. (2008). *Handbook of action research: Participative inquiry and practice* (2nd edn.). London: Sage Publications.

Smith, L.T. (2012). *Decolonising methodologies: Research and indigenous peoples* (2nd edn.). London: Zed Books.

Spaaij, R., & Jeanes, R. (2013). Education for social change? A Freirean critique of sport for development and peace. *Journal of Physical Education and Sport Pedagogy, 18* (4), 442–457.

21 Perspectives from the South

Sport and development as a priority on the international policy agenda

Marion Keim and Christo de Coning

Introduction

The opportunity to imagine what potential sport holds for the next few decades provides one with an exciting freedom to dream about what is possible. *What if* sport can fully come to its right not only because of its popularity as a competitive activity, but also as a major vehicle for development? *What if* sport and development initiatives in the South received their rightful focus from the South itself, but also their rightful support from the Northern Hemisphere?

Perspectives on the future of sport, from a Southern perspective, are certainly embedded and rooted in the notion of the broader development role of sport and recreation in communities. This vision shows that sport activities, recreation, game, play, and leisure are deeply embedded into the everyday lifestyle of African and other communities. Challenges related to health, social inclusion, gender, disability, physical education, youth, community development, and peace have been the basis for numerous sport development programs and projects over the past 25 years, many funded by the North and implemented in the South. The Millennium Development Goals (MDGs) were established as international development targets in 2001 and are presently reviewed, with Agenda 2020 on the rise.

This chapter will draw on the results of two recent studies, namely "The case for sport" (de Coning, 2014) and "Sport policy in Africa" (Keim & de Coning, 2014). The study will also draw on the research work of the International Network for Sport and Development, based at the University of Ghana under the chairperson-ship of Dr. Bella Bello Bitugu. The first publication focuses on socio-economic development benefits in sport and development, while the second publication focuses on African policy mapping research in 11 African countries. We will give a perspective from the South on sport and development issues, including emerging international policy developments.

The emergence of sport and development policies and programs on the policy agenda of multilateral organizations, corporations as well as NGOs and governments, is expected to become a major priority in the next period. This chapter shows that, increasingly, the interfaces between competitive and high-performance sport, on the one hand, and development programs aimed at increased activity of all citizens and focusing on socio-economic benefits of sport and recreation, on the other, are becoming major priorities. This chapter focuses on the increased attention that policy development is enjoying regarding sport and development in Africa and, more recently, in Brazil and the Caribbean, the emergence of results-based monitoring and evaluation, and the increased recognition by governments and multilateral organizations such as the UN and the IOC, for the role that sport and recreation play in socio-economic development. Attention will also be given to South–North relationships in this respect, as well as the role of universities in providing research support.

Sport and development

A recent workshop of the International Network for Sport and Development, held in Accra, Ghana during March 2014 showed that different views exist regarding the understanding of development and the relationship between sport and development. Whereas "sport and development" has emerged as a major new theme, with the emphasis on the use of sport as a vehicle to facilitate development priorities, the focus in the past has mainly been on sport science, sport nutrition, sport management, and sport psychology. Increasingly, more attention has also been given to the conceptual differences between the concepts "sport and development," "sport for development," and "sport development." Scholars such as Sanders, Phillips, and Vanreusel (2012) have also cautioned researchers and practitioners against misconceptions and the dangers of an advocacy approach where sport and development initiatives are promoted without proper consideration of the possible negative impacts of such initiatives.

It is clear that many Northern Hemisphere partners are struggling to understand that in countries such as South Africa, the concept of *development* has been mainstreamed in all government service delivery, and that in this country, but also many other Southern Hemisphere countries, poverty alleviation, socio-economic development, and the quest for sustainable development are closely linked with any association regarding sport and development. Increasingly, the developmental challenges of high-performance athletes from disadvantaged communities are also becoming an important area of emphasis.

The interpretations of concepts in the field of sport and development are, maybe more so than in other fields, dependent on geographical location and cultural context of scholars, researchers, and stakeholders of sport and development projects, since sport, recreation and play are so much part of our makeup. The emphasis in sport and development initiatives in the South has been on *sport* and *recreation*, as well as increasingly recognizing the important role of *game* and *play*. The following statement by a Kenyan respondent in the ICESSD Study of a Sport Policy Index (Keim & de Coning, 2014) illustrates this point.

[Traditional] sport and games enhance health and fitness of all citizens. They are crucial for physical, social, emotional growth and development of individual. They bring out important virtues such as honesty, tolerance, courage, confidence and enhance physical and spiritual well-being of people. They are part and parcel of the tradition way of life, games enhance skills to adult life, and youth acquires warfare tactics. Traditional sport and games activities included dance, wrestling, ajua, bao, foster social cohesion, communal, responsibility and group survival. Traditional sport and games form part of national heritage. They are symbols for our cultural diversity. They are means by which the young and old unite, show solidarity, and convey messages.

As is evident from the research report "The case for sport: Benefits of sport and recreation in the Western Cape" (de Coning, 2014), it is now generally accepted that sport and recreation have a direct impact on increased economic growth and development as well as a significant impact in social development areas, such as health, education, community safety, human and social capital development, and youth at risk. "The case for sport" showed that the contribution of sport and recreation to GDP per capita (more than 2.2 percent in South Africa and Rand 8 billion in the Western Cape) as well as to employment (60,000 jobs in the Western Cape) is significant, and that sport has impacted on social development and at-risk youth in significant ways (de Coning, 2014).

Human rights and cultural diversity in South–North relations

Although we assume that "The practice of physical education and sport is a fundamental right for all" (Article 1 of the International Charter of Physical Education and Sport; UNESCO, 1978), accessible to most and part of most children's upbringing, it is not the case. Out of about 122 million schoolchildren worldwide, only 60 percent are receiving a secondary education, many fewer are getting physical education (Zlotnik, 2005). Countries such as South Africa do not have physical education as part of their school curriculum, and in other countries increasingly less time is set aside for physical education and school sport. A recent study has shown, for example, that girls' participation in sport in the Western Cape is the lowest in the whole of South Africa (de Coning, 2014).

Although sport has developed into a huge field of business and an increasing field of research globally, the real impact of sport for development worldwide is still an issue of contention. In the sport and development field the number of scientific papers and books published by researchers in the North about sport and development is not at all comparable to the South, which is a strange phenomenon, considering that most sport and development projects are situated in the South.

Taking present local and global developments into consideration, we need to be cautious of mono-cultural/culturally dominant, one-sided research studies and interpretations of their results in the sport and development field, especially in terms of North–South collaboration. Our outcomes could be so much richer if they were based on mutually beneficial research collaborations between scholars from the North and South. In this context we ask for reflection on the following questions related to approaching sport and development differently:

- *What if* the North and South re-examine their relationship with respect to sport and development to develop future priorities to collaborate toward our common goals reflected in the MDGs and in Agenda 2020?
- *What if* there was a jointly owned strategic plan for sport and development initiatives?
- *What if* we revisit the developmental role of universities engaged in sport and development issues?
- *What if* we ensured that more South-driven and -conducted research initiatives take place, with publication output and PhDs supported by the North (co-authorship)?
- *What if* we contribute to the further development of a global sport policy index that has been started in Africa?

Challenges to partnerships and networking

Sport is seen to play an important role as a promoter for development, peace, and social integration (UN, 2005) in different geographical, cultural, and political contexts. Although one of the positive developments of the twenty-first century is that we have many important stakeholders on board already supporting the case for sport – from UN to grass-roots level – the challenge for many of these efforts is very often meaningful collaboration with mutual benefits and sustainability.

The last decade saw numerous sport and development projects implemented all over the world. Some only lately have received international recognition through initiatives like Sport for Social Change, Beyond Sport, Changemakers, SportAccord, UNICEF, Peace and Sport, or other international sports awards. These projects are often conducted in countries of the Global South, whereas funding generally comes from the Global North. These projects are conducted mostly by civil society organizations and volunteers in the South who cannot afford to attend national and international conferences on sport and development, including events such as Beyond Sport. However, they deliver the results on the home base, although they are often not empowered to monitor and evaluate their results properly, and need to rely on universities or outside stakeholders to measure their outcomes. This results in a lack of true empowerment and ownership by Southern grassroots partners, which impacts on the sustainability of sport for development projects, reflected in their program design, implementation, monitoring and evaluation (M&E) and research, publications, and tertiary education in the field, particularly in Africa.

If sport projects directed at social change are appropriately implemented, monitored, evaluated, and sustained, they hold promise to play a role in the process of development and transformation of a country (Keim, 2009). The importance of improved sport policy with a development focus, implemented with a development emphasis, as well as development priorities in M&E, are therefore obvious.

The importance of sport and development policy, implementation, and monitoring and evaluation

A recent study by the Interdisciplinary Centre for Sport Science and Development (ICESSD) at University of the Western Cape (UWC) has shown that an increased emphasis on the quality of public policies on sport is evident in Africa. This study, that included 11 African countries, also investigated the relationship between sport policy and planning and implementation levels. Various tendencies concerning the monitoring and evaluation of sport and development in these countries show that governments and NGOs are increasingly establishing such systems. Specific trends are also emerging concerning international protocols, gender issues, physical education as part of school curricula, the impact of sport and health, and other policy-related developments. It is thus clear that sport and development are increasingly part of the public policies of governments in Africa and that the potential exists to explore these priorities with partners in the Northern Hemisphere.

The research under discussion (Keim & de Coning, 2014) found that the existence and quality of public policy and legislation concerning sport and development varied greatly among the countries that were studied. In some instances, sport policy contains contemporary approaches and some of the world's cutting-edge approaches to sport and development; in other instances both policy and legislation on sport were found to be virtually absent. The study found that huge opportunities exist to share policy experiences across the continent and that collaborative action among African countries, which is at a very low level at present, may have a drastic impact on the improvement of sport policies and their support systems.

It was found that where good policies and legislation existed, public sector officials had far more guidance as to what to do and which priorities to pursue to ensure results and good performance. However, it was also found that countries where policies and legislation were virtually absent or of poor quality somehow still reported high levels of compliance with international protocols.

An exciting feature of the ICESSD African Sports Index study was that very valuable experiences on the various elements of sport policy and implementation were found in the different countries. These issues are briefly reported on below.

With regards to the topic at hand, namely the status and standing of sport policy and legislation in the selected African countries, it was found that other than great variance in policy content, an assessment of the policy system as a whole showed that severe weaknesses existed in the policy processes followed by African governments, and policy capacity, including policy analysis capacity, was of a poor standard and often non-existent. However, various good practices and successes existed in many dimensions of the policies, such as in the support for traditional games, the promotion of physical education in schools and special programs for vulnerable groups. The following section will present some of the key findings in this respect.

In terms of policy coherence it was found that the harmonization and coordination among different policies need to be improved. As limited results will be attained if sport policy is pursued and implemented on its own, it is essential that policy interfaces in other areas be realized, since the implementation of sport activities are often, if not usually, dependent on these. Good examples include infrastructure development that is usually developed by a department of public works, or the realization of physical education in schools, which is typically an education function. These linkages need to be consciously pursued.

Regarding policy process, the study showed that very few, if any, of the countries followed a sequential and comprehensive process to ensure not only good policy but also high levels of buy-in from stakeholders. Public policy processes are well developed and various models are in use in Africa, but these processes are seldom facilitated in a comprehensive manner, and this is very evident in the case of sport policy in Africa. Policy process models have been specially adapted for Africa (Mutahaba, Baguma, & Halfani, 1993; Cloete & de Coning, 2011) and have proven their worth in other sectors. In essence, the various steps in the policy process ensure that critical policy issues are addressed.

In terms of monitoring and evaluation, the African Sport Policy publication (Keim & de Coning, 2014) showed that although some macro-economic, public finance, and other government performance areas were being reported on in terms of normal government (public finance) reporting systems, government-wide, a Results-based Monitoring and Evaluation System (RBMES) was not yet established in the vast majority of countries that we studied. In fact, the only exception was South Africa, which has adopted a comprehensive approach (Maralack, Keim, & de Coning, 2013) and which has a Performance Monitoring and Review Department in the Presidency. This system includes M&E policies by the Presidency, National Treasury, and Department of Public Service and Administration. Although detailed monitoring frameworks with results-based outcomes and indicators have been developed at national and provincial levels, a detailed sport and development framework for monitoring has not yet been developed, and officials have reported work in progress in this respect. However, many other indicators, such as on social justice and gender, as well as education and health information, are available.

An RBMES for sport and development should thus be regarded as a bottom-up exercise, and support from multilateral agencies is possible, as some monitoring frameworks already exist at the level of the UNDP's Human Development Report, the World Bank and through the MDGs, where specific development goals and indicators have been developed that also relate to sport and development. Monitoring on sport and development at the continental level is also conducted by the AU through NEPAD and the African Peer Review Mechanism (APRM), although specific indicators on sport and development are still inadequate. It is proposed that a monitoring or tracking system be developed to monitor performance on sport and development initiatives, as such a system may feed directly into initiating M&E systems in member states.

The role of universities

Due to globalization in sport and multi-stakeholder involvement, including North–South collaboration, there is a great need for evidence-based sports interventions, programming, management, program monitoring, and evaluation of sport for development and peace programs, some geared towards the MDGs and Agenda 2020.

There is also a need for appropriate and sustainable approaches to sports programming, curriculum development, capacity building/training, research, advocacy, professional development, and delivery. When it comes to sport and sport development programs, universities in the South and the North therefore need to take as a point of departure the broader national context, as well as the realities of their country and the countries they work in, and in the case of African countries, the African continent as a whole.

There is evidence that African states, such as South Africa, have a sense of the significance of community development and outreach through university engagement. The 1997 DoE White Paper of South Africa on the transformation of higher education already speaks to national goals and gives to community engagement a central role in the life of our universities. It makes specific reference to the role that community engagement can play in transforming the higher education system. It is therefore important to start a conversation around the mandate of universities in the field, including the questions:

- What is the role of universities in sport, development, and peace individually, as partners, and as part of regional or international networks?
- Can universities play a leading role in initiating or even coordinating partnerships with government, NGOs, the private sector, and sporting organizations to harness expertise, leverage resources, and perform capacity building in the field of sport for development and peace?
- Are universities making intentional and appropriate use of their resources and human capital to support sport for development and peace research, teaching, and community development?
- Who would be the most suitable (not the most affluent or most scientifically privileged) partners nationally and internationally to support capacity building, and research for mutually beneficial and sustainable programs in the field?
- Which curricula should be used in sport for development and who defines and designs curricula and course contents?
- Where, how, and by whom are courses and degrees in the field designed and offered?

- Who are the leading publishers in the field compared to where sport and development programs are being conducted? How easy or difficult is it for young researchers in the South to do a PhD in the field and to be able to present internationally?
- Who is able to provide scholarships in the field to students, to study and conduct research, and where are these courses offered?

Looking at the world maps where sport and development programs are located and examining the research produced and published in the field, it seems as if the South is left (and even encouraged) to conduct the implementation elements at a grass-roots level, mostly with NGOs, and the North reaps the scientific rewards.

What if we offer our experience as knowledge partners rather than experts? This should include knowledge partners in the South working with partners in the South (like the Trinidad and Tobago–South Africa Project) around capacity building and M&E; partners in the South working with partners the North (like the VLIR university collaboration with South Africa (see Vanden Auweele, Malcolm, & Meulders, 2006)); and Northern partners working with partners in the South (for example the Leverhulme Trust UK and Ghana and Tanzania).

Can we imagine these kinds of partnerships as based on mutual appreciation and respect for the partnership, concern for the common good, and acknowledgment of local expertise as a guiding factor? Can we listen to each other, in a non-judgmental way, without preconceived attitudes and with a true appreciation of each other's expertise? Far too often, projects close down because a true feeling of equal partnership around the planning table is absent due to dependence or interdependence with regard to funding or resources, or due to a lack of awareness of the respective contribution, context, and culture.

This chapter is a call to reflect on the role of stakeholders in sport and development in the context of pressing global challenges and the central issue of human survival in an increasingly interdependent world.

We recently became even more aware that problems such as peace, poverty, health, environmental, and educational and developmental crises as outlined in the MDGs are no longer confined to one nation, but transcend local and national boundaries. It is therefore narrow-minded and presumptuous to assume that one group, be it a government, university, or NGO or network from the South, East, North, or West can deal with those issues in their own way, however experienced or scientific that way may seem, or that any sports and development approach can be the *best practice* model, as some like to call their programs.

Conclusion

The real impact of sport on development worldwide is still an issue of contention and its positive and negative impact, its criteria for success, including monitoring and evaluation, and its limits and challenges in terms of North–South and application and collaboration still raise serious questions.

This chapter also calls for mutually beneficial partnerships, multi-stakeholder collaboration, and coordinated efforts and interaction between civil society, communities, municipalities, sports federations, schools, clubs, tertiary institutions, and local and national governments with the national and international sporting fraternity, in helping to transform our society into a united and peaceful society. Sport can indeed play an important role in that regard, especially for the youth. The need exists to set a new vision to be inspired to facilitate a new relationship between the North and the South in terms of sport and development to the advantage of all of those concerned. Indeed, we have a new athlete on the track!

References

BMI Sport Info (2006). A case for sport in the Southern Africa Development Community (SADC) 2007, unpublished document.

Cloete, F., & de Coning, C. (2011). *Improving public policy, theory, practise and review.* Pretoria: Van Schaiks Publishers.

de Coning, C. (2014). The case for sport: Socio-economic benefits of sport and recreation in the Western Cape. University of the Western Cape, Department of Cultural Affairs and Sport (DCAS) and ICESSD.

Keim, M. (2009). Building peace through sport. *African Conflict & Peace Review Journal, 1* (1), 95–109.

Keim, M., & de Coning, C. (2014). Sport and development policy in Africa: Results of a collaborative study of selected country cases. University of the Western Cape, ICESSD.

Maralack, D., Keim, M., & de Coning, C. (2013). South Africa. In K. Petry *et al.* (Eds.), *Comparative sport development: Systems, participation and public policy* (pp. 253–268). New York: Springer.

Mutahaba, G., Baguma, R., & Halfani, M. (1993). *Vitalizing African public administration for recovery and development.* Sterling: Kumarian.

Sanders, B., Phillips, J., & Vanreusel, B. (2012). Opportunities and challenges facing NGOs using sport as a vehicle for development in post-apartheid South Africa. *Sport, Education and Society, 3* (1), 1–13.

South African Government (2001). *The white paper on sport and recreation.* Pretoria: The South African Government Printer.

UN (2005). *Report on the International Year of Sport and Physical Education.* Geneva: UN.

UNESCO (1978). *International Charter of Physical Education and Sport.* Paris: UNESCO.

Vanden Auweele, Y., Malcolm, C., & Meulders, B. (2006). *Sport and development.* Leuven: LannooCampus.

Zlotnik, H. (2005). Secondary education. Retrieved March 1, 2015, from www.worldmapper.org/posters/worldmapper_map200_ver5.pdf.

22 The concept of "development" and the sport-related (future) approach

Karen Petry and Marius Runkel

What do we mean by "development"?

As outlined in the chapter by Fred Coalter, the need for development is some-times not clear when it comes to the individual human being as well as to the wider social context. Therefore, the definition of development in a broader sense will be discussed and outlined in the following.

Until the early twentieth century, the term *development* referred to the advancement of thoughts, talents, and abilities in the context of early childhood development (Menzel, 2010). Thereafter, development also began to encompass the characterization and transformation of countries with regards to prevalent patterns of societies. Here, first meanings of development revolved around economic aspects comprising agricultural, industrial, and service sectors.

Today, the term is far more encompassing, and still suffers from a lack of a clear universal definition (Cornwall, 2007; Nelson, 2010). Consistently, Sachs considers development as "much more than just a socio-economic endeavor; it is a perception which models reality, a myth which comforts societies, and a fantasy which unleashes passions" (Sachs, 1992, 1).

The UN Declaration on the Right of Development of 1986 (UNHCR, 1986) attempted to capture all facets of development by condensing development as

> a comprehensive economic, social, cultural and political process, which aims at the constant improvement of the well-being of the entire population and of all individuals on the basis of their active, free and meaningful participation in development and the fair distribution of benefits there from.

According to Nelson (2010, 134), there is a growing consensus that development can be defined as "multi-faceted, multi-disciplinary and multi-sector set of actions, interventions and institutions aimed at improving the quality of people's lives."

Embedded in most definitions is the assumption that development is character-ized by positive change and a sense of progress, which is regarded as an ongoing process (Nuscheler, 2006). Also, the satisfaction of individual human needs appears to be at the center of attention while comprising the social engineering of emerging nations (Esteva, 1992; McMichael, 2004; Menzel, 2010). Whereas actors, most notably governments and businesses, have traditionally focused on macro-economic stimuli through mere influx of capital investments (top-down) to serve developmental demands (Korten, 1987), there has been a shift toward a more micro-oriented approach of communal or individual development embracing participation and empowerment at the ground level (bottom-up).

As a result, local requirements need to be set in place, so that affected individuals and communities may at best improve their life chances and satisfy personal needs of their own accord. By implication, developmental actors are able to actively shape these conditions. Accordingly, Menzel (2010) stresses political stability, economic performance, social justice, social participation, environmental sustainability, and cultural identity as beneficial conditions.

Burnett (2009) argues that developmental actions have to refer to individual and cultural meanings, and thus have to be interpreted in relation to respective social contexts. In cases where cultural identity and traditions are compromised, conflicts and political instability may surface and in turn severely impair individual development. Lastly, social participation is the overall presupposition for development, so that all other requirements and conditions can occur. Therefore, empowerment and participation are commonly regarded as key components, and development is generally considered as an active process of participation. Likewise, the South African Reconstruction and Development Program (RDP), launched in 1994, characterizes development as a people-driven process: "Development is not about the delivery of goods to a passive citizenry. It is about active involvement and growing empowerment" (Republic of South Africa, 1994, 8).

Summarizing the model, Woolcock (2009, 5) consequently defines development as the "internal and external processes that shape, in a given society or for a particular social group, the welfare, justice and opportunities of its members, but especially its poorest and most marginalized." The emphasis is on the principles of participation and empowerment. Such a form of development is more concerned with community or individual development taking place at the grassroots level. In detail, development is considered as a contextual process which targets underprivileged individuals and communities by promoting equal distribution of benefits and revealing opportunities through a focus on education, while taking into account environmental sustainability, social participation, and cultural identity issues.

Development and modernization: the engine of societies?

Modernization is broadly defined as a complex of closely coherent structural, cultural, mental, and physical changes shaping societies in a progressive sense (van der Loo & van Reijen, 1992). In this sense, the concept of modernization can be seen as a form of development and progress affecting individual and community improvement in terms of social and economic perspectives. In total, two strands of modernization theory exist: "There is an early, simplistic, rather capi-talistic, ideological strand and a modern, contextual one." The emergence of the "Early version of Modernization Theory (EMT)" coincided with the end of World War II (Knöbl, 2003). Poverty worsened in many countries and commu-nism posed a threat to capitalism during the Cold War (Inglehart & Welzel, 2009). In the course of time, mainly US economists and policy-makers harnessed the theory to present capitalist values as the cure for poverty worldwide and to launch a counter-communist movement (Ekbladh, 2010; Inglehart & Welzel, 2010). These traditional attributes were interpreted by proponents of EMT as internal shortcomings that were hampering the social and economic progress of less-developed countries. It was commonly assumed that, due to "traditional religious and communal values" (Inglehart & Welzel, 2009, 35), underdeveloped countries were not capable of prospering of their own accord. As a consequence, it was proclaimed that traditional societies had to abandon prevailing social and economic habitual systems as well as traditional customs, since these were regarded as being deficient and thus compromised development toward an ideal of modern prosperity (Woolcock, 2009). The main imperative of EMT was the reproduction of Westernized systems by actors such as Western governments and businesses since societies worldwide were generally regarded as coherent and interdependent (Kaya, 2004).

Beyond a doubt, it is not difficult to argue that the "early modernization theory" does not correspond with modern schools of thinking, but rather with ideological doctrines impacted by the conflict of capitalism versus communism. The theory was hence heavily criticized for oversimplifying vital relationships and issues such as the processes of linearity, consensus and convergence, and the dichotomy of tradition and modernity (Coetzee, Graaf, Heindricks, & Wood, 2007; Fourie, 2012; Inglehart & Welzel, 2010).

The idea of "New Modernization Theory (NMT)" continues to encompass the intended transformation of underdeveloped societies through the upgrading of social and economic institutions with the assistance of modern societies, but the concept of development can no longer be simplified by merely copying Western or Northern schemes (Inglehart & Welzel, 2010). Instead, the new modernization theory acknowledges that macro-level achievements of democracy and liberal economy do not suffice to attain welfare development of the whole population. Beyond these two approaches, transformation needs to stress micro-level relevant issues such as human development, equity, participation, empowerment, and enhancing people's capabilities through education and science (Zapf, 2004). Here, it is essential to embrace the whole population, including rural as well as urban areas, and underprivileged as well as privileged communities.

Development and sport: which relationship?

Bearing the previous relevant conceptualization of development in mind, sport in the context of development can be conceived. While being rather ignored in the development literature (Levermore, 2008a), development itself is regarded as an end that may be directly achieved through physical activity in sport-related contexts (Darnell & Black, 2011; Levermore, 2008b).

The notion of the concept of *sport and development* has emerged only recently and sport has lately become an integral part of socio-economic development agendas worldwide (Beutler, 2008; Coalter, 2010; Kidd, 2008). Yet, sport as an engine for development is commonly deployed by an ever-expanding range of local, national, and international actors comprising sports associations, multinational corporations, NGOs, development agencies, and governments (Giulianotti & Armstrong, 2011; Hartmann & Kwauk, 2011; Levermore, 2008a; 2008b; Spaiij, 2009b). Its recent emergence rests on the notion that common economic policies have failed to succeed in developmental achievements (Levermore & Beacom, 2009). The growing recognition of the need for new approaches and actors has led to a recent increase in projects interpreting sport as an actor for social change. Political claims and initiatives such as the United Nations' Millennium Development Goals (MDGs), the appointment of United Nations' first Special Adviser on Sport for Development and Peace in 2001, the 2005 proclaimed International Year of Sport and Physical Education, the Sport for Development and Peace International Working Group, as well as sporting initiatives such as the Olympic Aid program and other sports activisms were launched (Beutler, 2008; Coalter, 2010; Kidd, 2008).

Two main trends can be seen in the existing and predominant literature. First, there is a strong belief that sport might indeed be able to make a critical contribution to development goals; second, substantial criticism does exist directly linked to this optimistic supposition (Donnelly, Atkinson, Boyle, & Szto, 2011). In the first instance, sport is instrumentalized and it is believed that sport encompasses education, health, peace, and other social issues while addressing traditional sport ideologies of discipline, confidence, tolerance, leadership, social capital, and respect (Coalter, 2008). But as Coalter (2006, and in this book) points out, sport in development (SiD) projects continue where traditional objectives end, such as increased participation, development of sporting skills, and fun, but rather go one step further. Beyond those, it is supposed that sport may yield social and economic change in various forms (Coalter, 2010; Guest, 2009; Hylton, Braham, Jackson, & Nesti, 2007; Kidd 2008; Levermore, 2008b).

Supported by the international community, general policy statements, and the sports community itself, it is assumed that sport has the potential to fuel change and address objectives such as empowerment, equality, crime prevention, and environmental sustainability, *inter alia*, by harnessing the popular appeal and inherent properties of sport (Beutler, 2008; Burnett, 2006; Darnell, 2010; Fokwang, 2009; Kay, 2009; Kay & Bradbury, 2009; Giulianotti, 2004; Giulianotti & Armstrong, 2011; Lawson, 2005; Spaaij, 2009a; Vermeulen & Verwell, 2009; see also Keim and Cristo in this book).

Following this, Levermore (2008b) implements six categories referring to development outcomes: conflict resolution and intercultural understanding; strengthening physical, social, and community infrastructure; raising awareness, particularly through education; empowerment by means of developing employment, life skills, and other social investments; direct impact on physical and psychological health and general welfare; and economic development and poverty alleviation through encouraging business involvement. Correspondingly, Lyras and Peachey (2011, 1) define SiD as

> the use of sport to exert a positive influence on public health, the socialization of children, youths and adults, the social inclusion of the disadvantaged, the economic development of regions and states, and on fostering intercultural exchange and conflict resolution.

Likewise, Spaiij (2009b, 1115) broadly defines SiD as "all types of organized physical activity that may serve as a tool for development and peace." In short, the international community markets sport as an effective tool for development at great expense (Hartmann & Kwauk, 2011). However, these overly positive claims have to be treated with some caution when the criticisms below are taken into consideration. Although the extent of evaluation has increased (Levermore, 2011), many authors critically mention that there is still a grave gap in research and verification, entailing a lack of conceptualization, monitoring, evaluation, methodological considerations, organization, and structure of the sport and development area (Black, 2010; Coalter, 2006; 2010; Donnelly *et al.*, 2011; Hartmann & Kwauk, 2011; Levermore, 2008b; 2011; Spaaij, 2009b). Moreover, Skinner, Zakus, and Cowell (2008) as well as Darnell and Hayhurst (2011) and Mwaanga and Adeosun (in this book) comment critically that sport is often imposed on communities as a top-down approach without recognizing relevant contexts. Hence, based on rather anecdotal evidence, there is less understanding of the mechanisms by which sport might promote individual or community development. Beacom (2007) and Beutler (2008) point out that sport was linked to development in a rather ad-hoc and informal way. Furthermore, Coalter (2010), being a contributor to the field, explicitly criticizes claims about sport being a universal remedy, saying that they are based on rather broad policy legitimations arising out of failures of traditional instruments (Levermore, 2008b) and the notion that sport is regarded as a last resort. Likewise, Coalter (2010) states that these arguments seem to neglect respective local contexts and tend to overstate benefits without delivering sufficient proof. Consequently, there are a great number of unanswered questions and a crucial lack of research in the context of this sport-related "incredibly complex social intervention" (Donnelly *et al.*, 2011, 592).

"Beyond development": the potential of a new approach

"The SDP sector (sport for development and peace) is moving into a new phase" stated Giulianotti recently (2014, 15). But what does this mean for the concept of development? Do we still want to follow a top-down approach instead of a strong partnership approach with respect, autonomy, and influence in both directions? The future concept has to be based on the principles of building up a learning environment for all partners within a development cooperation process.

The post-2015 development agenda should have a broader approach with wider definitions of global learning in all geographical directions around the world.

But what does this mean for the use of the term "development"? It is proposed to avoid the term as much as possible, to be aware of one's own position and to realize alternatives (Ziai, 2014). One alternative approach could become the "global learning perspective." The term *global learning* is more related to the debate of sustainable education and it is based on the principle of a global responsibility. Global learning is possible at all levels, from the individual to the international, and is related to a democratic approach of partnership. It is already part of the SDGs (Sustainable Development Goals) and of the Post-2015-Agenda; it is said that "by 2030 [to] ensure all learners acquire knowledge and skills needed to promote sustainable development ... gender equality, promotion of a culture of peace and non-violence, global citizenship, and appreciation of cultural diversity and of culture's contribution to sustainable development" (United Nations, 2014).

This leads to a new beyond-development agenda in both contexts, in conflicting, economically challenged countries in transition as well as in the industrialized world. In other words: There is in the future a strong need for cooperation in both directions, North–South as well as South–North. The future approach should be based on the concept of "Beyond Aid" and should focus more on postmodernization patterns.

As outlined in this book by Mwaanga and Adeosun, as well as Keim and de Coning, the critical success factors in future development cooperation in sport are the mutual exchange of scientific knowledge, concepts, approaches, and experiences. Therefore, development as a concept should be redefined, and the discussion has to be led by the so-called countries in transition, using the words of the NMT. In this sense, development is subject to continual readjustments following reactions by social movements, modernizers, conservatives, and bystanders.

References

Beacom, A. (2007). A question of motives: Sport reciprocity and international development assistance. *European Sports Management Quarterly*, *7* (1), 81–107.

Beutler, I. (2008). Sport serving peace and development: Achieving the goals of the United Nations through sport. *Sport in Society*, *11* (4), 359–369.

Black, D.R. (2010). The ambiguities of development: implications for development through Sport. *Sport in Society*, *13* (1), 121–129.

Burnett, C. (2006). Building social capital through an active community club. *International Review for Sociology of Sport*, *41*, 283–294.

Burnett, C. (2009). Engaging sport-for-development for the social impact in the South African Context. *Sport in Society*, *12* (9), 1192–1205.

Coalter, F. (2006). Sport in development: Process evaluation and organizational development. In Y. van den Auweele, C. Malcolm, & B. Mulders (Eds.), *Sport and development* (pp. 149–162). Leuven: Lannoo Campus.

Coalter, F. (2008). Sport-in-development: Development for and through sport? In M. Nicholson & R. Hoye (Eds.), *Sport and social capital* (pp. 39–67). Oxford: Elsevier.

Coalter, F. (2010). The politics of sport-for development: Limited focus programmes and broad gauge problems. *International Review for the Sociology of Sport*, *45* (3), 295–314.

Coalter, F. (2012). What is the development in sport-for-development? In B. Segaert *et al.* (Eds.), *Sports governance, development and corporate responsibility* (pp. 88–104). New York: Taylor & Francis.

Coetzee, K.J., Graaf, J., Heindricks, F., & Wood, G. (2007). *Development: Theory, policy and practice*. Cape Town: Oxford University Press.

Cornwall, A. (2007). Buzzwords and Fuzzwords: Deconstructing development discourse. *Development in Practice*, *17* (4–5), 471–484.

Darnell, S.C. (2010). Power, politics and "sport-for development and peace": Investigating the utility of sport for international development. *Sociology of Sport Journal*, *27*, 54–75.

Darnell, S.C., & Black, D.R. (2011). Mainstreaming sport into international development studies. *Third World Quarterly*, *32* (3), 367–378.

Darnell, S.C., & Hayhurst, L. (2011). Sport for decolonization: Exploring a new praxis of sport for development. *Progress in Development Studies*, *11* (3), 183–196.

Donnelly, P., Atkinson, M., Boyle, S., & Szto, C. (2011). Sport for development and peace: A public sociology perspective. *Third World Quarterly*, *32* (3), 589–601.

Ekbladh, D. (2010). *The great American mission: Modernization and the construction of an American world order*. Princeton, NJ: Princeton University Press.

Esteva, G. (1992). Development. In W. Sachs (Eds.), *The development dictionary: A guide to knowledge as power* (pp. 6–25). London: Zed Books.

Fokwang, J. (2009). Southern perspective of sport-in-development: A case study of football in Bamenda, Cameroon. In R. Levermore & A. Beacom (Eds.), *Sport and international development* (pp. 198–218). Houndmills: Palgrave MacMillan.

Fourie, E. (2012). A future for the theory of multiple modernities: Insights from the new modernization theory. *Social Science Information*, *51* (1) 52–69.

Giulianotti, R. (2004). Human rights, globalization and sentimental education: The case of sport. *Sport in Society*, 7, 355–369.

Giulianotti, R. (2014). Sport for development and peace policy options in the Commonwealth. In O. Dudfield (Ed.), *Strengthening sport for development and peace. National policies and strategies*. London: Commonwealth Secretariat.

Giulianotti, R., & Armstrong, G. (2011). Sport, the military and peacemaking: History and possibilities. *Third World Quarterly*, *32* (3), 379–394.

Guest, A. (2009). The diffusion of development-through-sport: Analysing the history and practice of the Olympics Movement's grassroots outreach to Africa. *Sport in Society*, *12*, 1336–1352.

Hartmann, D., & Kwauk, C. (2011). Sport and development: An overview, critique and reconstruction. *Journal of Sport and Social Issues*, *35* (3), 284–305.

Hylton, K., Braham, P., Jackson, D., & Nesti, M. (2007). *Sports Development: Policy, Process and Practice*. London: Routledge.

Inglehart, R., & Welzel, C. (2009). How development leads to democracy: What we know about modernization. *Foreign Affairs*, *88* (2), 551–567.

Inglehart, R. & Welzel, C. (2010). Changing mass priorities: The link between modernization and democracy. *Perspectives on Politics*, *8* (2), 551–567.

Kay, T. (2009). Developing through sport: Evidencing sport impacts on young people. *Sport in Society*, *12* (9), 1177–1191.

Kay, T., & Bradbury, S. (2009). Youth sport volunteering: Developing social capital? *Sport, Education & Society*, *14*, 121–140.

Kaya, I. (2004). Modernity, openness, interpretation: A perspective on multiple modernities. *Social Science Information, 43* (1), 35–57.

Kidd, B. (2008). A new social movement: Sport for development and peace. *Sport in Society, 11* (4), 370–380.

Knöbl, W. (2003). Theories that won't pass away: The never-ending story of modernization theory. In G. Delanty & E.F. Isin (Eds.), *Handbook of historical sociology* (pp. 96–107). London: Sage.

Korten, D. (1987). Third generation NGO strategies: A key to people-centered development. *World development, 15* (1), 145–159.

Lawson, H.A. (2005). Empowering people, facilitating community development, and contributing to sustainable development: The social work of sport, exercise and physical education programs. *Sport, Education and Society, 10* (1), 135–160.

Levermore, R. (2008a). Sport in international development: Time to treat it seriously? *The Brown Journal of World Affairs, 14* (2), 55–56.

Levermore, R. (2008b). Sport: A new engine of development? *Progress in Development Studies, 8* (2), 183–190.

Levermore, R. (2011). Evaluating sport-for-development: Approaches and critical issues. *Progress in Development Studies, 11* (4), 339–353.

Levermore, R., & Beacom, A. (2009). Sport and development: Mapping the field. In R. Levermore & A. Beacom (Eds.), *Sport and International Development* (pp. 1–25), Houndmills: Palgrave Macmillan.

Levermore, R., & Beacom, A. (2012). Reassessing sport-for-development: Moving beyond "mapping the territory." *International Journal of Sport Policy and Politics, 4* (1), 125–137.

Lyras, A., & Peachy, J.W. (2011). Integrating sport-for-development theory and praxis. *Sport Management Review*, DOI:10.1016/j.smr.2011.05.006.

McMichael, P. (2004). *Development and social change: A global perspective.* Thousand Oaks, CA: Pine Forge Pass.

Menzel, U. (2010). Teil I: Entwicklungstheorie. In R. Stockmann, U. Menzel, & F. Nuscheler (Eds.), *Entwicklungspolitik. Theorien, Probleme, Strategien* [Development Policy. Theory, Problems, Strategies] (pp. 11–160). München: Oldenbourg.

Nelson, J. (2010). Development. In W. Visser, D. Matten, M. Pohl, & N. Tolhurst (Eds.), *The A to Z of Corporate Social Responsibility* (pp. 134–137), Chippenham: Rowe.

Nuscheler, F. (2006). *Entwicklungspolitik* [Development policy]. Bonn: Dietz.

Republic of South Africa (1994). White Paper on Reconstruction and Development. Parliament of the Republic of South Africa. Retrieved November, 15, 2012, from www.Info.gov.za/view/download.

Sachs, W. (1992). *The development dictionary: A guide to knowledge as power.* London: Zed Books.

SDPIWG (2011). Sport for Development and Peace International Working Group. Retrieved December, 11, 2014 from www.un.org/wcm/content/site/sport/pid/6229.

Skinner, J., Zakus, D., & Cowell, J. (2008). Development through sport: Building social capital in disadvantaged communities. *Sport Management Review, 11* (3), 253–275.

Spaaij, R. (2009a). Sport as a vehicle for social mobility and regulation of disadvantaged urban youth: Lessons from Rotterdam. *International Review for the Sociology of Sport, 44* (2–3), 247–264.

Spaaij, R. (2009b). The social impact of sport: Diversities, complexities and contexts. *Sport in Society, 12* (9), 1109–1117.

UNHCR (1986). Declaration on the Right to Development: Resolution adopted by the General Assembly. Retrieved December, 11, 2014 from www.refworld.org/cgi-bin/texis/vtx/rwmain?docid=3b00f22544.

United Nations (2014). https://sustainabledevelopment.un.org/focussdgs.html

van der Loo, H., & van Reijen, W. (1992). *Modernisierung. Projekt und Paradox* [Modernization. project and paradox]. München: Deutscher Taschenbuch-Verlag.

Vermeulen, J., & Verwell, P. (2009). Participation in sport: Bonding and bridging as identity work. *Sport in Society*, *12*, 1206–1219.

Woolcock, M. (2009). The next ten years of development studies: From modernization to multiple modernities, in theory and practice. *European Journal of Development Research*, *21* (1), 4–9.

Zapf, W. (2004). Modernization theory and the non-western World. *Welttrends: Zeitschriften für Internationale Politik*, *44*, 100–107.

Ziai, A. (2014). Post-Development-Ansätze: Konsequenzen für die Entwicklungstheorie. [Post-development-approaches: Conseqeunces for the development theory]. In F. Müller, E. Sondermann, I. Wehr, C. Jakobeit, & A. Ziai (Eds.), *Entwicklungstheorien* [Development theories] (pp. 405–434), Baden-Baden: Nomos.

Epilogue

The future of sport imagined

Yves Vanden Auweele, Elaine Cook and
Jim Parry

We start this epilogue with the warning from M. McNamee in the first chapter that each effort to look into the future should mention that due to the complexity of the sporting landscape in a globalizing world, all variables cannot be controlled and that therefore "predictions" aren't especially reliable. Projections and speculative judgment supported by reasoned argument and a reasonable body of evidence are therefore the most we have done.

This book has invited a selection of short and well-substantiated projections of sport into the twenty-first century, with clear messages that invite reflection and discussion.

In Part I, some authors address problems such as coaching attitudes, organizational norms, and the (alleged) ageing of the Olympism concept. These chapters can be seen as a set of open-ended challenges, proposing moves towards athlete-centered coaching; a never-ending effort to improve democratic representation and a renewing of the concept of Olympism as an inspiring social philosophy.

Other authors address more specific problems such as gender equity and the enforcing of gender quotas, corruption, migration of sports labor, inflation of athletes' rights, and the commercialization of sports medicine, not so much as open-ended challenges but in the context of a concrete integrity plan to be realized within a realistic time-frame.

Yet others doubt the efficiency of developing ad hoc solutions for particular problems, and suggest tackling the more fundamental causes of those problems (e.g. as side-effects of the commodification, globalization, and growing monoculture in sport), knowing that these proposals require long-term strategies directed to greater diversity in the context of a broader movement culture.

Summarizing all these positions, the imagined future of sport, that could provide the best possible answer to the major challenges of sport in the twenty-first century, will involve working and reflecting on different concepts, problems, and solutions, at all levels, with short- and long-term strategies simultaneously.

The common starting-point of the chapters of Part II is the observation that there is a clear lack of good governance in globalizing international sport, and all authors, in their different ways, present ideas on how to move forward in this matter.

Key proposals are the questioning of *sport specificity* – of sport's *state of exception* and claimed *autonomy*, and the development of more ethical governance, including social trust, democracy, consent, public support, legitimacy, control, accountability, and equity.

A major question addressed was whether the current structures and regulations of national and international sport systems are capable of ensuring the rights, (gender) equity, and accountability of all those affected by their decisions, in particular the athletes and the citizens of the countries organizing mega sport events.

An independent body for the control of the governance of sporting organizations worldwide has been suggested, as well as the organization of non-mega sport events to challenge the negative side-effects of the current gigantism.

Questions were raised as to which authority in the world has the normative power to direct global sport organizations toward more ethical governance, and whether the European Union can play a crucial role here.

Taken together, the authors present coherent and innovative thoughts and proposals on good governance in future world sport. Reading through these chapters it becomes clear that this is not just utopian thinking, but grounded and well-informed proposals.

Part III deals with the fairness of management, including the status of finances in future sport. The exceptional status of sports is also under discussion here, and a better *redistribution* of the financial income in *competitive sport*, since some sports bodies have such a societal impact that legal control should be the same as for any other large business. *Sport for All* is seen not only as a necessity but as a right.

In cycling, there is a suggestion to replace the *wealthy benefactors and powerful paternalistic oligarchs* with a new cycling institution representing all World Tour teams and riders, to get external financing from more responsible and sustainable brand sponsors.

The role of the EU as a normative power has been stressed because in the past EU law has proven to be legitimate and effective in addressing legal problems within the frameworks of sport bodies, even outside the EU, as the IOC and FIFA have experienced. Though the EU Treaty has recognized the specific characteristics of sport, it has also suggested that the sports world may face more governmental intervention. Sport has been seen as a phenomenon that must obey the legal principles of the (EU) market order. Public authorities such as the EU should not hesitate in using their hard legal competences to enforce transnational legal responses.

Part IV deals with one of the most discussed and controversial issues in sport – doping. To what extent is enhancing the potential of the athlete's body by drugs ethical, fair, and legal? Isn't there an overreaction by the authorities and WADA?

In this part, contrasting views have been presented. On the one hand, arguments are developed against the acceptance of performance-enhancing drugs (PEDs) in future sports practices; on the other hand, the failure of a zero-tolerance stance has been demonstrated. The latter pleads for a more relaxed stance, accompanied by harm-reduction strategies, to keep the individual and societal cost of such drug use lower.

Interestingly, a moral book has been opened on anti-doping regulators. Instead of the regular analytical methods, doping authorities have started using heavy pressure on athletes to testify against fellow sportsmen. They pit the athletes against each other and make an already highly toxic competitive athletic environment even more toxic, which is morally objectionable, and even treacherous.

The complexity of the moral problem has been disclosed and has taken away the hope for simplistic solutions in the future.

The starting point of the final section of the book, Part V, is the fact that sport has been linked to the realization of the Millennium Development Goals (MDGs), including the promotion of peace and human dignity, by the United Nations in 2003.

Controversial positions have been put forward in this part. Some have argued that it is naïve to think that current sport-for-development programs can approach the high (MDG) expectations placed upon them. Therefore, more research on outcomes and middle-range objectives is needed. Policy-driven enthusiasm is too fragile a basis to guarantee the expected outcomes and the quality, efficiency, and sustainability of sport-for-development programs.

Most sport for development programs are conceptualized in the North and may therefore be contaminated with elements of neo-colonialism. The future lies in a joint commitment from North and South. Issues in ideological, geographical, and academic inequities should be addressed and should be replaced by *global learning*, which means building up a learning environment for all partners within a cooperation process based on equality.

To conclude

Reflecting on the variety of these speculative suggestions, it is evident that some of them are far-reaching and we are aware that their realization will include systemic changes that will modify sports' DNA. This includes that some key players will lose power or at least will have to function in a different context, and that we no longer discuss problem solutions and innovations, but important societal and (sport) political challenges.

We are therefore realistic enough to grasp that what will be the driving force behind change and eventually implementation of some of these projections in the future will be the *pressure of necessity*, both in a negative and a positive sense. Negative, in the sense that a common outrage may unlock a demand for change as a reaction to fraudulent governance and management, bankruptcies of high-profile clubs, the disclosure of shameless abuses of power, and a continuous accumulation of incidents and scandals. Positive, in the sense of a worldwide pressing claim for *sport for all* based on universal human rights, such as the right to play, the right to participate in sport, and the right to develop a healthy life-style, based also on a growing need for relatedness, to feel a sense of belonging and support in an egocentric world; and based not least on the growing realization that sport and physical activity have the *potential* to facilitate development, social integration, education, and peace.

However, we are just as convinced that "necessity" will have to be combined with the effort of inspiring, convincing, and persuading individuals and organizations addressing these problems, needs, and claims each in their area of influence and responsibility. We have tried to offer some ideas as the first step in that important process.

After all, we would prefer to be called naïve rather than to be accused of culpable neglect.

Index